POLITICS AND SEX

POLITICS AND SEX

Exploring the Connections between Gender, Sexuality, and the State

Edna Keeble

Women's Press
Toronto

For Roy

Politics and Sex
by Edna Keeble

First published in 2016 by
Women's Press, an imprint of Canadian Scholars' Press Inc.
425 Adelaide Street West, Suite 200
Toronto, Ontario
M5V 3C1

www.womenspress.ca

Canadian Scholars' Press Inc. gratefully acknowledges financial support for our publishing activities from the Government of Canada through the Canada Book Fund (CBF).

Library and Archives Canada Cataloguing in Publication
Keeble, Edna, author
Politics and sex : exploring the connections between gender, sexuality, and the state / Edna Keeble.

Includes bibliographical references.
Issued in print and electronic formats.
ISBN 978-0-88961-585-4 (paperback).--ISBN 978-0-88961-587-8 (epub).--
ISBN 978-0-88961-586-1 (pdf)

1. Feminism--Political aspects. 2. Sex--Political aspects. 3. Sex role--Political aspects. 4. Women--Violence against. I. Title.

HQ1236.K43 2016 305.42 C2016-901449-5 C2016-901450-9

Text design by Aldo Fierro
Cover design by Em Dash Design

Printed and bound in Canada by Webcom

Canadä

MIX
Paper from responsible sources
FSC® C004071

TABLE OF CONTENTS

Acknowledgements • ix

Introduction • 1

Chapter 1: Politics and Sex: A Feminist Liberal Perspective • 9

Chapter 2: Body Politics • 39

Chapter 3: The Veiling of Women • 67

Chapter 4: Female Genital Mutilation/Cutting • 89

Chapter 5: Rape and Sexual Violence • 109

Chapter 6: Pornography • 135

Chapter 7: Prostitution and Trafficking • 157

Concluding Comments: Politics and Sex Revisited • 183

References • 203

ACKNOWLEDGEMENTS

I am fortunate to have had the best colleagues, the best students, and the best family. Among my wonderful colleagues and friends in political science, Meredith Ralston has always been an incredible supporter of my work as a feminist scholar and teacher ever since our days as graduate students working with the late and great political philosopher, and beloved mentor and dearest friend, David Braybrooke. Familiar with my approach in the classroom, Meredith put me in touch with Lily Bergh, the publishing director at CSPI/Women's Press. Lily expressed interest in my work and encouraged me to send a proposal to write a textbook based on my "Politics and Sex" course. That initial warm communication unfolded into a rewarding, positive experience with the press, particularly with Natalie Garriga, my developmental editor, who ensured five excellent peer reviewers for my manuscript and shepherded the book to completion. I would like to thank them all, along with Caley Clements, the production manager at CSPI/Women's Press, for being part of the collegial, congenial environment that led to the publication of this text.

There would never have been a textbook without my outstanding students at Saint Mary's University. Although they would recognize the organization and content of the book, they may not fully realize how much I learned from them. Since the first time I developed and taught this course in the 2008–9 academic year, I have made changes to the course because of my students' level of engagement with the material and with each other through class discussions. There are so many of my students who have impacted me and I want to thank, in particular, Katie, Kalina, Carolyn, Matt, Emma, Omar, Jeremiah, Julie, Glentine, Rebeca, Alison, Lauren, Chris, Kristen, Casey, Benjamin, Isalean, Jamie, Adrienne, Brad, Kathleen, Kirt, Chiedza, Callee, Tatiane, John, Marina, and, without a doubt, Rumbi. I will always be grateful to Rumbi Chimhanda for reminding me that students, far from wanting to be coddled, crave to be challenged.

Finally, I am indebted to my family for their support and hospitality during my year of leave from the university as I was finishing this book: Lydia, Richard, Edwin, Leony, Janice, Ian, and Kai in Chicago (with Alvin and Giselle in Miami); Edward, Agnes, and Rich in Laguna Niguel (with Rhianne in San Francisco); Jamie and Paul in Havana; Marie, Rose, Don, and Morgan in Halifax/Fall River; Raquel and Mark in Calgary; and Brett in Vancouver. My mother, Lydia Ward, and my children, Brett Keeble, Raquel (Keeble) MacKenzie, and (now) Mark MacKenzie, have given me unfailing encouragement. However, my greatest fan remains their father, my husband and confluent love, Roy Keeble, with whom I took a quantum leap 32 years ago and am continuing to cruise happily through life.

INTRODUCTION

When you picked up this book and saw the title, did a part of you think—or even perhaps hope—that it would be about political sex scandals? What more if this is an assigned or recommended text for a course in politics? As a professor of political science teaching undergraduate students, I can certainly understand. Who would not want to study illicit sexual desires, questionable individual choices, and damaging public scrutiny, which is why sex must be kept private, lest it erupt into a scandal? For many political observers, the most famous or, more appropriately, infamous case is former US President Bill Clinton's extramarital affair with Monica Lewinsky in the 1990s during his presidency while she was an intern at the White House, although this is far from being a contemporary, or a historical, anomaly. In 2015, DNA tests proved that Warren Harding, who was US president in the early 1900s, did indeed have a child while in office with his much younger mistress, more than 30 years his junior, who had written a tell-all book in 1928 detailing their affair, but whose story was never believed. Sex scandals are both titillating and ubiquitous, entangling all sorts of individuals, not only politicians but also celebrities, sports stars, and even everyday neighbours or co-workers, as was made public by the information released by hackers in August 2015 of the Toronto-based adultery website, Ashley Madison, infamous for its slogan: "Life is short. Have an affair."

Sex scandals, because they rest on ideas about the role of sexuality, individual choice, and the public-private in people's lives, resonate at a personal and not merely an intellectual level. These ideas are central to this book, so although it is not about political sex scandals, it is indeed about politics and sex.

More specifically, the book is about how *politics* and *sex* lead to focusing on *gender*, especially in terms of the challenges women continue to face, thus inviting inquiry into relations between women and men. This line of inquiry goes beyond being an important intellectual exercise. Focusing on the challenges faced by women can force us to think about our own personal values because our inquiry is not based on identifying as a woman and/or heterosexual. Rather, it stems from an understanding that sexuality, intimacy, and capabilities are at the core of what makes us human. Feeling desires for sexual pleasure; seeking attachments with others, specifically in bonding with another human being; and exercising capabilities in fundamental ways, particularly in terms of bodily integrity, are not particular to any one person based on gender, sexual orientation, gender identity, race, ethnicity, class, religion, or able-bodiedness. Human beings should be free to feel desire, seek attachments, and exercise capabilities. The problem, however, is that sexual pleasure has been subject to state regulation; pair bonding has been defined by norms of heterosexuality and masculinity; and capabilities have been undermined by forces of social conservatism. All of these have had harmful effects on women and sexual minorities, and all have to do with the exercise of power.

The study of politics is about the study of power. The overall objective of this book is to show how political science can look at issues of gender and sexuality in ways familiar to students in the discipline where the focus is on the state or the "public," while underscoring how central the study of gender and sexuality is to the discipline of political science. Conventional understandings of politics in the West centre on the governing features of the state, such as liberal democratic institutions (for example, parliamentary and presidential systems, federalism, and a Charter or Bill of Rights), processes (for example, elections, judicial decisions, and the influence of the women's rights and gay rights movements), and individuals (for example, prime ministers and presidents), and these are important to the analyses that follow. In the global context, conventional views of politics are evident in the focus on international security, international law, and international organizations, such as the United Nations and the World Health Organization, and these, too, are discussed in this book. The study of politics is founded on the public-private distinction, which is fundamental to classical liberal thinking, but this text shows how the "private" is also a site of power. Taking from the radical feminist insight that "the personal is political," I show how feminist critiques have "give[n] us a broader conception of the political and a sense of the questions that we confront," specifically in how power fuses gender in ways that focus on sexuality (Lacey 1993, 111). The way that I will be doing this is by framing analyses of particular topics from a feminist liberal perspective.

CHAPTER TOPICS

In Chapter 1, I introduce the feminist liberal perspective. This perspective points to the centrality of the individual and focuses on sexual freedoms, not only in the context of intimacy but also in terms of capabilities. Chapter 1 points out that the valorization of the heterosexual conjugal bond has not only marginalized sexual minorities, which is the primary concern of sexuality studies, but also disempowered women, which is the focus of this text. A feminist liberal perspective has four central ideas: the guiding principle of liberal individualism; the problem of systems of dominance that undermine individual autonomy; the transformation of intimacy; and the importance of progress and capabilities. Although this perspective is based on liberalism as a philosophy, the chapter is not a theoretical foray into either liberalism or feminism, and thus it does not offer a comprehensive account of differing interpretations of liberalism or feminism. There are other introductory texts that offer more wide-ranging treatments of liberalism (e.g., Bellamy 2000), feminism (e.g., Bromley 2012), and even feminist liberalism (e.g., Baehr 2004b), as well as more general texts on gender and sexuality, usually from sociological or psychological perspectives (e.g., Rahman and Jackson 2010; Naugler 2012; Rutter and Schwartz 2012). The goal is to introduce ideas centred on the importance of the individual and why this is a compelling way to analyze contemporary topics on gender and sexuality that should be of significant interest to students of political science.

The continuing challenges faced by women are evident in the next six chapters, which deal with body politics (Chapter 2), the veiling of women (Chapter 3), female genital mutilation/cutting (Chapter 4), rape and sexual violence (Chapter 5), pornography (Chapter 6), and prostitution and trafficking (Chapter 7). Although the chapters are topic-specific, they follow a particular logic because certain ideas from previous chapters inform subsequent chapters. In Chapter 2, I bring to bear the lives of four privileged women in Canadian and American politics to discuss body politics (a topic of significant interest to feminists) in the context of a changing body politic (a familiar term used in political science). Challenges to the valorization of the heterosexual conjugal bond are evident in a changing body politic, whereas the focus on women's appearance, particularly in the pathologizing of fat, is about body politics. We can rethink the focus on women's appearance by looking at body-as-process as opposed to body-as-object, leading to discussions of body confidence.

The appearance of women, however, is an essential part of the debates on the veiling of Muslim women, which is the topic of Chapter 3. The veiling of Muslim women has been constructed as a prime example of cultural differences between the West and Islam, a religion that has been placed front and centre in the post-9/11 security environment, in the context of concerns about gender equality. This chapter looks at calls for veil bans in the West, particularly the burqa and the niqab, and extends the discussion beyond Canada and the United States to other immigrant-receiving countries in the West, namely those in Europe as well as Australia. On the one hand, I highlight that conservative arguments against the veil, although appropriating feminist discourse, have less to do with gender equality and more to do with security concerns and anti-immigrant sentiments in the West. On the other hand, arguments centred on the veil as a symbol of resistance against Western imperialism, particularly against the perceived oppressive beauty culture of the West, tie rather than divide many Western and Muslim women. The veiling issue is not about the cultural differences between the West and Islam, but rather, as I argue, about systems of dominance that undermine individual autonomy.

Problematic arguments about Western imperialism and cultural difference (leading to cultural relativism) also inform discussions about female genital mutilation/cutting (FGM/C), which is the topic of Chapter 4. Global efforts and changing attitudes have undermined the arguments of cultural relativists because FGM/C rests on the control of women's sexuality. Although FGM/C is largely found in the region covering the Atlantic coast to the Horn of Africa, the practice is also found in many Western countries, including Canada and the United States, given increasing immigration from this region. Criminalizing FGM/C in the West has opened up questions, not only about the accommodation of cultural practices in a liberal democratic society, but also about women's choices regarding their bodies, particularly in light of the increasing popularity of female genital cosmetic surgery (FGCS). I point out in this chapter that we have to be mindful about two matters regarding the banning of FGM/C in the West: one, that representations of the oppressed African immigrant and the liberated Westerner are not being perpetuated; and two, that cultures are seen as dynamic so that a traditional practice need not be eradicated if its original meaning and intent, such as the control of women's sexuality, has lost social force, thus giving credence to what is referred to, in the case of genital cutting, as the "ritual nick." The global consensus against FGM/C has arisen because it has been recognized as a form of violence against women, which, in turn, is seen as a human rights violation.

Sexual violence is a form of violence against women, and rape and sexual violence is the topic of Chapter 5. Here, the focus shifts specifically again to Canada and the United States, particularly because sexual assault on Canadian and American university campuses has (rightly so) been receiving a great deal of attention. This chapter discusses not only the persistence of rape myths despite three decades of rape law reform in Canada and the United States (where we see shifts in language from rape to sexual assault), but also the prevalence of acquaintance rape in society, particularly on university campuses. I argue that "affirmative consent" should be the standard adopted in all universities, where the burden of proof in disciplinary hearings is shifted to the accused as opposed to the complainant. Rape is a sexualized form of violence that is traumatic and alienating, often taking away the capacity for sexual desire by those who have been victimized, and it remains a gendered phenomenon.

Pornography and prostitution represent deep divisions between feminist groups on what sexual liberation has meant for women, and these are the topics of Chapter 6 and Chapter 7, respectively. Because freedom of expression is protected under the constitution in both Canada and the United States, adult pornography is not illegal in either country, but the harmful effects of the sexual representation of women have been at the heart of feminist opposition to pornography. Chapter 6 discusses how these harmful effects can be recognized without condemning all hard-core, raunchy representations of sex (i.e., pornography), which, for some women, may be important to their sexual agency. Here, I talk about "egalitarian pornography," as found particularly in the genre of feminist porn, and why sexualization, which can be seen as a process of recognizing sexual agency as a result of the sexual revolution in the West, is not the same as objectification. Prostitution is also not the same as trafficking. Chapter 7 shows how the problematic conflation between prostitution and trafficking, grounded in the idea that all sex workers are trafficked and therefore are all victimized, has dominated discourses in both Canada and the United States. This has led to Canada adopting an abolitionist system, or the Nordic model, in 2014 after the Supreme Court struck down the country's existing laws on prostitution. Instead of moving toward decriminalization, which is the best system for protecting the rights of sex workers, Canada has effectively outlawed prostitution with the criminalization of the buying of sex and has further limited the choices of women, particularly poor women.

The final chapter revisits the meanings of gender and sexuality, showing that a feminist liberal perspective can extend beyond an examination of the challenges faced by women in heterosexual relationships. Here, I argue that by paying attention to women's equality, we set the stage for equality in other ways. This is evident not only in the legal recognition of same-sex marriage in Canada and the United States, but also in the greater acceptance of transgender people. Sexual orientation and gender identity have redefined what we mean by sexuality and gender, demonstrating the kind of progress evident in the transformation of intimacy. This transformation points to how the ideals of individual autonomy and equality can be realized in private relationships, namely the democratization of personal life, which must occur alongside democratizing processes in the public arena.

PEDAGOGICAL FEATURES

This book is directed primarily to an undergraduate audience, specifically to students in political science. Because chapters are topic-specific, they can be read in a different order from how they are presented. (I do state above, however, that the chapters follow a particular logic.) Although I bring in examples from different countries, the primary focus of the book is Canada and the United States. The point is not to compare the two countries but to illustrate particular ideas about each topic from Canadian and American politics and to engage readers in topics not normally discussed in conventional political science courses.

Each chapter is an exploration of the topic at hand (I make no assumptions of previous knowledge of the topic), and the introductory section of each chapter is organized around a set of questions. The ways in which I address these questions in each chapter are by no means definitive, which is why I make clear the particular perspective that I take in the book. I have supplemented each chapter with a brief list of films, video clips, or websites to provoke discussions on the topic. With the advent of social media platforms like Facebook, YouTube, Instagram, Twitter, and Snapchat, it is clear that communication—and thus learning—occurs through both words and images. In some instances, these films, video clips, or websites are in keeping with the perspective of the chapter, but in many others, they offer an opposing view, provide a different approach to the topic, or have such popular appeal (e.g., web presence, or have gone viral) that it makes sense to look at *why*. I encourage readers to find more current or more relevant materials, many of which are web-based, to further enhance their learning on each topic. Although the academic sources referred to in each chapter are ones that I think should be read first-hand, I end each chapter with a short list of additional readings on the topic.

A FEMINIST LIBERAL PERSPECTIVE

The foundation of this book is a feminist liberal perspective, which points to the centrality of the individual. As you will read in the first chapter, the guiding principle of liberal individualism is not only about respecting individual separateness in which each individual is recognized as an end, and not as a means to the ends of others, but also about recognizing who we are as individuals and how we can think critically about ourselves and the world around us. The importance of the individual—the individual as the moral centre—permeates this entire text because I believe that it helps students to learn, to understand, and to think critically about the topics at hand. This is the heart of a university education.

At the same time, I also believe that seeing the importance of the individual will help students in their lives outside of the classroom. As a political science professor who has taught undergraduate students for over a quarter of a century and as a mother of two adult university-educated children whose working lives have recently begun, I am aware that many students are in university for both intrinsic and extrinsic reasons. Intrinsically, students are motivated because they want to learn, to understand, and to develop critical thinking, reading, and writing skills. Extrinsically, students are motivated because they want to find a job and to achieve independent economic means. Even before they graduate, students should read Sheryl Sandberg's (2014) *Lean In (for Graduates)*, a bestselling book advising women to put themselves forward in leadership positions despite the many gender biases and obstacles that still exist. Sandberg is the chief operating officer of Facebook, and her book, first published in 2013, generated a great deal of criticism. As Anne-Marie Slaughter (2013) argues, Sandberg identifies "lack of ambition" (i.e., women stepping back instead of leaning in) for the paucity of women in leadership positions as opposed to "lack of support" by workplaces, which are responsible for obstacles to women's success. Slaughter, an accomplished Princeton University professor who held a significant position in the US State Department under then Secretary of State Hillary Clinton, authored "Why Women Still Can't Have It All," which compellingly details the systemic obstacles that women continue to face in society, particularly in the workplace (Slaughter 2012). Young feminists, too, have been highly critical of Sandberg's work, linking what they see as her brand of privileged white feminism to the rise of Hillary Clinton, accounting for why young feminists are unenthusiastic about Clinton's candidacy for the presidency (Mirhashem 2015). Their focus is less on the individual woman overcoming gender barriers to potentially become president of the United States, and more on the continuing obstacles that other women continue to face based on race, class, sexual orientation, gender identity, ethnicity, religion, and/or able-bodiedness. However, I am struck by the words of a recent graduate on the importance of the individual. Writing in *The Atlantic*, she relates why, after critiquing Sandberg while in university, she has a change of heart:

> Oddly enough, I ended up taking a second look at Sheryl Sandberg, whose neglect of the pervasiveness of racial, socioeconomic, and gender-based social barriers sparked such criticism from my college self (then safely at school on my parents' dime). Not so (or not so much) anymore: What I needed now, far more than feminist theory, was someone to tell me that I did have the personal strength to respond to the vast, impossibly complex challenges of finding meaningful work in this economy and preparing to navigate the professional world as a young woman. I needed an example of someone who had the audacity to consider the individual, not society, the center of paradigm shifts. I needed a reminder that I owed it to myself to respect the power of my own agency. (Barthel 2014)

Chapter 1
POLITICS AND SEX: A FEMINIST LIBERAL PERSPECTIVE

INTRODUCTION

Many students growing up in Canada and the United States cannot help but think about themselves as sexual beings, about their erotic desires and need to couple, if not for love, then for sex. This is because they have been introduced to sex education as part of school curriculum (Public Health of Agency Canada 2008), have grown up as part of the "hook up" culture (Claxton and van Dulmen 2013), and have largely been freed from the sexual mores of the past. Not only are they products of the sexual revolution in the West, where casual sex has become relatively commonplace, but they have also been bombarded with sexual imagery that, with the rise of the digital age, has become a pervasive part of their lives. Students are not alone in experiencing that "sex sells" in Western consumption-oriented societies. The sexualization of the film, television, music, fashion, gaming, and sports industries, coupled with new media platforms, has meant that sex is *literally* everywhere.

At the same time, the term *sex* has another meaning. Sex is a reference not only to erotic desires and experiences, but also to differences between women and men. Most people identify as one or the other, evident, for example, in references to the "opposite sex," but many students today are the least likely to see that such differences matter. Partly why feminist ideas are seen as outdated is because women's rights in the Western world have progressed to the point that overt discrimination against women in political institutions, work environments, and even university classrooms has arguably become a relic of the past. Indeed, the idea that "politics is a man's game" has few adherents in the 21st century. Women throughout the West and in many parts of the world are becoming national leaders, cabinet members, legislators, judges, and diplomats. For example, although men still dominate the highest echelons of government, the need to have a greater, if not equal, number of women in the legislature and/or the executive is becoming more overt. When the 30-member cabinet of newly elected Liberal prime minister Justin Trudeau was sworn into office in November 2015, it was composed of an equal number of women and men. When Trudeau was asked by reporters why his executive was composed in this way, his pithy reply of "Because it's 2015" not only resulted in greater international attention for the new Canadian prime minister but also demonstrated societal acceptance of gender equality. In addition, although both Canada and the United States have yet to be governed for a sustained period of time by a female national leader (Canada's Conservative prime minister Kim Campbell governed for a little over four months until she lost in the October 25, 1993, federal election and, as of February 2016, the United States has never had a woman president), women are becoming Canadian provincial premiers and US state governors in greater numbers. When Premier Kathleen Wynne of Ontario was sworn into office in February 2013, she became not only the first woman to lead Canada's largest province but also the first openly lesbian premier in the country. Moreover, in their own lives, many students do not see work opportunities limited simply because they are female, nor do female students find themselves overshadowed in university classrooms by their male peers. Indeed, not only are more women becoming the primary breadwinners in Canadian and American households, but more women than men are also attending university in Canada and the United States across many undergraduate and postgraduate programs.

Politics is about power, and power speaks to conflict, co-operation, and change among and within entities such as intergovernmental or transnational bodies, sovereign states, levels of government, market agents, civil society actors, and individuals. Traditional understandings of power centre on conflict and relationships of dominance where one group or individual changes the behaviour of another by means that range from persuasion using words to violence using guns. Less conventional understandings, including feminist ones, centre on co-operation and relationships of collaboration and partnership where groups or individuals work together for change to the mutual benefit of all. Students of political science understand that power is the key concept in their discipline, and the extent to which power infuses both understandings of "sex" is the focus of this book. At its simplest, sex in terms of erotic desires and experiences speaks to sexuality, and sex in terms of differences between women and men speaks to gender. Many students of political science may have been exposed to the notion of gender, either in a "Women and Politics" course or as a component of a course, such as feminist critiques of international relations, but explicit discussions of sexual desires and experiences are rarely found in the work of mainstream political scientists, and yet sexuality is highly political. As Veronique Mottier (2008, 1–2) explains, "sexuality, understood as the way in which people experience their bodies, pleasures and desires, … is shaped by social and political forces and connects in important ways to relations of power around class, race, and, especially gender." Mottier (2008) provides an excellent introduction to sexuality, and students in political science unfamiliar with the term would benefit from reading her concise treatment of the field.

The objective of this book is to show how power infuses gender in ways that focus on sexuality. As evident in the analyses of topics in this book, the linkages between politics, gender, and sexuality draw attention to continuing challenges faced by women, inviting further inquiry into relations between women and men. This is not a primary source of interest these days in feminist academic circles, in large part because gender theory has given way to queer theory, patriarchy to intersectionality, liberalism to post-colonialism, and feminist empiricism to postmodernism. Yet, being a woman or a man remains at the heart of how the vast majority of people live their lives in the world, so that from high-level governmental discussions of power and gender to everyday conversations, the focus continues to be on women and their relationship to men.

Underpinning analyses in this book are four key ideas. First of all, women and men matter as individuals because they share a common humanity, which not only makes them more similar than different, but also cautions treating "women" and "men" as fixed or essentialist categories. This is because there are multiple systems of dominance, and alongside sexism are racism, classism, heterosexism (including homophobia and transphobia), and ableism. This second idea shows that individual women face differing obstacles to equality and that human dignity, if it is to be realized, must account for how some women are privileged and other women are disadvantaged because they are subject to differing—and intersecting—systems of dominance. Thirdly, captured by the radical feminist slogan that "the personal is political," power in the home has to be recognized because it is the home where women have historically been relegated, and there is nothing more "personal" than sexuality. At the same time, sexual relations are changing due to what Anthony Giddens (1992) has observed as the transformation of intimacy in the West. This leads to the fourth idea, which centres on women's sexual freedoms brought about by the sexual revolution, specifically in Western liberal democracies. Here, although notable progress in gender and sexual equality has been evident, the challenges from socially conservative, if not fundamentalist, circles both at home and abroad stand to undermine the progress that has been made.

Egalitarianism is a central principle of a liberal democracy, and although historically individual rights were limited to white, propertied, heterosexual, able-bodied men in states like Canada and the United States, the advancement of individual rights continues to be evident. Governments in liberal democracies have played an important role in specifically ending discrimination, but scholars today are divided on whether government is instrumental or detrimental to the realization of equality. For example, critical feminist scholars drawing from Marxism, anti-racism, or postmodernism would not only offer differing ideas about politics, gender, and sexuality than are offered here, but also critique and reject that a liberal democracy holds any real promise for marginalized groups and individuals. Scholars from these perspectives largely see government as the problem, and because liberal democracies are rooted in the West, many also see the West as the problem. This is because underpinning many of their critiques is an anti-capitalist stance, encapsulated in their understanding of liberal ideas primarily in terms of neo-liberalism or neo-liberal globalization, which means that they see capitalism as a fundamental part of the problem of liberal democracies.

It is clear that more needs to be done to reconcile the universal ideals of equality, freedom, and justice, and the actual material conditions of peoples, particularly racial or ethnic minorities. For example, within Canada and the United States, the impoverished situations of Aboriginal Canadians and black Americans, their higher rates of being murdered or incarcerated, and the deterioration of their family and community structures can be directly attributable to a legacy of systemic racism. From a global perspective where economic and racial injustices have been perpetuated by the West both as colonial and neo-colonial powers, many peoples throughout Africa, Asia, Latin America, and the

Middle East remain subject to a globalized capitalism that disproportionately benefits the West and core economic elites in their regions of the world. Problematically, however, arguments that stem from the injustices created by global economic inequalities have extended to charges of Western cultural imperialism where it is argued that, under the guise of protecting individual rights, liberal democracies have imposed their values on the post-colonial world. Specifically, human rights are seen as Western cultural values as opposed to universal ones. Moreover, with the changing face of immigration in Western states like Canada and the United States due to the countries of origin of immigrants shifting from Europe to many parts of the post-colonial world, similar sorts of critiques about racism and cultural imperialism have also taken hold within liberal democracies. In particular, feminism rooted in liberal ideas, commonly known as liberal feminism, has been implicated as reflecting the experiences of the privileged few, namely white, Western, heterosexual, middle-class women.

These sorts of critiques have their adherents, but these are not the approaches taken here in the examination of politics, gender, and sexuality. The purpose of this introductory chapter is to show why a *feminist liberal* perspective is a compelling way to organize thinking around six topics that will be examined in this book: (1) body politics, (2) the veiling of women, (3) female genital mutilation/cutting, (4) rape and sexual violence, (5) pornography, and (6) prostitution and trafficking. The shift in terminology from *liberal feminism* to *feminist liberalism* is deliberate because of the importance of liberal ideas of equality and rights, specifically as they pertain to gender and sexuality. As Ruth Abbey (2011, 8–9) points out, using the term *liberal feminism* has in many ways become problematic. It invites comparisons to other types of feminisms, which have resulted in unfounded characterizations of what liberal feminism entails. For example, critics have pointed out that, according to liberal feminism, women's equality with men means sameness, which it does not, given that "liberalism's promise of equal dignity as persons … makes no *a priori* commitment to masculine standards of judgement and achievement and provides, moreover, normative grounds for criticizing their wholesale application to women" (Abbey 2011, 9). Critics have also argued that the idea of rights is simply a Western construct, which it is not, given that peoples throughout the world use rights language to fight against injustice and demand for equality (Nussbaum 1999, 66–67). Abbey (2011) explores the works and ideas of three significant feminist liberal thinkers: Susan Moller Okin, Jean Hampton, and Martha Nussbaum, asserting that "their feminism is an extension of their liberalism" (8).

For the purposes of this book, the ideas in Nussbaum's *Sex and Social Justice* (1999), complemented by the ideas in Anthony Giddens's *The Transformation of Intimacy* (1992) and Jeffrey Weeks's *The World We Have Won* (2007), provide the basis for the perspective presented in this chapter. Nussbaum is an American political philosopher whose significant contributions, as exemplified by Abbey (2011), are widely read, cited, and debated. Because Nussbaum's work addresses the great philosophical issues in political science regarding justice, equality, and liberty, it rightly serves as a foundation for others in articulating their particular perspective. Giddens is a British sociologist whose work has made notable impact beyond both his discipline and academia, and Weeks has been recognized as the most important British intellectual in the study of sexuality. All three have been extremely prolific in their writings, and those who are well acquainted with their contributions would see why their ideas are in many ways complementary, particularly the three texts drawn for the perspective for this book.

A feminist liberal perspective rests on the importance of sexual freedoms, particularly for women and, accordingly, it stems from a particular moment in time, namely women's sexual liberation in the West beginning in the 1960s. This was an important moment, precipitated in many ways by the revolutionary impact of the birth control pill; the delinking of sexual intercourse and reproduction resulted in "a radical transformation of the conditions of female sexuality with, in turn, profound consequences for male sexuality" (Mottier 2008, 56). Without the fear of pregnancy, women were better able to take control of their lives. Being sexually active no longer had to be within the confines of marriage, and sexual permissiveness along with a rethinking of love, sex, and relationships dramatically altered Western understandings of sexuality (Mottier 2008, 56). "The Pill has achieved mythological status as the harbinger of women's liberation," as Weeks (2007, 69) has pointed out, but "it is difficult to see how better contraception, in women's hands, could have been so effective without an accompanying transformation in women's sense of their sexual freedom to choose" (70). Although the sexual revolution came to be seen as a heterosexual revolution, "the loosening of moral control over sexuality, combined with the weakening of legal regulations against deviant sexualities, created societal conditions" for the gay liberation movement (Mottier 2008, 76). The women's and gay liberation movements shared a great deal in common. "Both movements were concerned with freeing individuals from the burdens of history, whether of tradition, patriarchy, homophobia or heteronormativity, and at their heart is the assumption of individual autonomy" (Weeks

2007, 84). This idea of individual autonomy ties together the works of Nussbaum, Giddens, and Weeks.

A feminist liberal perspective has four central elements:

1. Understanding the guiding principle of liberal individualism,
2. Identifying systems of dominance that undermine individual autonomy,
3. Accounting for the transformation of intimacy, and
4. Recognizing progress and the focus on capabilities.

In discussing this perspective, the next section examines the "feminist sex wars," which were particularly acute during the 1980s, and the "culture wars" of yesteryear and today. Women's sexual liberation has not only created a divide between certain feminist groups but, more problematically, also emboldened conservative reactionary movements both within and outside the West. These conservative groups have, under the guise of protecting "family values" or defending culture, sought to reverse or, in the case of more traditional societies, reject sexual reforms. It has also spawned strange bedfellows between radical feminists and religious conservatives in the West, not only in their focus on male aggression, specifically expressed in the uncontrolled male sexual appetite, but also in their common opposition to the sex industry, particularly pornography and prostitution. The topics studied in this book are concerned primarily with heterosexual relations because of the continuing valorization of the heterosexual conjugal bond, which centres on the uncritical acceptance that sex must always be relational (ruling out self-satisfaction), dyadic (ruling out multiple partners), heterosexual (ruling out sexual minorities), and meaningful (ruling out pure carnal pleasure). This has resulted not only in the marginalization of sexual minorities, which has been the primary concern of many scholars of sexuality, but also in the disempowerment of women, which is the primary concern here. As Nussbaum (1999, 17) asserts, "the desire to control women's reproductive functioning and to maintain control over their sexuality has been a major impetus behind various restrictions on women's public role." Gender and sexuality are intricately connected in the way power has been exercised over women's public and private lives.

At the same time, there has been a "gender revolution," one in which "millennia of male dominance over women have been fundamentally and almost certainly irreversibly undermined, even as on a global scale the impact is still uneven" (Weeks 2007, 7). Although Weeks recognizes that gender equality is far from being realized even in the

West, he stresses that "the real achievement is that inequality has lost all its moral justification, and this has profoundly shifted the debate.... The starting point has to be the full human equality of men and women, and from this flows all the other forms of equality" (7). Indeed, Giddens (1992) argues that there is even more reason to be optimistic about gender relations, specifically in the West. The feminist movement has brought about the democratization of personal life, which has paralleled the democratization of politics in the 20th century, resulting in the "pure relationship," which is void of hierarchy, patriarchy, and structure. This "transformation of intimacy," as Giddens calls it, is where the democratic ideals of personal autonomy and responsibility are realized, and it can be seen in conjunction with the transformation of the polity.

Fundamentally, focusing on gender does not have to pit women against men. There is little credence to the idea that "the record of injustice [in which men have dominated women] erodes, practically speaking, all possibilities of sympathy, trust, and love between women and men" (Nussbaum 1999, 14). In addition, focusing on sexuality is not about studying sexual behaviour outside of the context of human longing for meaningful relationships. The right to choose to have sex whenever, however, and with whomever individuals want should be fundamental, but exercising that right does not mean that they also do not want intimacy, love, and family. Conservative reactionaries and cultural defenders in particular do not, and should not, have a monopoly on defining marital love or "family values." Conservative arguments rest on the heterosexual conjugal bond as the foundation of family and society, which has both condemned sexual minorities and undermined gains made by women. The sexual revolution has indeed been a turning point, but sexuality is not simply about sex and erotic fulfillment, but also about love, intimacy, and partnership characterized by autonomy and equality. As Giddens (1992) argues, the "pure relationship" is characteristic of both opposite-sex and same-sex couples where "gay women and men have preceded most heterosexuals in developing relationships ... in conditions of relative equality between partners" (15). Intimacy can be transformed, but the problem is that for many women, inequalities persist in their private and public lives and their individual autonomy is far from being realized. The four central elements of a feminist liberal perspective are outlined in the remainder of this chapter.

THE GUIDING PRINCIPLE OF LIBERAL INDIVIDUALISM

Liberal ideas are out of fashion among many feminists in academia because, as Amy Baehr (2004a, 1) points out, the idea that "liberalism and feminism are incompatible has been arguably the *dominant* view among feminist scholars over the past thirty years." Part of this perceived incompatibility stems from the importance of the individual in liberal thinking, and the belief that individualism necessarily means egoism or self-sufficiency (Nussbaum 1999, 59). These traits are seen as incongruent with the lives of women whose reproductive and caregiving roles make them more attached to others. However, there are many liberalisms, just as there are many feminisms (Baehr 2004b), but, too often, the liberalism that is criticized is that associated with contemporary neo-liberal or neo-classical economic thinking. Neo-liberalism is a set of ideas "developed by economists in the global North and imposed there and on the global South" (Peterson and Runyan 2010, 20), underpinning economic globalization, where governments relinquish their responsibilities to provide health, education, and other social services to their citizens; where they compete with other states to lower tax, wage, labour, and environmental standards in order to attract investment; and where they suppress political opposition and restrict civil and political rights in order to provide a corporate-friendly environment. Neo-liberal globalization is "a major source of structural violence" (Peterson and Runyan 2010, 19) where there is "a total faith in the market, unfettered by state regulation and protection for its citizens" (20). Although there have been debates, for example, on the continuing strength of neo-liberal thinking in the Canadian context because of the rise of the "social investment perspective," which recognizes that the government has become more interventionist in the economy, it is clear that "Canadian women, in general, have not fared well under neo-liberalism and ... certain groups of women have had a much harder time than others" (Dobrowolsky 2009, 4). Neo-liberalism is incompatible with feminist liberal thinking. Rather, feminist liberal ideas align with "enlightened capitalism" (Cudd 2011) or "Marxian liberalism" (Reiman 2012).

Liberal individualism, as Nussbaum (1999, 59–67) argues, is not about egoism or self-sufficiency. Liberalism is about individual separateness where each individual is recognized as an end, and not as a means to the ends of others. It is the recognition of the separateness of one life from another and the equal importance of each life. This recognition does not mean that women do not or should not put others before themselves. Nussbaum asserts that many liberal thinkers have made compassion, care, and love an essential part of their normative understandings (10), but what concerns her is not that women sacrifice their well-being for others, such as their husbands or children, but that they are forced to do so out of a care and love that have been constructed under unjust conditions, such as convention, tradition, or worse yet, coercion and violence.

Women must be able to freely choose for themselves, but too often women are treated not as individuals but as merely extensions of their husbands and children. That is why Nussbaum emphasizes the importance of understanding how preference and desire are shaped by social norms that, in some instances, may be unjust, and of how "women's propensity to care for others veers over into an undignified self-abnegation in which a woman subordinates her humanity utterly to the needs of another or others" (13). As Nussbaum argues:

> The central question of politics should not be, How is the organic whole doing?, but rather, How are X and Y and Z and Q doing? The central goal for politics will be some sort of amelioration in the lives of X and Y and Z and Q.... Putting things this way does not require us to deny that X might love Y intensely and view his life as worthless without Y; it does not require that Z and Q do not plan their lives together and aim at shared ends.... It just asks us to concern ourselves ... to see how well *each and every one of them is doing*, seeing each and every one as an end, worthy of concern. (62)

The importance of the individual becomes even clearer in the context of sexual freedoms in the West, where the individual in question is you, me, your partner, or my partner, speaking to how individuals live their lives. As Weeks (2007, 125) points out, "one of the most striking features of contemporary sexuality is the emphasis many put on self-invention, on the creation of a viable sense of self, which has become a key element of the individualizing process." Individuals are engaged, as Giddens states (1992, 8) in "everyday social experiments" where, in the course of living their lives, they deal with "wider social changes" related to marriage, family, and sexuality. In the introduction to *The Transformation of Intimacy*, Giddens (1992, 1–2) writes that he had "set out to write on sex [but he] found [himself] writing just as much about love; and about gender ... [because] women—ordinary women, going about their day-to-day lives, as well as self-consciously feminist groups—have pioneered changes of great, and generalizable, importance." With the democratization of personal life brought about by the feminist movement, the "capacity of individuals to be self-reflective and self-determining," to be autonomous, has become more of a reality (Giddens 1992, 185). Sexuality today has been "made meaningful through language ... [and] among the most powerful terms are those associated with self-making and self-invention" (Weeks 2007, 126). At the same time, individualism is also about "reciprocity and care," that is, it "is about more than doing your own thing" (133). It is a self-reflexive process whereby individuals focusing on themselves and realizing their freedoms to decide their fates also demand it for others: "If the end of the individual is self-determination, then the higher purpose to which the individual is committed is likely to be the self-determination of others" (Heller and Feher 1988, 36 as quoted in Weeks 2007, 133).

The idea that each individual is the starting point for understanding others also helps to provide insight into the value of a university education. Universities are places to develop critical thinking skills, and research is at the heart of that endeavour. That is why many students at the undergraduate level are encouraged to write research papers. Because a methodology refers to the theory and analysis of how research does or should proceed, it is from a methodological viewpoint that feminists have critiqued dominant views in the social sciences (Tickner 2005). Feminist critiques include questioning the assumption of an unbiased, objective, detached researcher whose goal is to understand the reality "out there" with little reflection on how she or he may be an integral part of that reality. "Whereas personal experience is thought by conventional social science to contaminate a project's objectivity, feminists believe one's awareness of one's personal position in the research process to be a corrective to 'pseudo-objectivity'" (Tickner 2005, 9). A feminist methodology demands self-reflexivity on the part of the researcher because not only does it matter who the researcher is, for example, in terms of gender, sexual orientation, gender identity, race, ethnicity, class, or disability, but the research also has impact on both the research subjects and what society considers important as research. For too long women, sexual minorities, racial or ethnic minorities, poor people, and disabled people have all been left out of research, both as researchers and research subjects.

This demand for self-reflexivity on the part of the researcher is crucial for understanding differences between individual women. Just as the experiences of women and men are differentiated because of gender, so too are the experiences of women differentiated because of sexual orientation, gender identity, race, ethnicity, class, and/or disability. The concept of intersectionality has arisen in feminist thinking, not only because of the multiple identity markers that women have, but also because of the interconnection of multiple systems of dominance or oppression. For example, a black woman can face inequalities based on both her gender and her race. Indeed, *intersectionality*, a term coined by black feminist Kimberle Crenshaw, originally pointed to how both feminist theory and anti-racist policy discourse marginalize the experiences of black women. As Crenshaw (2011) has argued, "the intersectional experience is greater than the sum of racism and sexism [and] any analysis that does not take intersectionality into account cannot sufficiently address the particular manner in which black women are subordinated" (26). Crenshaw's critique of feminist theory brings out two key arguments: first, feminism has reflected only the experiences of white women and, thus, it has not taken into account the experiences of others; and second, white women have been speaking for all women and, thus, they have appropriated the voices of others. These sorts of arguments are also made by post-colonial feminists who extend the critique further, often identifying the problem as white, Western, middle-class women (for example, see Kempadoo's [2012] critique of the abolitionist approach to anti-trafficking).

Although the problems with these critiques have been identified elsewhere, not least that perhaps what should worry many feminists more are patriarchy, homophobia, transphobia, racism, global economic inequality, and ableism, and that they should place less focus on the problem as white women (Ralston and Keeble 2009), the self-reflexive researcher needs to be aware of her privilege in relation to her research subjects.

> Reflexivity is important not only for explaining agency … but also for explaining how we come to be gendered and sexual subjects who take part in the interactive processes through which we produce a shared sense of reality and get the business of everyday life done.… The self cannot exist outside of the social and that human social action is founded on interpretive processes.… To have a sense of self is to be aware of ourselves as both separate from others and situated *in relation to* others. (Rahman and Jackson 2010, 165–66)

The critiques around appropriation of voice stem from the difficulties of knowing and representing others, but it cannot be the case that knowledge is limited to those who experience it. An individual does not have to be a woman to know that sexism exists, or gay or lesbian to know that homophobia exists, or a racialized person to know that racism exists. A university education teaches individuals to learn, to know, to understand, and to think critically about the ways in which different sorts of people are dominated and empowered, and to do so in a way, according to liberal thinkers, to see their common humanity. Moreover, the issues raised by intersectional analysis can be incorporated in a feminist liberal perspective. As Abbey (2011) argues, there is a difference between moral and methodological individualism. "The individual is the moral, rather than the analytical, center of much current liberalism, with the promise of equal freedom for all being its regulative ideal" (215). The individual is the point of moral concern, where each individual is recognized as an end, and not as a means to the ends of others. The individual is not the sole unit of analysis, which means that feminist liberals have not only seen, in the first instance, women as a whole based on their subordination, but have also recognized "the sort of systematic disadvantage based on poverty and race that members of minority groups might also face" (217). In other words, moral individualism does not preclude critiques of multiple and intersecting systems of dominance or oppression, "for a society that permits individuals to be disadvantaged in these ways fails to respect the dignity and equal personhood of all its members" (217).

At the same time, students have to be careful not to confuse feminists' questioning of research objectivity in the social sciences, which is about methodology, with the premise that there are no standards for research. Understanding an individual's personal position in the research process does not mean that learning is simply about individual experiences or opinions. There is a difference between methodology and methods. Research methods are the techniques for gathering and analyzing evidence to substantiate assertions, and these techniques include qualitative interviews, statistical surveys, discourse analyses, and philosophical arguments. These techniques are referred to as primary research, and this is what academics do. As Tickner (2005, 3) argues, "there is no unique feminist method" because feminists regularly use the same methods as conventional social scientists in their work, although they differ in their methodology. Undergraduate students engage in research as part of their university education, but primarily in secondary research. This means that they read academic books and articles, as well as sources from the non-academic or popular press, such as newspapers or newsmagazines, and use the arguments of these sources to substantiate their assertions. Students do research in order to learn, to know, to understand, and to think critically. In that way, the guiding principle of liberal individualism is not only about respecting individual separateness where each individual is recognized as an end, and not as a means to the ends of others, but also about students being aware of who they are as individuals and how they can think critically about themselves and the world around them. A university education is crucial to developing that kind of critical thinking.

SYSTEMS OF DOMINANCE THAT UNDERMINE INDIVIDUAL AUTONOMY

Not everyone is in a position to have a university education, or to be self-reflexive and self-determining, or to be autonomous. Power is the currency of politics, and inequality is predicated on the exercise of power as traditionally understood in the study of political science, leading to focus on those who have it over those who do not. Governments have used laws and regulations to eliminate inequalities based on gender, sexual orientation, race, class, and able-bodiedness, yet despite laws recognizing equality, which, in Canada, is constitutionally entrenched in the Charter of Rights and Freedoms, sexism, heterosexism, racism, classism, and ableism still exist in every country throughout the world. The United Nations Development Program, in its annual *Human Development Report*, includes a Gender Inequality Index to capture the continuing inequalities between women and men globally. As Nussbaum (1999, 5) states: "Many women all over the world find themselves treated unequally with respect to employment, bodily safety and integrity, basic nutrition and health care, education, and political voice. In many cases, these hardships are caused by their being women, and in many cases laws and institutions construct or perpetuate these inequalities."

One of the charges against liberalism is that it cannot account for systems of dominance that undermine equality because of its focus on the individual. The argument here is that by "viewing people primarily as autonomous individuals, liberalism is incapable of analyzing oppression in class or group terms" (Abbey 2011, 15). For example, women are seen as individuals and not as a group who are oppressed by men as a group, leading women to believe that they may have achieved equality when, in fact, they remain subject to male-dominated structures. This critique posits that liberal feminism is the "add women and stir" approach, and by focusing on women, and not gender, liberal feminism rests on the assumption that male dominance can be corrected by incorporating women into historically male-dominated roles in society, be it in government or in the workplace (Steans 2006, 12). In the study of international relations (IR), liberal feminism is considered a limited and highly problematic approach. It has been characterized as simply dealing with legal remedies to address inequality, so that by failing to recognize that "gender inequalities continue to exist in societies that have long since achieved formal legal equality," such as in Western liberal democracies, this approach is rejected by many contemporary feminist scholars in the IR discipline (Tickner 2011, 266). These international relations scholars call themselves "post-liberal feminists" because of their characterization of liberal feminism as being unable to use gender as a category of analysis (Tickner 2011, 266).

However, drawing from the ideas of Nussbaum, a feminist liberal framework can account for systems of dominance that undermine equality, using gender as a category of analysis. Nussbaum "insist[s] on doing what feminist critics of liberalism insist it cannot: enquiring into the social forces that affect women as a group or collective" (Abbey 2011, 215). Nussbaum is interested in identifying the forces that undermine women's agency, such as the social shaping of preference and desire in order to illustrate how women's preferences have been formed under conditions of inequality. She integrates radical feminist insights into her thinking, arguing that far from turning women into victims, these insights are grounded in "a demand for equal respect, asking that laws and institutions truly acknowledge women's equal worth in ways they have not previously done" (Nussbaum 1999, 20). In order to bring out gender as a category of analysis in this way, it is important to understand the distinctions not simply between sex and gender, but also, more importantly, between "gender-as-difference" and "gender-as-power" (Beckman and D'Amico 1994, 3–8). This will lead to an examination of the "feminist sex wars."

The conventional distinction between sex and gender is often understood as one between "nature," which is about biology, and "nurture," which is about culture or society. The term *sex* refers to the biological and physiological differences that define male and female, whereas *gender* refers to the socially constructed roles, behaviours, activities, and attributes that a given culture or society considers appropriate for men and women, specifically in defining what is masculine and what is feminine. The most common biologically accepted traits that differentiate males from females stem from their physical differences, notably their genitalia (a male has a penis; a female has a vagina), their reproductive roles (only a female can bear children), and their chemical or hormonal levels (a male has more testosterone; a female has more estrogen) (Beckman and D'Amico 1994, 3). Sex differences are, generally speaking, accepted universally, although they are not immutable categories given that intersex people who, like other sexual minorities, have faced widespread discrimination and, problematically, have had to face the surgical removal or modification of their genitals in order to force conformity to a particular sex. Gender differences may vary greatly throughout the world because societies or cultures may differ in how they construct roles, behaviours, activities, and attributes that they consider appropriate for men and women. "Male" and "female" are sex categories, while "masculinity" and "femininity" are gender categories, and they relate to each other because men (namely those with male physical attributes such as a penis) are expected to be masculine and women (namely those with female physical attributes such as a vagina) are expected to be feminine. Yet these, too, are not immutable categories given the discrimination also faced by transgender people, namely those who gender identify as men, but do not have male genitalia and those who gender identify as women, but do not have female genitalia. Although it is important to recognize that intersex and transgender people do not fit conventional distinctions between sex and gender, accounting for the discrimination they face as sexual and gender minorities, understanding what these conventional distinctions mean for women explains the significance of gender as a category of analysis. The classic example to bring out the distinctions between sex and gender is: women give birth because of their sex, but they take care of children because of their gender (see Vickers 1997, 25).

However, taking care of children is not simply a statement of gender differences between men and women where, for example, masculinity is defined as being rational and detached, and femininity as being emotional and caring, thus explaining why it is women who take care of children. The idea of "gender-as-power" brings out the unequal relationship between men and women where men dominate women. In this case, gender is not merely about what defines masculinity and femininity, but also about the hierarchical relationship between the two, which has led to the perpetuation and normalization of masculine roles, behaviours, activities, and attributes as superior to feminine ones. This translates to valuing men and what men do, and devaluing women and what women do. That is why, historically speaking, taking care of children has been either unpaid work because it has been done primarily by women as mothers or grandmothers, or low-wage work because it has been a female-dominated profession. The devaluing of feminine roles, behaviours, activities, and attributes (however *feminine* may be defined in any given culture or society) is an aspect of gender that not only has not differed greatly throughout the world, but also has been evident throughout history.

The importance of gender as a category of analysis is crucial in the study of sexuality. For too long, the norm of study has been male sexual behaviour, with abnormality being defined at various points as either women's excessive sexual urges or women's lack of interest in sex. Furthermore, because the norm has been heterosexuality, homosexuality has been seen as a perversion. Given that large-scale sexuality studies have shown, for example, that there is more of a continuum between normal and abnormal sexual practices for both women and men, and that same-sex relations are a common feature in many people's lives, questions have been raised about the idea of "natural" sexual instincts and the conception of "normalcy," and this questioning has been fuelled by anti-essentialist perspectives in the social sciences and the humanities beginning in the 1970s (Mottier 2008, 25–48). These perspectives "reject the idea of sexuality as natural or biological, emphasizing instead the social nature of the sexual experience … [so that] sexual identities are not merely the expression of natural instincts, but are social as well as political constructs" (Mottier 2008, 47). These ideas arose out of the sexual liberation movement with greater attention being paid to female sexuality.

Many feminist groups have been divided on what sexual liberation has meant for women, resulting in the "feminist sex wars," which were particularly prominent in the 1980s. On one side are those who assert that sexual liberation has been crucial for women's liberation, arguing that women have as much right to sexual pleasure as men, and by exercising that right, they can free themselves of male domination. As feminist sex researcher Shere Hite famously remarked, "Lack of sexual satisfaction is another sign of the oppression of women" (as quoted in Mottier 2008, 61). These ideas are part of sex-radical or sex-positive feminism. On the other side are those who argue that "the [sexual] revolution was less an increase in sexual freedom for women [and more] about the fulfillment of male fantasies about female availability [so that] the rhetoric of sexual liberation [merely] legitimized male control of women's sexuality" (Mottier 2008, 57–58). These are ideas associated with radical feminism.

Sexuality has become the battleground between radical feminist and sex-radical feminist groups, and their positions on pornography and prostitution crystallize their differences. Radical feminists regard sexuality (and thus any kind of sex work, such as pornography and prostitution) as inherently exploitative within male-dominated systems. The focus of radical feminists is on male sexuality, which they see as fundamentally grounded in violence. Catherine MacKinnon, a prominent leader and thinker of radical feminism, has argued that the social meaning of sex is created by the sexual objectification of women where women are treated merely as objects for satisfying men's desires. She asserts that masculinity is defined as sexual dominance, and femininity as sexual submissiveness, so that gender differences are created through the eroticization of dominance and submission. Gender is by definition hierarchical, and this hierarchy is fundamentally tied to sexual power relations where the hierarchy has been internalized by both men and women. Accordingly, men eroticize domination and learn to achieve sexual satisfaction; and women eroticize submission and learn to find sexual satisfaction in being dominated. As MacKinnon (1989) has stated:

> To be clear: what is sexual is what gives a man an erection. Whatever it takes to make the penis shudder and stiffen with the experience of its potency is what sexuality means culturally.... What is understood as violation, conventionally penetration and intercourse, defines the paradigmatic sexual encounter.... All this suggests that what is called sexuality is the dynamic of control by which male dominance—in forms that range from intimate to institutional, from a look to rape—eroticizes and thus defines man and woman, gender identity and sexual pleasure. It is also that which maintains and defines male supremacy as a political system. (137)

Sex-radical feminists, in contrast, regard sexuality (and thus any kind of sex work, such as pornography and prostitution) as undermining male-dominated definitions of how femininity has been traditionally understood. They focus on female sexuality as the realization not only of the sexual freedoms of women, but also of greater equality between women and men. To them, the radical feminist position is not only anti-sex, but also anti-men. They refer to themselves as "sex-positive" feminists who not only have "rejected the 'depressing' views of sex that reduced female sexual pleasure in intercourse to the result of male brainwashing," but also have condemned the "disturbing political alliances" that radical feminists make with conservative religious groups who have been fighting the women's and gay rights movements (Mottier 2008, 70).

It is important to understand, however, that both radical and sex-radical feminist groups are equally concerned with the realization of women's sexual freedoms, but given the radical feminist perception of the intractable nature of patriarchy, particularly evident in women's sexual lives, they simply cannot see how male dominance can be overcome. That is why radical feminist groups appear to be anti-sex and anti-men. Gender is not the only category of analysis where it is not simply about difference but about power; the exercise of power is seen in differences in sexual orientation, gender identity, race, ethnicity, class, disability, and other identity markers. Although radical feminist critiques focus on gender, these critiques can be seen in conjunction with multiple and intersecting systems of dominance that undermine individual autonomy and perpetuate inequality. The valorization of the heterosexual conjugal bond stems from the intersecting hierarchies of gender and sexual orientation, privileging men and heterosexuality. However, gender relations can and do change. That is why Nussbaum (1999) wants "to combine a radical feminist critique of sex relations with an interest in the possibilities of trust and understandings" between women and men (14). In other words, Nussbaum puts forward a conception of feminism that highlights structures, systems, laws, and institutions that have perpetuated male dominance, aggression, and even violence toward women, without blaming individual men; and in the case of hierarchical sexual relations that rest on male control of female sexuality, without rejecting sex. As she states: "Even in societies that nourish problematic roles for men and women, real men and women can also find spaces in which to subvert those conventions, resourcefully creating possibilities of love and joy" (14).

THE TRANSFORMATION OF INTIMACY

The idea that liberalism simply looks at political institutions and laws, accounting for critiques that liberal feminism offers only legal remedies to rectifying gender inequalities, stems from the public-private distinction central to classical liberal thinking. Although the term *public* has traditionally been understood as a reference to activities associated only with the government, feminists have regarded the public more broadly to include activities associated with businesses or corporations as well as those associated with non-governmental or non-profit organizations. They do so because the government, business, and civil society sectors are all workplaces that can provide waged labour, and feminists reserve the term *private* to refer only to the household or domestic sphere where women have historically been relegated (Squires 2003). Focusing on the private in this way leads feminists to highlight two principal problems with the public-private distinction. First, there is the problematic assumption that the family is necessarily composed of a breadwinner father who undertakes waged work outside of the home to support the family, and a stay-at-home mother who takes care of the children and undertakes other household tasks, such as cleaning and preparing meals for the family. Second, there is the problematic assumption that politics occurs only in the public realm so that liberal ideas of equality and rights are seen as irrelevant to the private domain because it is assumed that love, not power, is exercised in the home.

The heart of radical feminism is identifying the extent to which the home has also been a site for male dominance. What can be more private than sex? "Feminist critique has exposed the ways in which sexuality, an area of life traditionally constructed as private, impacts upon women's lives in an adverse way which should not be beyond the sphere of politics" (Lacey 1993, 110). Arguing that "the personal is political," radical feminists have focused on issues revolving around male control of female sexuality, such as domestic violence and marital rape, in order to bring out how power is exercised in the home. They have regarded the family as a patriarchal institution, evident in the view of the father as the head of the household, and they did not see the sexual revolution leading to women's sexual freedoms but rather to men's greater access to women's bodies. As stated earlier, Nussbaum (1999) incorporates these radical feminist insights into her thinking. As she argues further, the construction of the family as a non-political entity with congenial interests characterized by "organic unity and harmony" is not reflective of the reality that families are sites of "competition for resources, divergent interests, and differences of power" (Nussbaum 1999, 65). Male dominance in the private sphere is just as unacceptable as in the public sphere. That is why Nussbaum points out that "what we see here is not a failure intrinsic to liberalism itself [but] ... a failure of liberal thinkers to follow their own thought through to its socially radical conclusion" (65).

A feminist liberal perspective accounts for inequalities in the home, but the hierarchical structure of the family has been changing in the West. In large part, this is due to more women working outside of the home—and controlling their income (keeping in mind that many women in poor families have always needed to work outside of the home)—because economic dependency has been a primary reason for women's inequality. That is why Nussbaum (1999) highlights the importance of waged labour outside of the home, and the necessity for governments to eliminate barriers and ensure equal pay. This gives women the freedom to exercise choices in their lives, from leaving an abusive relationship to realizing their own worth and dignity. This does not mean that women who choose not to work outside of the home are making choices that should not be valued; rather, it is the fact that they are able to make a choice that must be the subject of attention. Many women throughout the world simply do not have these choices because of the laws and institutions that they are under, or the cultural or societal attitudes that they face. One of the surest ways for women to protect themselves and their children is to have independent economic means.

At the same time, this argument goes well beyond changes in women's economic activities and greater presence in the public sphere. The hierarchical structure of the family in the West has been fundamentally undermined because of the realization of women's sexual freedoms. The sexual revolution has led to both intimacy and masculinity being redefined, undermining the valorization of the heterosexual conjugal bond and creating the conditions for the "pure relationship" in which, according to Giddens (1992, 58), "a social relation is entered into for its own sake, for what can be derived by each person from a sustained association with another; and which is continued only in so far as it is thought by both parties to deliver enough satisfactions for each individual to stay within it." This type of relationship rests on "confluent love" as opposed to romantic love, the latter "plainly allied to women's subordination in the home" but also "an expression of women's power" (43). Giddens argues that this "contradictory assertion of autonomy in the face of deprivation" (43) stems from romantic love perpetuating the idealization of motherhood where women's control of child rearing leads men to recognize them as "different, unknowable—concerned with a particular domain alien to men" (42). Romantic love is a Western cultural construction, a "feminised love," which is differentiated from passionate love, a universal phenomenon that connects love and sexual attachment (37–38). Giddens sees passionate love as potentially subversive of society, and that is why it is constrained by cultural or societal institutions.

According to Giddens, romantic love in the West is problematic because it is "held in check by the association of love with marriage and motherhood; and by the idea that true love, once found, is for ever" (46). Female sexuality is kept within the confines of marriage, at least for the "respectable" woman. Getting and staying married becomes the preoccupation of women, particularly if the marriage is "sustained by a division of labour between the sexes, with the domain of the husband that of paid work and the wife that of the home" (46). According to Giddens, men have been cynical of romantic love, and have dealt with the tensions between romantic love and the sexual compulsions of passionate love "by separating the comfort of the domestic environment from the sexuality of the mistress or whore" (43). Male sexuality is defined by "the division between unsullied and impure women," and even for those few romantic men who reject this division, they do not see women as equals because of gendered understandings of the relationship (59). Romantic love is predicated on the association of motherhood with femininity and breadwinner with masculinity because "for men self-identity was sought after in work" (60). It is rooted in conceptions of two individuals coming together to make a whole "strengthened by established differences between masculinity and femininity, each defined in terms of an antithesis" of the other (61). Although romantic love has "an egalitarian strain, intrinsic to the idea that a relationship can derive from the emotional involvement of two people, rather than external social criteria," in practice it is "thoroughly skewed in terms of power" (62).

In contrast, according to Giddens, confluent love is egalitarian and it can only develop when two people are thoroughly "prepared to reveal concerns and needs to the other and to be vulnerable to that other" (62). A crucial feature of confluent love is that it is grounded in the individual, and intimacy is sought as part of self-development. Unlike romantic love, it is not based on the idea of two halves making a whole. There is no "she or he completes me" in confluent love because if one partner perceives that the relationship is undermining the self, she or he ends the relationship. There is no "forever" in confluent love; it is contingent on both parties finding satisfaction, and a key part of that satisfaction is "reciprocal sexual pleasure" (62). Sexual satisfaction by both partners is a key component, and although Giddens is silent on whether masturbation is a recognized means, his focus on the individual does not preclude its use in the context of a relationship.

Confluent love, then, rests on women's sexual freedoms brought about by the sexual revolution. As Giddens argues, the severing of reproduction from sexual intercourse has freed women to pursue their sexual pleasures without fear of pregnancy or dying from childbirth. He talks about "plastic sexuality" to capture the extent to which sexuality has become "malleable, open to being shaped in diverse ways, and a potential 'property' of the individual," and he sees the emergence of reproductive technologies as "the final 'liberation' for sexuality" because "reproduction can occur in the absence of sexual activity" (27). Sex has clearly become about pleasure for both women and men, but Giddens's concerns are not only about sex and erotic fulfillment. As he makes clear, "the transmutation of love is as much a phenomenon of modernity as is the emergence of sexuality" (34). Love and sex go hand in hand, and both are grounded in the individual. "Confluent love develops as an ideal in a society where almost everyone has a chance to become sexually accomplished; and it presumes the disappearance of the schism between 'respectable' women and those who in some way lie outside the pale of orthodox social life" (63). It is not necessarily dependent on sexual exclusivity because even monogamy is negotiated between the two partners. Moreover, it "has no specific connection to heterosexuality," and indeed opposite-sex couples should look to same-sex couples because the latter are more exemplary of confluent love (63).

More importantly, confluent love undermines the valorization of the heterosexual conjugal bond by unsettling conventional understandings of masculinity in heterosexual relationships, demanding that men participate as emotional equals in the same way that women participate as sexual equals. Giddens argues that although romantic love has been infused with gender imbalances, it nevertheless has pointed to a woman's desire for intimacy, to be close to another individual, while "the desirable man has often been represented as cold and unapproachable" (62). Since confluent love "dissolves these characteristics, which are revealed as a front, recognition of male emotional vulnerability is evidently present" (62). The transformation of intimacy places both partners on an equal plane, engaging in a pure relationship as part of their individual self-development, and in the process, it disrupts problematic features of masculinity, particularly in the desire of men to prove their manhood to other men. This is where men look to other men for affirmation of their identity. Referred to as "homosocial enactment" by Michael Kimmel (2005, 33), this component ties in two other features of masculinity, namely repudiation of femininity and homophobia, evident in Western society. The connection here is that men have sexually objectified women in order to ward off any suspicion by other men that they are homosexual. "Homophobia, the fear of being perceived as gay, as not a real man, keeps men exaggerating all the traditional rules of masculinity, including sexual predation toward women. Homophobia and sexism go hand in hand" (Kimmel 2005, 37). When men engage in "pure relationships," they no longer abide by "external social criteria," focused as they are, just like women, on their self-development through the creation of intimacy. As Giddens argues, dominant understandings of masculinity and femininity no longer become relevant in defining one's self. This is the democratization of personal life brought about by the feminist movement in the West. Alongside democratizing processes where feminists and gay rights activists have impacted governmental laws and institutions, including legal remedies ending discrimination, the transformation of intimacy points to how the ideals of individual autonomy and equality can be realized in private relationships.

PROGRESS AND CAPABILITIES

Weeks (2007) states that the world now is very different from the world of the past because of a "long, convoluted, messy, unfinished but profound revolution," one that "has given rise to discourses of individual autonomy, right and sexual justice that have set new standards for judging sexual wrongs, and can empower new forms of agency" (3). It is, as Weeks's 2007 book title states, "the world we have won," and the changes that have come about "have been overwhelmingly beneficial to the vast majority of people in the West, and increasingly to people living in the South" (3). Although there are compelling grounds to be optimistic about the future, Weeks puts forward three world views that can become what he calls "traps" when assessing the future, and he refers to them as the progressive, declinist, and continuist views.

The progressive view is one that sees "the transformation as automatic or inevitable, a journey from the darkness of sexual repression into sexual freedom" (3). Weeks admits that this view is closest to his own thinking, but he argues that progress is not automatic or inevitable even in Western liberal democracies, let alone in many parts of the world where gender and sexual injustices persist. He also does not want to downplay the struggles of feminists and gay rights activists who have fought long and hard to create changes in the West, emphasizing instead that they are indicative of the kinds of grassroots movements that can move many parts of the world forward to embrace sexual pleasure, desire, diversity, and choice. In contrast, the declinist view is held by those who "lament the awful state of the present ... and to compare that with some golden age of faith, stability and family values" (5). Many of those who espouse this view frame their outlook in terms of religion, and their belief in "the truth of the gendered body, heterosexual sex, the horrors of perversity and the sanctity of faith" has compelled them to act in the political arena, and for some, to do so violently (6). Finally, the continuist view rests, fundamentally, on the argument that "nothing has really changed" (6). Composed, for example, of radical feminists who focus strictly on the unchanging nature of male violence and aggression, queer theorists who see "same sex-marriage [as] simply an assimilation into heteronormative structures," and critical political economists who see change as simply "the latest ruse of power, fully complicit with the strategic need of neo-liberalism," Weeks finds that their work is arguably out of touch with the realities of people's lives (6). As he puts plainly:

> Progressively between the 1960s and 2000s the automatic unity between sexual activity and reproduction, between sex and marriage, and between marriage and parenting, had been severed. Marriage had become, for the majority of population, a matter of choice, carrying rights and responsibilities certainly, but entered into voluntarily as and when the individuals decided largely as a sign of commitment.... [With the adoption of same-sex marriage by more and more states throughout the world] the automatic link between marriage and heterosexuality [has also been] severed. This is a profoundly symbolic rupture. It is perhaps the most dramatic illustration of this new world we have made. (15)

At the same time, there are clearly conservative forces at work throughout the world seeking to curb, reverse, or reject sexual reforms. Although Weeks recognizes that the term *culture wars* is associated with the rise of the moral majority, or the religious right, in the United States, particularly after the AIDS crisis in the 1980s, these clashes can be seen more broadly as conflicts between progressive liberal ideas and social conservative reactionary ones, including more fundamentalist iterations, all of whom "seek to restore demarcations between men and women, reaffirm heterosexual relationships and extirpate perversity" (Weeks 2007, 14). Culture is about a way of life, and the sexual revolution precipitated changes in the Western way of life that have led not only to clashes between more liberal and more conservative forces within the Western world, but also to claims of difference between Western and non-Western cultures. The contested terrain—the site of the "culture wars"—is control of sexual behaviour, specifically that of women and sexual minorities. That is why the idea of "culture wars" is evident both within states and in the global context. According to conservative critics, the Western liberal way of life has undermined the traditional family, marginalized religion, and sanctioned sexual permissiveness, if not sexual perversity. Conservative critics in the West have placed the blame on the women's rights and gay rights movements for the decline of Western society, while those outside of the West have painted women's rights and the rights of sexual minorities as Western values imposed on their way of life. Many feminists throughout the Third or post-colonial world reject Western feminism because they see it as a movement of white, middle-class, heterosexual women, but as Uma Narayan (1998) points out, Third World or post-colonial feminists often rest their view on essentialist understandings of "Western" culture and "traditional" (or Third World or non-Western) culture. Arguing that cultural essentialism is just as problematic as gender essentialism, Narayan (1998) states:

> The resulting portraits of 'Western women', 'Third World women', 'African women', 'Indian women', 'Muslim women', or the like, as well as the pictures of the 'cultures' that are attributed to these various groups of women, often remain fundamentally essentialist. They depict as homogenous groups of heterogeneous people whose values, interests, ways of life, and moral and political commitments are internally plural and divergent.... While gender essentialism often

> proceeds to assume and construct sharp binaries about the qualities, abilities, or locations of 'men' and 'women', cultural essentialism assumes and constructs sharp binaries between 'Western culture' and 'Non-western cultures' or between 'Western culture' and particular 'Other' cultures. (88)

Narayan sees cultural essentialism as "[posing] particular problems for Third World feminist agendas" (87). Although white, Western, middle-class, heterosexual women have undoubtedly played a dominant role in constructing the concerns of women as universal, which, to Narayan, is problematic, she is also concerned that Third World feminists end up validating "Third World fundamentalists who share the views of Western cultural supremacists that all such notions [like equality and human rights] are 'Western ideas'" (97), thus undermining the fight for gender equality within their own specific cultural contexts.

Widespread evidence of a transformation of intimacy, along with democratizing processes transforming the polity, can move societies forward toward gender equality. The ideals of individual autonomy and equality are universal ones, and they underpin Nussbaum's model of capabilities. According to Weeks (2007, 222), her model shows that a "universal account of social justice need not be insensitive to the variety of traditions that shape human lives, nor is it a mere projection of particularist Western values onto parts of the world with different concerns." Nussbaum lists 10 capabilities, arguing that these capabilities are central to "a life in which fully human functioning, or a kind of human functioning, will be available," a life predicated on the "dignity of the human being," and not one of "mere survival" (Nussbaum 1999, 40; see also Nussbaum 2011). These 10 capabilities are:

1. Life
2. Bodily health and integrity
3. Bodily integrity
4. Senses, imagination, and thought
5. Emotions
6. Practical reason
7. Affiliation
8. Other species, namely "being able to live with concern for and in relation to animals, plants, and the world of nature"
9. Play

10. Control over one's environment (political and material)

Nussbaum differentiates between "bodily health and integrity" and "bodily integrity" as a way to highlight the importance of both reproductive health, which includes bodily nourishment and shelter (bodily health and integrity), and freedom from sexual violence, opportunities for sexual satisfaction, and reproductive choice (bodily integrity). She states that the central goal of public policy should be to ensure that people have the necessary capabilities to function, and the distinction between "capability" and "function" is crucial. Every individual must have these capabilities, but it is her or his choice if she or he wants to exercise any particular capability (i.e., make it function). As she points out:

> Whether for religious or for other reasons, a person may prefer a celibate life to one containing sexual expression … [but] capability, not functioning, is the political goal. [Although] it is perfectly true that functionings, not simply capabilities, are what render a life fully human … for political purposes, it is appropriate for us to shoot for capabilities, and those alone. Citizens must be left free to determine their course after that. (44)

Understanding the difference between the absence of sexual freedoms and celibacy, Nussbaum goes on to make the distinction between starving and fasting to illustrate the importance of individual autonomy, highlighting that governments have a role to play in creating conditions where choice can be exercised. Clearly, the kind of control of sexual behaviour desired by social conservative critics directly undermines the central human functional capabilities of bodily integrity and emotions, which are necessary for the realization of women's rights and the rights of sexual minorities. The capability for bodily integrity includes "having opportunities for sexual satisfaction and for choice in matters of reproduction," and the capability for emotions includes "being able to have attachments to things and persons outside ourselves; being able to love those who love and care for us … [and] not having one's emotional developing blighted by fear or anxiety" (41). At the very least, from a public policy perspective, this means that efforts to threaten both reproductive rights, such as limiting access to abortion, and same-sex rights, such as defining marriage as strictly between a man and a woman, undermine individual capabilities.

Women's control of their own sexuality is central to Nussbaum's capabilities model, and this cannot be realized in an environment that valorizes the heterosexual conjugal bond. The capabilities model rests on the centrality of human dignity, and it constitutes the final aspect of a feminist liberal perspective. The question of whether women have the necessary capabilities to function as individuals, are able to choose for themselves, and are free from unjust conditions, fuels the examination of body politics, the veiling of women, female genital mutilation/cutting, rape and sexual violence, pornography, and prostitution and trafficking. This book draws from Nussbaum's (1999) *Sex and Social Justice*, not only because of the richness of her philosophical ideas, but also because of the cogency of her specific cases. It builds on her work not only by providing more contemporary examples but also in seeing how her ideas are informed by, and can more greatly inform, work on sexuality. In looking at how the study of sexuality can lead to a "better world," Ken Plummer (2008), then editor of *Sexualities*, has pointed out that "[Nussbaum's] relevance to sexualities remains unexplored" and yet her list of capabilities are "all there at the heart of sexual life," pointing to how individuals may foster "the ability—an attitude—to sense and empathize with a range of different positions in the world … and to seek out some common ways of living around them" (20). As Plummer states, only Jeffrey Weeks (2007) has explored the significance of Nussbaum's ideas to the study of sexuality, and that is why this chapter has focused on her work. By offering a feminist liberal perspective, this book encourages students to think about, debate, and conduct research on how power infuses gender in ways that focus on sexuality. As Weeks (2007, 203) states: "Globalization has made us aware of sexual wrongs across the world, has swept us up in global flows, and has awakened us to the significance of sexual rights." Individuals lead what he calls "connected lives," and fuelled by advancements in global travel and information and communication technologies, the ability of students of politics to learn what is happening to others should lead them to reflect not merely on their own privileged lives but also on the kinds of ideas and actions that can best address injustices, particularly against women, both in their own backyard and throughout the world.

RECOMMENDED FILMS, VIDEO CLIPS, AND WEBSITES

Examined Life: Martha Nussbaum. 2008. Excerpt from *Examined Life*, directed by Astra Taylor. www.youtube.com/watch?v=cbcGbflpFzI.

Sandberg, Sheryl. "Why We Have Too Few Women Leaders." 2010. TED Talk. www.ted.com/

talks/sheryl_sandberg_why_we_have_too_few_women_leaders?language=en#t-105781.

ADDITIONAL READINGS

Anderson, Eric. 2009. *Inclusive Masculinity*. New York: Routledge.

Bryant, Christopher G. A., and David Jerry. 2001. *The Contemporary Giddens*. New York: Palgrave Macmillan Press.

Cudd, Ann E., and Nancy Holmstrom. 2011. *Capitalism, For and Against: A Feminist Debate*. New York: Cambridge University Press.

Jónasdóttir, Anna G., Valerie Bryson, and Kathleen B. Jones. 2011. *Sexuality, Gender and Power*. New York: Routledge.

Katz, Jonathan Ned. 2007. *The Invention of Heterosexuality*. Chicago: University of Chicago Press.

Kimmel, Michael. 2007. *The Sexual Self*. Nashville: Vanderbilt University Press.

———. 2010. *Misframing Men: The Politics of Contemporary Masculinities*. New Brunswick, NJ: Rutgers University Press.

McClain, Linda. 2006. "Some ABCs of Feminist Sex Education (In Light of the Sexuality Critique of Legal Feminism)." *Columbia Journal of Gender and Law* 15, no. 1: 63–88.

Nussbaum, Martha. 2003. "Capabilities as Fundamental Entitlements: Sen and Social Justice." *Feminist Economics* 9, no. 2–3: 33–59.

———. 2012. *Philosophical Interventions*. New York: Oxford University Press.

Okin, Susan Moller. 1989. *Justice, Gender, and the Family*. New York: Basic Books, Inc., Publishers.

Reiman, Jeffrey. 2012. *As Free and as Just as Possible: The Theory of Marxian Liberalism*. Chichester: Wiley-Blackwell.

Weeks, Jeffrey. 2009. *Sexuality*. 3rd ed. London: Routledge.

Chapter 2
BODY POLITICS

INTRODUCTION

Many students of political science are familiar with the term *body politic* because it is often used as a reference to the citizens of a particular state, such as Canada or the United States, highlighting the system of government (democratic or authoritarian, federal or unitary, parliamentary or presidential) characterizing the state. Elections are crucial for maintaining the legitimacy of democratic states, and in terms of election years, 2008 was a banner year for students of Canadian and American politics. Although Canada has a parliamentary system and the United States has a presidential one, there are many reasons to compare the two systems of government, not least because they are both Western, immigrant-receiving, and historically male-dominated liberal democracies; and for Canada, being the neighbour of the United States has had significant impacts on its foreign and domestic policies. They are also both federal systems: this means that the 10 provinces in Canada and the 50 states in the United States hold constitutional jurisdiction over key areas, such as education in Canada (including sex education in schools) and marriage in the United States (including the legalization of same-sex marriage). On October 14, 2008, the Canadian federal election was held, resulting in the re-election of yet another minority government for the Conservative Party under Prime Minister

Stephen Harper. Less than a month later, the American presidential election was held on November 4, resulting in the election of Democratic candidate Barack Obama, the first African American president in US history.

The contrast in excitement between the two countries during the 2008 electoral cycle was startling: Canada's election led to the same outcome after Canadians went to the polls less than three years earlier in January 2006, whereas the United States stood to elect its first African American president after the gruelling presidential primaries for the Democratic Party between Obama and Hillary Rodham Clinton, the candidate who could have been the country's first woman president. In addition, had the Republican Party won the election, the United States stood to elect its first woman vice-president, Sarah Palin, who was on the Republican ticket with presidential candidate John McCain. The excitement over the historic election in the United States could not help but spread beyond American borders, particularly into Canada, where Canadians lamented that they had only the same sort of political leaders from whom to choose: all middle-aged, heterosexual, white men, none of whom could capture the mood of voters with slogans such as "Hope We Can Believe In" or "Yes, We Can," so skillfully articulated on the campaign trail by then presidential hopeful Barack Obama.

Years later, Stephen Harper, Barack Obama, Hillary Rodham Clinton, and Sarah Palin remained significant actors in the political arena, and there was little doubt that their spouses played an important role in their successes. Prime Minister Harper went on to win a majority government on May 2, 2011, and his wife, Laureen Harper, was considered his greatest political asset, including by the American embassy in Ottawa, as revealed by WikiLeaks (*CBC News* 2011). President Obama went on to win a second term after the November 6, 2012, federal election, and his wife, Michelle Obama, was instrumental to his success, even polling higher public approval numbers than the president (Brown 2014). Hillary Rodham Clinton, who was appointed as secretary of state in the first Obama administration, announced that she was running in the 2016 Democratic presidential primaries. Her husband, former US president Bill Clinton, remained a crucial asset in realizing her political aspirations, despite being the protagonist of likely the most well-known political sex scandal of all time (a topic briefly discussed at the end of this chapter). Finally, Sarah Palin, the Republican vice-presidential candidate, after losing the November 2008 election, stayed on as governor of Alaska until her resignation in July 2009 before her term ended. Since then, she has stayed in the public eye as a bestselling author (Palin 2009), reality show personality, political commentator, and avid campaigner for the right-wing, libertarian Tea Party movement in the United States (Tyrrell 2013). Her husband, Todd Palin, was a stay-at-home dad while she was governor of Alaska, embracing the title of "First Dude," and being known for "[backing] his wife's ambitions, if not always her politics" (MacGillis and Vick 2008).

For too long, only men have been involved in politics, and it took feminists to ask, "Where are the women?" to show that women have always been present. Cynthia Enloe's (1989) landmark work in international relations reveals, for example, how diplomatic wives in their unpaid, private capacity had been central to the functioning of the international system, illustrating clearly how the apparent stay-at-home wife/mother was often pivotal to the working success of the breadwinner husband/father. As discussed in Chapter 1, this dichotomous relationship was central to the maintenance of the heterosexual conjugal bond rooted in romantic love, which reinforced traditional understandings of masculinity and femininity. In the contemporary context, many women not only work outside the home but also are becoming the primary breadwinners, with a significant number, like Clinton and Palin, becoming successful politicians in their own right. However, although women as well as racial, sexual, and other minorities remain under-represented in the body politic of both the United States and Canada, getting more women like Sarah Palin into office would only undermine the gains made by women after the sexual revolution.

According to Schreiber (2008, 136), because Palin stood to become the first woman vice-president had the Republican Party won in 2008, questions were raised about feminism and whether conservative women like Palin would be considered feminists. There is a difference between women and gender in politics. Palin represents the declinist view held by conservatives who want to return to some fictitious past of faith and family values, and who work to curb or reverse sexual reforms. Although Schreiber recognizes that feminists distinguish between "elected officials [who] support feminist goals … [and] elected officials [who happen to] be female" (133), too often this distinction gets lost in terms of what this means for progress. Sarah Palin, Hillary Rodham Clinton, Michelle Obama, and Laureen Harper are all privileged women living in the West, exercising individual autonomy and representing women's progress with their lived realities, but that does not mean that as individuals they use their privilege to work for the progress of others. This speaks to their role in the body politic.

At the same time, as high-profile women in the public arena, regardless of whether they are the politicians (Clinton and Palin) or the spouses (Harper and Obama), they have generated public interest because of their looks, specifically in maintaining a fit, toned body, although in the case of Clinton, it has been a source of criticism because she is perceived as not living up to a fit, or any, body ideal. The idea that women are judged by their looks has become a truism in Western society. Although women have become a normal part of public life in the West and their progress in the political arena continues to be evident, they remain scrutinized and criticized, particularly in terms of having to meet culturally constructed ideals around the "slender body" perpetuated by the celebrity, fashion, beauty, and weight-loss industries (Bordo 2003, 185–212). Naomi Wolf (1991) pointed out nearly a quarter of a century ago that what she calls the "beauty myth" is the "last, best belief system that keeps male dominance intact" (12). Whether in political life or the corporate sector, women continue to be judged by their looks, and the slimmer they are, the better. This stems from Western understandings of femininity, which have been steeped in patriarchal norms, leading to "the feminine body-as-object 'beauty trap'" (Franzoi 1995, 433). Moreover, the focus on women's appearance has been exacerbated by the digital revolution, where images have come to dominate communication and information. From the prevalence of Facebook and Instagram, to the ubiquity of the strategically shot, if not photoshopped, selfie, social media is dominated by images. Individuals with smart phones can take and share pictures almost instantaneously for any and all to see; conventional media news outlets often follow what is trending in social media; and words have given way to pictures, and pictures, no longer the sole purview of professional photographers or artists, have become the medium of choice. For someone like Hillary Clinton, whose political competence was unbelievably questioned during the 2008 presidential primaries because of an unflattering picture published in the *Drudge Report* (the comments, not surprisingly, were sexist and ageist), tweeting pictures like her selfie with her daughter, Chelsea, in June 2013 (received positively by many observers) was arguably a way to regain control of what has been evident throughout her political career: being judged by her looks. On April 12, 2015, when she announced her candidacy for president through a 2-minute, 18-second YouTube video, the images were primarily of a diverse representation of women and men, and her image was but a small part of the video. Unlike Michelle Obama and Sarah Palin, her body had been judged harshly in the past. No longer simply about the "body politic," this is the terrain of "body politics"—or the politics of the body—a topic of significant interest to feminists (Davis 1997; Gimlin 2002; Bordo 2003).

The body has been an important component of feminist thinking in part because of the mind-body dichotomy in Western political thought that not only has justified keeping women out of political life, but also has treated women's bodies as needing to be controlled, both by societal norms and by medical science. Underpinned by ideas of masculinity (associated with the mind and science) and femininity (associated with the body and nature), men have been seen as governed by rationality and women by emotions. This has led to two sorts of arguments: first, the exclusion of women from the public arena, including voting, holding office, or obtaining higher education, because they do not have the capacity for reason; and second, the requirement of society and science to tame and control the female body because it is seen as more susceptible to pathology than the male body, from the identification of hysteria and nymphomania in past centuries to more contemporary problems of postpartum depression, premenstrual syndrome, anorexia nervosa, bulimia, and menopause (Davis 1997, 5–6). In the contemporary context, the taming and controlling of the female body has led to the pathologizing of fat. This has led not only to eating disorders and dangerous yo-yo dieting, but also to women's self-loathing and body shame.

It is difficult to talk about sexuality without talking about the body, and this chapter focuses on women's bodies in the context of changes in the body politic. As discussed in Chapter 1, progress has occurred with the advent of the sexual revolution in the West, calling into question traditional norms around masculinity, femininity, and heterosexuality. By weaving stories of the lives of individual women in political life—namely Hillary Clinton, Michelle Obama, Sarah Palin, and, to some extent, Laureen Harper—this chapter looks at the extent to which traditional understandings of women's sexual roles centred on motherhood have been reshaped due to women working outside of the home. At the same time, does emphasizing motherhood and family necessarily mean that women subscribe to the primacy of the heterosexual conjugal bond rooted in romantic love? In terms of body politics, why is there an argument to be made that the four women are all body confident given that their appearance has been subject to public interest? How does the "feminine body-as-object 'beauty trap'" undermine women's body confidence, particularly in terms of defining beauty along the lines of thin body ideals? Why is it important that efforts to end fat stigma not be seen as a rejection of fitness as a form of physical activity or challenge? Why does it make sense to differentiate between body-as-object and body-as-process? How does a focus on body confidence lead to a rethinking of body politics and understandings of intimacy, femininity, and masculinity? These are the sorts of questions that will be examined in this chapter. It is divided into five sections: changing gender relations, motherhood and family, body ideals, fat stigma, and body confidence. If intimacy is to be transformed and the ideals of individual autonomy and equality are to be realized, then women—and men—need, at the minimum, to have body confidence.

Figure 2.1: (*Left to right, top to bottom*): Laureen Harper, Michelle Obama, Hillary Rodham Clinton, Sarah Palin

Sources: Laureen Harper: Federal Government (Germany)/REGIERUNGonline/Steins; Michelle Obama: Official White House Photo by Chuck Kennedy; Hillary Rodham Clinton: US Department of State; Sarah Palin: Gage Skidmore.

CHANGING GENDER RELATIONS

Growing up in the 21st century, students would find it hard to believe that the idea of married women being in the workforce was ever an unusual, let alone a controversial, phenomenon, but in 1992 when Bill Clinton became president of the United States, Hillary Rodham Clinton, a Yale Law School graduate who was an accomplished partner in a well-known law firm, was the first career woman to become First Lady. She had initially retained her own surname and went by Hillary Rodham when she first married Clinton in 1975, but changed it when her husband ran once again for governor of Arkansas in 1982. After being elected in 1978, Bill Clinton lost re-election in 1980 (the term in office for Arkansas governors was two years until 1986 when it changed to four-year terms), and whether her name change helped his attempt to get re-elected again in the southern state, "it probably didn't hurt" (Page 1993). She challenged the American public's view of what the First Lady should be like and often suffered because of it.

> Much of the reaction to Hillary stemmed from deep-seeded [*sic*] unconscious and conscious biases against independent women who perform their gender identities in professional and independent ways, and are not sufficiently submissive to their husbands. Hillary Clinton's identity performance was a threat to men and to those women who had made a choice to live in more traditional marriages. These women viewed their work lives outside of the home, if they worked outside of the home at all, as secondary to their husbands' careers, and they spent a large percentage of their time caring for their husbands and children. (McGinley 2009, 716)

Despite being a product of the women's movement, Hillary Rodham Clinton (born in 1947) was part of the first wave of the baby boom generation (the generation born in the years 1946–64) and encountered more resistance initially as an independent, working wife than later baby boomers Laureen Harper (born in 1963), Michelle Obama (born in 1964), and Sarah Palin (born in 1964).

Women's decision to keep their surnames was a practice that made news in the 1970s and the 1980s in the United States and Canada precisely because it represented women's greater education, particularly in completing advanced studies, such as law and graduate degrees; their increasing economic independence as laws eliminated discrimination based on gender; and their demands to be free of societal norms that categorized women depending on their marital status (Golden and Shim 2004). Despite the debut of Gloria Steinem's *Ms. Magazine* in 1972, "Ms." became acceptable for widespread use only in the mid-1980s, and before then women's honorifics were either "Miss," if single, or "Mrs.," if married; there was no equivalent to "Mr.," which has no connection to the marital status of men (Golden and Shim 2004, 144–45). Clinton's negative experience of initially keeping her surname was mirrored in Canada with that of Maureen McTeer (born in 1952) during the brief time that her husband, Joe Clark, served as Canada's prime minister for nine months (June 1979–March 1980). McTeer made headlines in 1979 by becoming the first prime minister's wife to keep her surname, and decades later, she remained primarily defined by that decision, despite her many accomplishments, including receiving a law degree in 1976, running for member of Parliament in 1988 (although she lost, she was the only prime minister's wife to have run for office), and living an activist life (McTeer 2003). In today's society, the practice of a woman keeping or changing her surname has much less salience politically, with "the desire to share a last name with [her] children appear[ing] to be at the heart of a growing trend among heterosexual women who identify as feminists [taking the names of their husbands]," and some, particularly same-sex couples who have not been governed by patriarchal norms, simply choosing a different common surname altogether (Bernstein 2013).

Women working outside of the home have changed gender relations between heterosexual couples. Oriel Sullivan (2006) argues that although "the phrases 'the dual [or double] burden', 'the second shift', and the 'stalled revolution' are concepts that have made an important contribution to our understanding of inequalities in domestic labour and related issues of gender power within the household," she sees notable progress in the domestic or private sphere in the West in the latter half of the 20th century (1–2). Looking at empirical, cross-national data from the mid-1960s to the late 1990s, she points to a complex process of change based on increasing gender consciousness of women and men, differing relational resources over time within couples, and changing material circumstances of the household. She argues that differences in attitudes regarding gender equality, including a more equitable distribution of household labour, are important to study between generations (such as between baby boomers born in the years 1946–64 and millennials, like students today, born in the years 1980–2000). However, it is also crucial to pay attention to the significance of research on intragenerational, or intracohort, shifts in thinking, and not only intergenerational ones. This is because this research points to "a more rapid process of change, in which the same individuals display changing attitudes over time" (29). Sullivan notes, in particular, the changing attitudes of men in terms of their family roles as well as "the significance of changing images of masculinity and fatherhood and for the real existence in gender practice, particularly in relation to masculine caring behaviour" (36). Indeed, not only do women not leave the labour market when they have children, but more and more women are becoming the primary breadwinners in their families.

Recent findings show that nearly a third of women in the United States and Canada earn more than their husbands, and more and more men are staying home to take care of the children and do housework (Gulli 2012, Boesveld 2012; Marshall 2006). As an example, the extent to which political wives in the West leave paid employment these days appears to have less to do with traditional family structures and more to do with the practical realities of political life. Laureen Harper was building a successful graphic design and desktop publishing business when she married Stephen Harper in 1993, and she became the breadwinner of the family when he left his job as head of the National Citizens Coalition in 2002 to run for the leadership of the Canadian Alliance (Kingston 2007). She left the job market when she moved to Ottawa after her husband became the leader of the Opposition, changing her surname from Teskey to Harper only when the Conservative Party (created after the 2003 merger of the Canadian Alliance and Progressive Conservative parties) won its first minority government in 2006 and Stephen Harper became prime minister. She then told the Canadian Press that "she wished to be known publicly by her husband's last name" only "to defray any potential confusion now that her husband was Prime Minister" (Carlson 2013). There was little or no media attention to her name change.

In contrast, when Justin Trudeau became prime minister after the October 19, 2015, federal election, there was some outcry when his wife, Sophie Grégoire, decided to hyphenate her name to include his surname. Critics pointed out that the choice of Sophie Grégoire-Trudeau puts her "at odds with the couple's home province of Quebec, where adopting your husband's name is neither customary nor legal [because] under Quebec's Civil Code, women are not allowed to formally change their name at marriage and they can't tether their husband's names to their own either" (Peritz 2015). Quebec is the only province in Canada to enact legislation (in 1981) prohibiting a woman from adopting her husband's surname apart from an "exceptional situation." Whether this provides legal protection from an anachronistic traditional practice or only limits married women's choices further in Quebec, is a question that invites inquiry into the changing nature of Western culture. As Chapter 4 points out, a traditional practice need not be eradicated if its original meaning and intent has lost social force. That likely explains why the issue of a heterosexual woman taking her husband's name in Canada and the United States has ceased being an important matter for gender equality. In Grégoire-Trudeau's case, the problem was arguably not that she changed her name, but *when* she did it. Like Laureen Harper, she adopted her husband's surname only when he became prime minister, leading observers to ask if "most high-profile women [namely, politicians' wives] don't have the same range of options" as most women when it comes to changing (or keeping) their names (Kingston 2015).

Wives of Canadian prime ministers do not perform formal roles like wives of US presidents, and thus are not constantly in the public eye, but Laureen Harper had proactively stayed out of the limelight. She had not been the subject of many interviews, preferring to keep a lower public profile than would be expected of the prime minister's wife, and had claimed to have a "self-professed ability to fly under the radar" (Levitz 2013). That is why, although married to a Conservative prime minister whose party members held many socially conservative views around reproductive rights and the rights of sexual minorities, it is not clear how conservative her views were and the extent to which she subscribed to traditional understandings of masculinity, femininity, and heterosexuality. However, in April 2015 she was appointed as the ambassador for the "Day of Pink" anti-bullying campaign by the Canadian Centre for Gender and Sexual Diversity, and instead of demonstrating that she may hold different views from that of the former prime minister and the Conservative Party, her appointment caused outrage by some lesbian, gay, bisexual, trans, queer (LGBTQ) activists *because* she is married to Harper. Many came to Laureen Harper's defence, arguing that it is generally accepted that "marriage does not, or should not, strip a woman of her individual identity, opinions or perspective ... [except perhaps] when a woman is married to, say, an odious political figure" (Urbach 2015).

EMPHASIZING MOTHERHOOD AND FAMILY

In contrast to Laureen Harper, Michelle Obama is well known in the popular press not only in the United States but worldwide. A graduate of Princeton University and Harvard Law School and an accomplished professional who worked at a well-known Chicago law firm (where she met Barack Obama in 1989 because she was assigned to supervise his work), she was not subject to the same type of scrutiny in the 2008 presidential election about her career success as Hillary Rodham Clinton was in the 1992 election (McGinley 2009, 722). Taking Obama's name when they married in 1992 appeared to be a non-issue, reflecting a trend in the 1990s even among heterosexual women who identify themselves as feminists (Golden and Shim 2004; Bernstein 2013). However, unlike Clinton, she has had to negotiate her racial identity along with her gender, and having been depicted as an "angry black woman" in her husband's first campaign for the presidency, Michelle Obama has taken "a radically different tack in her public appearances, embracing and celebrating her roles as mother and wife and refashioning herself into the role of 'Mom-in-Chief,'" causing consternation for many feminists who have been "disturbed by Obama's retreat to the conservative positions of wife and mother" (Cooper 2010, 50). Indeed, some have argued that she has become a "feminist nightmare" because although her husband is now in his second term and there are no longer any worries about re-election, she does not forcefully speak out on issues of gender, racial, and class inequalities in the United States, including the specific challenges faced by women in poor minority communities. According to one of her recent critics:

> So enough already with the pining for a Michelle Obama who simply doesn't exist. The woman is not going to morph into an edgier, more activist first lady. The 2012 election did not set her free. Even now, with her husband waddling toward lame duck territory, she is not going to let loose suddenly with some straight talk about abortion rights or Obamacare or the Common Core curriculum debate. Turns out she was serious about that whole 'mom-in-chief' business—it wasn't merely a political strategy but also a personal choice. (Cottle 2013)

Not surprisingly, the intersection of gender and race has become a minefield for feminists so that the reactions to the First Lady's critics have been grounded in part by demanding that white feminists "should be quiet" because "it is race that shapes black women's access to [the narrative] of womanhood, and the protection that comes with femininity," a "narrative that has been the sole and privileged access of heterosexual, middle-class white women … [who] do not want to acknowledge that this narrative has given them a particular kind of white female privilege" (Cooper 2013). Brittney Cooper (2010) argues that black women have historically been depicted as "bad mothers," and given that the children of enslaved black women could be sold and disciplined without their consent, "Michelle Obama's proactive, positive brand of mothering performs important cultural work for the embattled imagery of the black mother" (50–51).

Cooper is right to point out that both gender and race define Michelle Obama, and her criticism of white feminists is a reminder that Michelle Obama has indeed faced racial barriers not encountered by First Ladies of the past. Understanding that individuals (women and men; black and white; heterosexual and gay, lesbian, or bisexual; rich and poor; able-bodied and challenged) all have multiple and intersecting identities is part of a feminist liberal perspective. Michelle Obama's critics are right that the First Lady has made a choice. Not only is it the fact that she can make a choice, irrespective of her race and gender, which is relevant to feminist liberalism, but her choice to focus on motherhood must also be understood in the context of her support of reproductive rights and sexual diversity. In that way, she is starkly different from Sarah Palin, who has also focused on her role as wife and mother.

Despite the reversal of traditional roles with Todd Palin being, at one point, a stay-at-home dad and Sarah Palin working outside of the home, Palin embraces and propagates socially conservative ideas about sexuality. This was particularly evident when she was running as a vice-presidential candidate for the Republican Party in 2008 when her positions on women's reproductive rights and same-sex marriage even put her at odds with her running mate, John McCain, and indeed with many Republicans (Stein 2008; Conroy 2008). She is avowedly pro-life and opposes abortion in all circumstances, including pregnancies resulting from rape or incest; the only exception is when a woman's life is in danger. She also supports amending the US Constitution to define marriage as between a man and a woman, in effect creating a constitutional ban on same-sex marriage and undercutting equality rights as they have been upheld by the courts, including the US Supreme Court. Palin has been described as the "belle of the ball among religious conservatives" (Stein 2008) and her attitudes regarding sexuality are part of her status as a "celebritician" (i.e., celebrity-politician), remaining a significant figure in large part because of her endorsement of specific right-wing candidates (Kucinich and Henderson 2014), including controversial Republican presidential candidate Donald Trump in 2016. Although she likely will never run for political office again, and she uses primarily social media as opposed to conventional media outlets to propagate her views, Palin is popular in socially conservative circles. For example, during the 2013 Conservative Political Action Conference (CPAC), she gave a speech extolling the virtues of gun ownership in the context of the right to bear arms found in the Second Amendment of the US Constitution. She then related a story about her husband, Todd, giving her a gun rack for Christmas and she, in turn, gave him a gun.

She ended with the punchline: "He's got the rifle, I got the rack" (quoted in Peoples and Thomas 2013).

Palin's remark shows that today's conservatives are not reluctant to talk about sex in the public arena. The problem is that social conservatives see sex as properly occurring only within a marriage between a man and a woman, condemning premarital, extramarital, and same-sex sex and working to put these views into practice through opposition to sex education in schools, public persecution of infidelity (and even prosecution, as in former US president Bill Clinton's case), and disapproval of same-sex relations, particularly same-sex marriage. Rooted in early Christian ethics, which demands that individuals overcome what St. Augustine, one of the founding fathers of Western Christianity, called the "corruptions of the flesh," sexual desire has been seen as an obstacle to spiritual salvation. Only procreative sex in marriage resting on monogamy and fidelity is allowed because of the need to propagate the human race, leading to families becoming the backbone of society (Mottier 2008, 24). That is why conservative reactionary forces within and outside the West have pointed to "both feminists and gays and lesbians as underminers of the traditional social order," an order predicated on heteronormativity, femininity as motherhood, and masculinity as provider for the family (Nussbaum 1999, 15). As discussed in Chapter 1, with the advent of the sexual revolution the severing of linkages between sex and reproduction has been crucial to the advancement of women's rights and the rights of sexual minorities. Indeed, when the AIDS crisis of the 1980s led to the resurgence of the moral or religious right in the West, "the moral agenda of the Right was shaped in response to the claims of gay rights activists and the perceived threat from feminist critiques of dominant understandings of femininity and female sexuality" (Mottier 2008, 77). Jeffrey Weeks (1985) explores why the conservative reactionary movement gained ground in curbing sexual reforms at a time when more liberal sexual attitudes had become more widespread in Western societies. He argues that the mass support for the moral or religious right had come from two principal constituencies: embattled Christians, and largely middle-class, morally concerned women, where the primary battleground has been the family.

Weeks (1985) points out that the conservative interpretation of the role of women in the heterosexual bond has undergone a major shift. Generally speaking, conservatives see male sexuality as uncontrolled and rampant, but whereas in the 19th century, they perceived women as little more than receptacles for male urges, reflecting women's submissive role, conservatives today celebrate women as nurturers who assertively curb male sexual appetites and "civilize" men into accepting their role in the family. Weeks looks to the influential work of conservatives Roger Scruton and George Gilder to capture this shift in thinking. He states that Scruton highlights the "unbridled ambition of the phallus" and the need for women "to quieten what is most vagrant" (42). He points out that, according to Gilder, "a married man ... is spurred by the claims of the family to channel his otherwise disruptive male aggressions into his performance as a provider for his wife and children" (42). As Weeks pointedly argues, "By a skilful theoretical manoeuvre, the feminist case against male violence is turned into a defence of conservative forms" (42). In other words, men are seen as weak beings because they so easily succumb to their sexual appetites. Women, on the other hand, are put forward as strong nurturers who act as the foundation of the family and, as wives and mothers, take care of men and their children. Thus, male-dominated structures, such as the traditional family arising out of the valorization of the heterosexual conjugal bond, are perpetuated under the guise of seeing women as powerful because they are the saviours of men. Socially conservative women, like Palin, may and do work outside of the home, but instead of calling into question problematic conceptions of heterosexuality, femininity, and masculinity, embedded in ideas of the traditional family, they only reinforce them. This is the danger faced by radical feminists who, in sharing the views of conservatives on the nature of male sexuality and aggression, may undermine progress on sexual reforms and the acceptance of sexual diversity. Ironically, while looking at the socially constructed nature of female sexuality, radical feminists treat male sexuality as unproblematic. Arguably their "portrayals of male sexuality had echoed biological models of sexuality in taking for granted its naturally aggressive, triumphant, and, at times, violent nature ... [but] it would be a mistake to conclude this is also the only way in which individual men experience sexuality" (Mottier 2008, 73). Indeed, as discussed earlier, the nature of masculinity and fatherhood is changing in the West.

In contrast to Palin, Michelle Obama's choice to focus on motherhood is not embedded in the reinforcement of traditional sexual roles around heterosexuality and femininity. Not only does she support same-sex marriage and urged the president to publicly support it well before he decided to do so (Becker 2014), but she also embodies changing conceptions of femininity evident in both the nature of her relationship to the president (Kantor 2012), which seems to rest more on confluent rather than romantic love, and the ways in which her intersectional identity as a black woman challenges dominant Western understandings of femininity in terms of the ideal female body.

BODY IDEALS

Women's body ideals have changed throughout history. Unlike the celebration of the "Rubenesque" woman in the 1600s, named after Flemish painter Peter Paul Ruben, where the ideal female body was full-figured and plump, the thin body ideal has dominated the latter part of the 20th and the 21st centuries in Western society. This is evident in fashion runways, which are dominated by thin, waif-like models; in magazines, which continue to feature inordinately slim women; and in online pictures that celebrate the "thigh gap," which have been circulating as part of "thinspiration" around the web. However, the thin body ideal is no longer critically unaccepted. Over a decade ago in 2004, Dove launched its "Campaign for Real Beauty" to showcase women's differing body shapes, even inviting both Susie Orbach, author of the classic *Fat Is a Feminist Issue* (1978), and Naomi Wolf, author of the bestselling *The Beauty Myth* (1991), to contribute to "a large-scale, multinational survey of women's conceptions and practices" around beauty and appearance (Johnston and Taylor 2008, 951). In today's society, fat-shaming is being brought to the forefront and challenged, not only by huge corporations like Unilever (of which Dove is a subsidiary), clearly motivated as much by profit as by concerns to challenge the thin body ideal, but also by everyday women on social media. For example, in August 2014 a mother of five in Edmonton posted a message on Facebook, along with a picture of her stomach, directed to two men and one woman who had ridiculed her body while she was suntanning on a beach in a bikini. Bringing out that her "stomach isn't flat and tight … [and her] belly is covered in stretch marks … [because her] body has housed, grown, protected, birthed and nurtured FIVE fabulous, healthy, intelligent and wonderful human beings," the message was "shared over a million times and generated tens of thousands of comments" of support (Zabjek 2014). Less than a week later, women who were similarly sized as, or larger than, the mother of five showed up in their bikinis in downtown Edmonton for a rally to vividly show that no woman should be shamed for, nor be ashamed of, her body (Purdy 2014). Pictures and videos accompanied the news coverage, highlighting challenges to thin body ideals.

It is an inspiring story in large part because the bikini has become an iconic piece of clothing reserved only for young, slim women who have the confidence to put their bodies on display. From the *Sports Illustrated* annual swimsuit edition to the Victoria's Secret Fashion Show, from pictures of famous stars in the music and film industries to selfies of self-made celebrities such as Paulina Gretzky, the daughter of hockey legend Wayne Gretzky, it is not difficult to find pictures of beautiful, perfectly shaped, slim, bikini-clad women. Yet, as Saguy and Ward (2011) point out, some women who are part of the fat acceptance movement have purposely worn bikinis in order to claim a "'normal life'" where they see it as "an important step in becoming more socially integrated" (68). Rather than flaunting their size, they see it as fitting into society. Indeed, in August 2014 women wearing a "fatkini" had become the latest trend on Twitter and Instagram as they "bravely outed their big and beautiful bodies by shedding their beach cover-ups and posting shots of themselves" in two-piece bathing suits (McNally 2014).

The connection between body confidence and sexuality is an important one because, although both women and men may be self-conscious about their bodies during sex, women are more likely not to desire sex because of body confidence issues than men. Even if issues of size are applicable to both women and men, the effects on their sexual behaviour have an important gender component. Women's sexuality is more affected by their satisfaction with their body, so that as a number of studies have pointed out (for example, Woertman and van den Brink 2012; Donaghue 2009), there is a correlation between body shame (or body dissatisfaction) and sexual dysfunction. Indeed, as women get older and gain weight, they lose interest in sex, but whereas physiological explanations focus on hormonal changes, more psychological ones look at women's outlook on their heavier bodies (Clarke 2010). Interestingly, as men get older and gain weight, they do not necessarily have the concomitant loss of interest in sex. Women's views of their bodies are related to societal constructions of the body ideal, and these constructions can often affect their sex lives.

The fat acceptance movement, often associated with the US-based National Association to Advance Fat Acceptance, has been critical to raising fat consciousness and working to end fat stigma in society (Kirkland 2008; Farrell 2011; Saguy and Ward 2011). The movement has also been crucial to fat women in accepting, and indeed celebrating, their size. Fat stigma in Western society stems from the association of fatness with laziness, unattractiveness, excessive eating, poor personal hygiene, and ill health (Elliott 2007, 141). Unlike other societies "where food is scarce and where fatness signals health and high status" (Saguy and Ward 2011, 55), in affluent societies like the West, fat people are regarded as unmotivated, lacking self-control, and draining the health care system; accordingly, they are seen as failing society. That is why Charlene Elliott (2007) argues that the narrative of the failed citizen is constructed around the framing of the fat body. She points out that the distinction between the classical body (controlled, ruled by reason, autonomous, and disciplined) and the carnivalesque body (uncontrolled, ruled by passion, dependent [on health care], and undisciplined) underpins the construction of the "failed" (fat) citizen. She argues that governments, like those in Canada and the United States, use discourses such as the "war on fat or obesity" to frame the larger body as a lesser citizen, noting that "the obese body is, ironically, democratic—open to all, regardless of gender, race, or class" (140).

Fat activists use *fat* deliberately because just like gays and lesbians who have rejected the term *homosexual* and have appropriated the term *queer*, fat activists "are reclaiming the term *fat*, commonly used as an insult, as a neutral and positive descriptor … [and are] rejecting the terms *obese* and *overweight* as pathologizing normal human variation" (Saguy and Ward 2011, 54). The medical community, which uses the terms *obese* and *overweight* based on the body mass index (BMI), has noted the rise of a global "obesity epidemic," labelling it as "a major public health concern," which is getting worse for most countries, including Canada and the United States (Sassi 2010, 26). However, fat studies scholars dismiss research on obesity regularly reported in the popular press as alarmist, misleading, and perpetuating fat stigma (Elliott 2007; Kirkland 2008; Farrell 2011; Saguy and Ward 2011; Rothblum 2012). For example, Anna Kirkland (2011, 471) points out that BMI standards were actually lowered for overweight (25 or above) and obese (30 or above) in 1998, "creating millions of new people by definitional fiat" to fit those categories. She calls into question the objectivity of lowering the standards, given that "the decision-making organizations are funded by drug companies for whom pathologizing fat would be enormously profitable" (Kirkland 2011, 471). The pathologizing of fat has been particularly directed to, and felt by, women so that it is not surprising that most fat activists are women. Amy Farrell (2011) describes the story of one woman's struggle to illustrate the ways in which fat women overcome their challenges.

> She has used the tools of a feminist perspective to allow herself to see the ways that the life of a fat woman is especially 'painful and dangerous, compared to either thin women or even fat men', who experience, she argues, a level of tolerance not given to fat women. Indeed, the fat acceptance world that Deborah inhabits is one largely made up of women. Ironically, then, women are in the majority both at the weight

> loss centers *and* at the fat acceptance bashes. It is probable that the extraordinary stigma U.S. culture attaches to female fat propels women either to be adamant about taking off the weight *or* to challenge that stigma that so oppresses them. (167)

There is a difference between fat stigma and fat (or weight) discrimination. Both Canada and the United States have anti-discrimination laws based on categories, such as gender, race, sexual orientation, age, ethnicity, religion, and disability, but with the exception of the state of Michigan and a handful of US municipalities, there are no laws preventing discrimination based on weight (Immen 2010; Rothblum 2012; Rudd Center for Food Policy and Obesity 2013). Although there have been some court cases in both countries that have treated obesity as a disability, and therefore subject to protection under the law, very few fat people facing what could be regarded as weight discrimination, such as by employers (for example, being passed up for a promotion) or doctors (for example, facing refusal to be treated), do not see themselves as having rights to be protected. A "civil rights consciousness" arguably does not fit because despite wanting to end fat stigma in society and be accepted for their size, many fat people struggle with the extent to which their size has been a matter of personal choice caused by a lack of discipline or control over their eating (Kirkland 2008). Although for some scholars this struggle is clearly indicative of fat people internalizing their own oppression due to the "cultural production of the unhealthy and morally decrepit fat person" who is "undeserving of rights protection" (Kirkland 2008, 399), or the societal framing of the fat body as "the failure of personal responsibility," referred to as "responsibilization" (Elliott 2007, 135), many of those who struggle with their weight state that they want to take responsibility for their lives. Are they simply being duped into wanting to lose weight, or are they making a choice about their bodies? For those who do lose weight, should they be pitied for succumbing to societal pressures, or should their efforts be applauded? Shouldn't individual motivation for wanting to lose weight matter so that there is a difference between an individual who is motivated by health reasons and one who wants to lose weight in order to meet some thin(ner) body ideal imposed by society?

ENDING FAT STIGMA AND THE BODY-AS-PROCESS

Being motivated by health reasons as a fat person is not as uncomplicated as it first seems. Focusing on a healthy and active lifestyle instead of weight loss has been met with a great deal of trepidation by fat activists and scholars in large part because of the ways in which health and fitness have been equated with thinness and leanness. Elliott (2007) argues that juxtaposed to the framing of the fat body as a failed citizen has been the valorization of the "fit" body as the ideal citizen, where fitness is equated with leanness. Although Elliott argues that this is wrong, the association of fatness with lack of discipline, control, and motivation only perpetuates the view that being healthy and active means not being fat. This is further evident in arguments to be "fit, not fat," found in an Organisation for Economic Co-operation and Development report (Sassi 2010). The problem with this binary opposition is that there are healthy individuals who are in the BMI categories of being overweight or obese just as there are unhealthy ones who are in the ideal weight range and below it. In essence, one can be fat and fit.

That is why some doctors are using different measures for health, such as looking at waist circumference (or abdominal fat) as opposed to BMI, and the Health at Every Size (HAES) movement is gaining attention where "health is defined as physical, emotional, and spiritual well-being," the emphasis is on "improving nutrition and enjoying food," and greater focus is paid to "the joy of movement instead of adherence to a structured exercise program" (Rothblum 2012, 4). Clearly, having a healthy, active lifestyle stems from purposeful acts regarding nutrition and physical activity where the problem is not food, but the kind of dieting centred on the need to control eating, which can lead to disorders like anorexia and bulimia. At the same time, for those promoting health, it makes little sense to identify the problem as structured exercise; rather, the problem is a sedentary lifestyle where the lack of activity can lead to greater likelihood of diabetes, heart disease, and even cancer. In this way, the conflation of fitness with thinness or leanness has only undermined an important way to maintain an active lifestyle, particularly in Western affluent societies where work often does not require strenuous physical labour. The HAES movement is endorsed by fat studies scholars because people within the movement "underscore the fact that we cannot tell people's health and fitness level just from looking at them" (Rothblum 2012, 4), but dismissing the utility of a structured exercise program only feeds into thinking that fitness is about leanness.

To illustrate the purposeful nature of a healthy, active lifestyle, Ann Cahill (2010), an American feminist philosopher, has written an interesting piece about her weight loss. She explains why her weight loss was not because she had succumbed to "the tyranny of femininity and its emphasis on bodily control and thinness," but because she wanted to "[maximize her] ability to *move*, quickly, effectively, strongly[, which] was entirely conducive to [her] feminist aspirations and activities" (486). She relates that she developed guidelines so that food was not her enemy, took up food journaling, and started lifting weights. She found that the more intentional she was about her eating, the more she wanted to keep up her workouts, and the more purposeful she was about her workouts, the less appealing she found food that was unhealthy. She ended up losing 35 pounds in a year, and although this "significant bodily transformation" affected her "sense of self," she "couldn't find a ready-made story to tap into" to explain her weight loss (491). She points out that she did not have body shame and never saw herself as a "thinner-person-needing-to-be-liberated," nor did she feel bad that she had nothing to wear, or dislike pictures of herself (491). Yet, she could not deny the positive consequences of her weight loss. She writes:

> I'm living in a body that I experience as *fast*. I like that. I'm living in a body that falls asleep quickly and deeply, craves a raised heartbeat, and loves the taste of chocolate and risotto and steamed broccoli. I'm living in a body that reacts with distress when I put too much food into it, and I'm still learning what that line is. I'm living in a body that treads a bit more lightly on the earth, both literally and figuratively. (Cahill 2010, 491)

Although Bordo (2003) argues that the slender body is a "tightly managed body" and it matters little for the cultural oppression of women in the West whether it is a "sleek, minimalist" (thin) one or a body with "firmly developed muscles" because both speak to "a contemporary ideal of specifically female attractiveness" in a white, male world (211), body ideals that are governed by fitness and athleticism are arguably different from ideals based on standards of extreme thinness. The ideal woman's body that is fit and strong can challenge, if not overcome, what Davis (1997) describes as "cultural images in the media [which] normalize women by presenting images of the female body as glamorously affluent, impossibly thin and invariably white" (6). Grounded in research studies that demonstrate that "women who participate in sports are more likely to be tough-minded, self-sufficient, assertive, autonomous, and emotionally stable" (Gimlin 2002, 51), a fit, strong, active body can be empowering. Epitomizing this fit ideal is Michelle Obama, who, despite initial calls for her to dress more modestly, has claimed her "right to bare arms" (a clever take on the Second Amendment to the US Constitution) by wearing sleeveless tops and dresses. This began with her one-shouldered, white silk chiffon gown (now on display at the Smithsonian National Museum of American History) at the first presidential inauguration ball in January 2009, when she first drew public attention to her toned, sleek arms (Abraham 2011). Moreover, as African American feminist Brittney Cooper (2010) argues:

> Obama's muscular arms signal different possibilities for black women than those signaled by Sojourner Truth's muscular arms. [Sojourner Truth was born into slavery in 1791. She was an African American abolitionist and women's rights activist, famous for her "Ain't I a Woman?" speech in 1851 at the Ohio Women's Rights Convention.]…. Sojourner Truth's muscular arms signaled a life of unpaid labor, chattel slavery and inhumane working conditions. Obama's muscular arms symbolize her economic capacity to prioritize herself and her health and her access to the privileges of work/life balance. (53)

The recognition of a fit and strong body ideal can be crucial for changing women's perceptions of their body. Stephen Franzoi (1995) points out that there are gender differences in body esteem because women subscribe to the view of body-as-object, judging themselves in terms of appearance, and men subscribe to the view of body-as-process, judging themselves in terms of performance or functioning. Both of these views result from socialization processes that value women for their looks and men for their actions. The problem, according to Franzoi, is that, to the detriment of women, "the cultural fixation on their bodies as objects results in a standard of feminine ideal that is not only extremely salient, but also virtually impossible to attain. [Moreover,] even if a woman cognitively resigns herself to the fact that she cannot match the attractiveness standard, or even if she rejects the standard outright, the larger culture often still judges her by it" (420). In contrast, not only is the masculine standard focusing on performance or functioning less pressing for men as dictates of culture, but they are also more likely to have positive body esteem because they see their bodies in a more dynamic, rather than static, fashion. However, Franzoi points out that the feminist movement has created possibilities for women to break free of "the feminine body-as-object 'beauty trap'" and if women "pay more attention to their body-as-process … it may not only change female body attitudes [in Western culture], but it may restructure their body esteem as well" (433). As Wasylkiw et al. (2009) have argued, "engagement in exercise is beneficial for body image [and] women involved in regular exercise tend to be less anxious about their physiques than women not involved in regular exercise" (137). In other words, by focusing on what her body can do (performance) as opposed to what her body looks like (appearance), a woman can not only increase her body confidence, but also impact Western societal attitudes that focus on women's appearance.

Michelle Obama, Laureen Harper, Sarah Palin, and Hillary Rodham Clinton have all generated public interest because of their looks, particularly (with the exception of Clinton) in maintaining a fit, toned body. Michelle Obama has become well known in the popular press for her active lifestyle and commitment to fitness. It is not surprising that in her role as First Lady she has led a high-profile, anti-obesity initiative focused on schools, launching the "Let's Move" campaign in 2010 to "end childhood obesity within a generation." Laureen Harper, too, has received positive attention regarding her fitness because she is often described as an "avid motorcycle enthusiast" who is physically active and stays fit by running, hiking, snowshoeing, and canoeing (Gunn 2012). Sarah Palin has also attracted attention because she is physically active, has been a "runner all her life," and has even stated that she is writing a book on fitness as a way to deflect media concerns about her weight loss (Reese 2012). A former beauty queen contestant, Palin was described as "the hottest governor from the coldest state" when she exploded onto the national political scene in 2008, leading conservative shock radio host Rush Limbaugh to claim during the election: "We're the ones with the babe on the ticket."

In contrast, Hillary Rodham Clinton was portrayed as unattractive, if not asexual, due to her fashion choices of wearing pantsuits when she ran against Obama in 2008 (McGinley 2009). However, she disarmed her fashion critics when she appropriated a well-known 2005 girl-bonding movie during her concession speech at the Democratic National Convention that August: "To my supporters, to my champions—to my *sisterhood of the traveling pantsuits*—from the bottom of my heart: Thank you. You never gave in. You never gave up. And together we made history" (italics added). Interestingly, Clinton has publicly stated that she has an exercise regime (Tanabe 2011). She has remarked that although she has a personal trainer three times a week and she also does yoga with an instructor, her appearance has not necessarily changed, stating: "Not that it shows ... but it does energize me" (as quoted in Tanabe 2011). Unlike Obama, Harper, and Palin, Clinton has rarely received positive attention regarding her looks, but her fit, active lifestyle has arguably instilled her with body confidence. This perhaps helps to explain why she has been able to readily deal with critiques of her appearance, which, when she became secretary of state, changed from criticisms of her fashion choices to her choices of hairstyles and accessories. Similar to her clever quip regarding her pantsuits, she has stated that she should have titled her second political memoir detailing her years as secretary of state as "The Scrunchie Chronicles: 112 Countries and It's Still All About My Hair" (Chozik 2014).

BODY CONFIDENCE

Hillary Rodham Clinton is running for the presidency in 2016 and she may well become the first woman president of the United States. This is arguably exciting for feminists of all stripes because there is a chance that she can actually win. Even Kim Campbell, Canada's only female prime minister, became so only because she took over a declining party that was in power and there was really little chance that she would win the 1993 election (her governing Progressive Conservative Party went from 156 to *2* seats, and she lost her own seat, leading many to believe that she won the party leadership only because party stalwarts knew that the party was in steep decline). Despite Hillary Rodham Clinton's many accomplishments, many observers continue to be fixated on why she stayed with her husband after he had an affair with an intern when he was president. Indeed, when asked by reporters about her years in the White House as she promoted her second political memoir (Clinton 2014; see also Clinton 2003), she responded that she has "moved on" from the Lewinsky scandal (Chozik 2014).

There have been many political sex scandals in the United States, and the list is long: former senator and Democratic vice-presidential candidate John Edwards, former New York governor Eliot Spitzer, former South Carolina governor Mark Sanford, former congressman Anthony Weiner, former California governor and actor Arnold Schwarzenegger, former CIA director and retired army general David Petraeus, and countless more. These are all stories of men in public office in the United States behaving badly, and these stories are nothing new (Dagnes 2011), but the Clinton-Lewinsky scandal stands out. It is a story that has entered our popular imagination for two good reasons. First, the president unbelievably stated his denial that he had sex with Monica Lewinsky, then a 22-year-old White House intern, not simply because there was no sexual intercourse, but also because, although they had oral sex, it was strictly fellatio. As President Clinton famously remarked, "She had sex with me, but I did not have sex with her." Second, the scandal also led to the impeachment of Clinton in 1998, one of only two presidents impeached in US history (the other was Andrew Johnson in 1868), and it has been immortalized in *The Starr Report: The Independent Counsel's Complete Report to Congress on the Investigation of President Clinton*. Notably, the juicy, titillating details about the affair are captured in what is an official US government publication where there are sexually explicit passages such as the following:

> There [in the private study of the Oval Office], according to Ms. Lewinsky, they kissed. She was wearing a long dress that buttoned from the neck to the ankles. 'And he unbuttoned my dress and he unhooked my bra, and sort of took the dress off my shoulders and … moved the bra.… He was looking at me and touching me and telling me how beautiful I was.' He touched her breasts with his hands and his mouth, and touched her genitals, first through underwear and then directly. She performed oral sex on him. (*The Starr Report* 1998, 83–84)

Although the House of Representatives voted in December 1998 to impeach President Clinton on charges of perjury and obstruction of justice, he was acquitted by the Senate in February 1999. Shortly thereafter, Hillary Rodham Clinton announced her intention to run for, and then would eventually win, a Senate seat from New York in the 2000 election, which meant that she was campaigning while still in her role as First Lady. The Lewinsky affair remains a defining moment of Bill Clinton's presidency, and sex scandals appear to be a regular feature of American politics. However, these scandals reveal more about American attitudes regarding monogamy and their expectations of male political leaders than they do about continuing challenges faced by women resulting from how power infuses gender in ways that focus on sexuality. Lewinsky has never seen herself as victimized by President Clinton; indeed, she has reiterated that her relationship with the former president was consensual, that "at the time—at least from [her] point of view—it was an authentic connection, with emotional intimacy, frequent visits, plans made, phone calls and gifts exchanged" (Lewinsky 2014).

Over two decades after Lewinsky's first sexual encounter with her husband on November 15, 1995, Hillary Rodham Clinton's rise to political prominence as a New

York senator, secretary of state, and perhaps president of the United States has been used to explain why she stayed with the former president after the affair. Although explanations range from a "genuine, intellectually and emotionally stimulating partnership" to a "colder, mutually advantageous political arrangement" (Eggertson 2012) and many books have been written about the Clintons and their marriage (see, for example, Chafe 2012), no one can really know why she has stayed with Bill. What is known is that Hillary Rodham Clinton is smart, independent, self-assured, and body confident. A more charitable, albeit controversial, explanation is that her relationship with Bill is perhaps an example of confluent love, which, as discussed in the first chapter, is grounded in the individual where intimacy is sought as part of self-development. It is an egalitarian, "pure relationship," undergoing monitoring and negotiation by both partners so that if one partner perceives the relationship as undermining the self, she or he ends it. Confluent love rests on a woman's control of her sexuality, and how she understands sexual satisfaction, and it is not necessarily dependent on sexual exclusivity or monogamy. An even more compelling example of confluent love is likely the relationship between the Obamas and, interestingly like Hillary, Michelle Obama is smart, independent, self-assured, and body confident. Unfortunately, Obama has given no indication that she wants to run for office after the end of her husband's second term as president. Although her "Let's Move" campaign has been criticized for focusing more on personal responsibility as opposed to addressing the obesogenic environment in a meaningful way, including tackling big food manufacturers and junk food advertising, she is clearly a role model, particularly for young, racialized women.

Body confidence is part of the creation of the viable sense of self crucial to confluent love. If intimacy is to be transformed and the ideals of individual autonomy and equality are to be realized particularly in heterosexual relationships, as Giddens (1992) has argued, women—and men—need to be more body confident. Although, as discussed above, a way to do this is for women to embrace the body-as-process associated with masculinity as opposed to the body-as-object associated with femininity, those lines have become increasingly blurred. In some instances, the fit, toned body has become more about appearance even for men, which is problematic. The point here is that although a fit, toned body may *appear* more attractive by societal standards than one that is not, the individual's motivating factor in taking care of his or her body should be performance or functioning (i.e., body-as-process), and not appearance (i.e., body-as-object). That is why body size is irrelevant, and being fit and fat makes a great deal of sense. Bodies that move come in all different sizes because the ideal is a healthy, active body, and not a thin, sleek one.

Unfortunately, women are not the only ones focusing on their appearance. Mark Simpson, who coined the term *metrosexual* to capture the changing nature of masculinity two decades ago when young heterosexual men living in urban centres began caring about, and spending money on, their clothes and personal comforts, has introduced the term *spornosexual* to illustrate more recent trends (Simpson 2014). Male body obsession has arguably reached a new level because "sport and porn are mashed together to produce men who want to be desired for their bodies and love to expose their rock-hard abs" (Richard 2014). Using British soccer star David Beckham as an example, the spornosexual has raised body image concerns, particularly for young men. According to Pepper Schwartz (as quoted in Richard 2014), "the conscious product of hours at the gym straining and heaving for just the right muscle definition, rather than as just having nice bodies from keeping in shape as athletes or because they need to be strong to carry a fire hose, is a major cultural change." As more and more men are becoming concerned about their appearance, body dissatisfaction and body shame are increasing. Wasylkiw et al. (2009) argue that

> when adolescent boys viewed images of men promoting performance, they experience positive self-perceptions and when they viewed images of men promoting appearance, they experience negative self-perceptions. Thus, muscular ideals produced very different effects as a function of whether appearance or performance was emphasized. (140)

The focus on appearance is nothing new for women. This emphasis on appearance is why Bordo (2003) did not distinguish between the "sleek, minimalist," thin body and the body with "firmly developed muscles" as resulting in the cultural oppression of women in the West (211). The focus on body-as-object by men, even as they are achieving it through sports and exercise, only reinforces body ideals based on appearance. This is a troubling trend because it not only undermines body confidence, but also threatens the progress of changing cultural norms in the West.

RECOMMENDED FILMS, VIDEO CLIPS, AND WEBSITES

"Fat Girl Tinder Date (Social Experiment)." 2014. www.youtube.com/watch?v=2alnVIj1Jf8.

"Fat Guy Tinder Date (Social Experiment)." 2014. www.youtube.com/watch?v=iUy3_kBme4M.

"Getting Started—Hillary Clinton." 2015. Published on April 12, 2015. www.youtube.com/watch?v=0uY7gLZDmn4.

Miss Representation. 2011. Documentary directed by Jennifer Siebel Newsom. www.filmsforaction.org/watch/miss_representation/. See also: therepresentationproject.org/about/.

ADDITIONAL READINGS

Coulombeau, Sophie. 2014. "I'm Getting Married: Should I Change My Surname?" *The Guardian*, December 12. www.theguardian.com/books/2014/dec/12/im-getting-married-should-i-change-my-surname.

Gailey, Jeannine. 2012. "Fat Shame to Fat Pride: Fat Women's Sexual and Dating Experiences." *Fat Studies* 1, no. 1: 114–27.

Hamilton, Laura, Claudia Geist, and Brian Powell. 2011. "Marital Name Change as a Window into Gender Attitudes." *Gender and Society* 25, no. 2: 145–75.

Hawkesworth, Mary. 2012. *Political Worlds of Women*. Boulder: Westview Press.

Mills, Sara. 2003. "Caught between Sexism, Anti-sexism and 'Political Correctness': Feminist Women's Negotiations with Naming Practices." *Discourse and Society* 14, no. 1: 87–110.

Moore, Sarah E. H. 2010. "Is the Healthy Body Gendered? Toward a Feminist Critique of the New Paradigm of Health." *Body and Society* 16, no. 2: 95–118.

Norman, Moss E. 2011. "Embodying the Double-Bind of Masculinity: Young Men and Discourses of Normalcy, Health, Heterosexuality, and Individualism." *Men and Masculinities* 14, no. 4: 430–49.

Scott, Linda M. 2005. *Fresh Lipstick*. London: Palgrave Macmillan.

Swami, Viren, and Martin Tovee. 2009. "Big Beautiful Women: The Body Size Preferences of Male Fat Admirers." *Journal of Sex Research* 46, no. 1: 89–96.

Thistle, Susan. 2006. *From Marriage to the Market*. Berkeley: University of California Press.

Weitz, Rose, ed. 2003. *The Politics of Women's Bodies: Sexuality, Appearance and Behaviour*. 2nd ed. New York: Oxford University Press.

Chapter 3
THE VEILING OF WOMEN

INTRODUCTION

In March 2015 when then prime minister Stephen Harper explicitly weighed in on why his government was appealing a federal court's ruling that overturned a 2011 directive made by one of his ministers and allowed the niqab—a face-covering veil worn by some Muslim women—to be worn while taking the oath during Canadian citizenship ceremonies, he entered a contentious debate on the veiling of Muslim women. Although women belonging to other religious traditions, such as Catholicism, Judaism, and Hinduism, have also worn head coverings as a symbol of their faith, the dominant understanding today when we talk about the veiling of women centres on Islam. This is not only because Islam has been placed front and centre in the post-9/11 security environment, but also because the veiling of Muslim women has been constructed as a prime example of cultural differences between the West and Islam. The difference stems from a common Western understanding that Muslim women, unlike liberated women in the West, are oppressed. With changing immigration patterns in both Europe and North America, where Muslim-minority communities have become more visible to the larger society, veiled women have become part of everyday realities in the West. Calls to ban the veil stem from concerns about gender equality and the need for limits to accommodating cultural differences. As then prime minister Harper stated in the House of Commons on March 10,

2015, "Why would Canadians, contrary to our own values, embrace a practice at that time that is not transparent, that is not open and, frankly, is rooted in a culture that is anti-women?"

It has been almost two decades since Susan Moller Okin (1999) first posed the question: "Is multiculturalism bad for women?" This was not a normative judgment, as some critics of Okin have suggested, that Western culture is superior to other cultures, or that the experiences of white, Western, heterosexual, middle-class women are universal, but rather a pressing question that Okin directed to liberal theorists who were advocating special rights for minority groups in liberal societies in cases where groups were internally illiberal, namely, violating the rights of women in the group (see Abbey 2011, 83–102). Although Okin (1999) opened her landmark essay with discussion of a controversy in the 1980s on whether French Muslim girls should be allowed to wear headscarves in schools, she saw polygamy as the real problem for gender equality within multicultural communities in France. She pointed out that whereas "the public was virtually silent about a problem of vastly greater importance to many French Arab and African immigrant women," caused by the French government's decision at the time to allow immigrant men to bring in multiple wives, it was the veil issue that generated a great deal of public attention and outcry (9). That attention continues, but coloured by security concerns caused by the 9/11 terrorist attacks, more contemporary debates about the veil in the West have not simply been about issues of multiculturalism and gender equality. Indeed, Western governments' identification of the terrorist threat as not merely outside of, but more importantly, within, the state's borders has created a climate of fear and suspicion of others, namely Muslims.

It is not simply that the 9/11 attacks happened on US soil, immediately prioritizing the importance of homeland security and the need for governments to police their borders, but also that subsequent high-profile attacks in the West have been all religiously motivated (see Bramadat and Dawson 2014), such as the 2004 Madrid train bombing and the 2005 London bombing, as well as more recent lone-wolf attacks such as the 2009 Fort Hood shooting, the 2013 Boston marathon bombing, and the 2014 Ottawa shooting. In addition, there have been other potential terrorist attacks that were prevented by police and security agencies, such as the arrests of the Toronto 18 in 2006. Just as with 9/11, Islamic extremism has been identified as the prime motivation for these terrorist attacks. Not only has this raised concerns about religious radicalization in the West, leading to debates about home-grown terrorism, but this has also brought back to the fore the role of religion in secular Western societies. For Western feminists, the role of religion adds a further complication to discussions of multiculturalism and gender equality because many reject organized religion, which has historically been and largely remains male-dominated. However, many women, particularly in Muslim-minority communities, are embracing their religious identities and, clearly, part of a woman's Muslim identity may be wearing the veil.

The Muslim veil comes in many forms because Islam, like Christianity and Judaism, is grounded in multiple traditions that have emerged from a variety of historical, economic, cultural, and political forces. Although it is common to assume that the inviolable core of any religion is its philosophical set of beliefs associated with transcendence, morality, and existential issues (i.e., its theology), religious studies scholars point out that all religions are historically contingent and socially constructed because, in practice, the religious lives of most people centre on human relationships, relationships with a divine figure, and everyday emotions, ideas, and convictions evident in the way people live their lives (see Bramadat 2000). Religion is understood not merely in terms of its ideas and proclamations around the divine, often discovered through key texts such as the Christian Bible, the Jewish Torah, and the Muslim Quran, but more importantly through its practices as rooted in particular cultures. That is why the question of whether the Quran requires the veil for women is more about theology (i.e., ideas and beliefs) than it is about religion (i.e., practices). In that way, the fact that some Muslim women wear the veil in the way that they do has less to do with the dictates of Islam and more to do with the dictates of culture. The various forms of the Muslim veil reflect specific cultural traditions as they have developed in different parts of the world.

Figure 3.1: Different Types of Muslim Veils

Source: Copyright © 2016 by Facing History and Ourselves. Reprinted with permission. www.facinghistory.org.

Although there are various forms of the Muslim veil, including the khimar, chador, shayla, and jilbab, the most common type of veil worn by Muslim women in the West is the hijab, a headscarf that is loosely worn to cover the hair, ears, and neck, and may be wrapped in the back. The al-amira hijab consists of two pieces—a larger headscarf and a smaller scarf that resembles a tube cap—and is also commonly seen in the West. These types of headscarves do not cover the face and are the kind seen in Tunisia, Egypt, Turkey, Iraq, and Iran. At different historical periods, these Muslim-majority countries have legislated banning the wearing of veils in public places largely to modernize the state, and in the case of Turkey, to uphold its tradition of secularism, although Iran, after the shah was deposed in 1979, has reinstituted the veiling of women under its theocratic regime.

In contrast, the burqa (or burka) and niqab cover the body from head to toe, and in the case of the burqa, the entire face is also covered except for a mesh screen for women to see through. Women in Afghanistan wear burqas, mandated under the former Taliban regime, which ruled the country from 1996 until 2001. The regime was deposed after 9/11 by United States–led military forces for sheltering Osama bin Laden and al Qaeda, but the Taliban remains an insurgent force in Afghanistan and has found refuge in neighbouring Pakistan. Brave 17-year-old Pakistani activist Malala Yousafzai (2013), the youngest winner of the Nobel Peace Prize when she was awarded it in 2014, was shot by a Taliban gunman in 2012 because she championed the education of girls. The niqab, which leaves the area around the eyes uncovered, is widely worn by women in Saudi Arabia. Women in Taliban-controlled territories and women in Saudi Arabia have faced the most restrictions on their movements in public places. For example, women and girls under Taliban-controlled territories have been largely confined to their homes and prohibited from attending schools or working, and Saudi women do not leave the house without a male chaperone, do not drive, and cannot vote, although because of a 2011 royal decree, they have been able to vote in local elections since 2015 (Dewey 2013). Muslim women wearing the burqa or niqab are also in the West, and these two types of veils have proven to be the most controversial, often resulting in conservative politicians in the West, like then prime minister Harper, making what appears to be a feminist case to ban their use in public places. Former French President Nicolas Sarkozy, a fellow conservative, was even more categorical in June 2009: "The problem of the burka is not a religious problem, it's a problem of liberty and women's dignity. It's not a religious symbol, but a sign of subservience and debasement. I want to say solemnly, the burka is not welcome in France. In our country, we can't accept women prisoners behind a screen, cut off from all social life, deprived of all identity. That's not our idea of freedom" (quoted in Chrisafis 2009).

To what extent are the cultural differences between the West and Islam as expounded by conservative opponents of the veil less about concerns for gender equality and more about security concerns and anti-immigrant sentiments? If the Muslim veil, specifically the burqa and niqab, does symbolize women's oppression, why are feminists divided on condemning it outright? Do efforts to ban the veil constitute reasonable limits in a liberal democratic society? Does the veil undermine women's control of their sexuality and their integration in Western society? What normative assumptions underpin the connection between liberalism and secularism, and how do these assumptions affect feminist liberalism? These are the questions that are addressed in this chapter. The chapter is divided into three sections: first, the debates around veil bans, including the former Parti Québécois government's failed Charter of Values (introduced in 2013), illustrate that the veiling of Muslim women cannot be understood outside of the current post-9/11 security environment; second, current discussions are underpinned by the relationship between women's dress, sexuality, and social harmony; and third, the connection between liberalism and secularism perhaps points to another system of dominance for feminist liberalism to consider. As argued in the chapter, the veiling issue is not about cultural differences between the West and Islam, but about systems of dominance that undermine individual autonomy.

THE POST-9/11 ENVIRONMENT AND VEIL BANS

The terrorist attacks on the World Trade Center in New York City and the Pentagon in Washington, D.C., on September 11, 2001, not only resulted in the quick passage of anti-terrorism legislation in both the United States and Canada, allowing for increased governmental surveillance and detention powers to thwart potential terrorists within their respective states (Keeble 2005), but also reinforced Western ideas about Islam as different from the West, prone to violence with its calls to jihadism and grounded in gender and sexual oppression. This conflation of Islam with both terrorism and women's oppression has led to dominant perceptions of Muslim men as terrorists and Muslim women as oppressed, so that the men need to be watched and detained and the women to be educated and saved. Not only does the question of individual liberty lie at the heart of both understandings, but in both instances Muslims are also unfairly singled out. In terms of anti-terrorism legislation, individual rights are curtailed in the name of security. Often referred to as the liberty-security conundrum because the expansion of government powers is seen as necessary to keep individuals safe, this has led to concerns about racial and religious profiling. The concerns are not unfounded, not only because many Muslims in their everyday lives find themselves singled out in airports, train stations, and even shopping malls, but also because the case of Maher Arar, a Syrian Canadian whose subsequent detention in the United States and deportation to and torture in Syria in 2001–2 were due to the actions of Canadian security officials, has become a cause célèbre for people concerned about injustices perpetuated against Canadian Muslims in the post 9/11 context. Although it was the Harper government that apologized to, and compensated, Arar in 2007 after a long and exhaustive judicial inquiry led by Justice Dennis O'Connor found that the Royal Canadian Mounted Police (RCMP) mislabelled Arar as an Islamic extremist with suspected ties to al Qaeda, that did not stop the former Conservative government from proposing further anti-terrorism measures, such as the recent Anti-Terrorism Act (Bill C-51), introduced in January 2015, or stating that the security threat to Canada is "violent jihadism" (McGregor and O'Malley 2015), thus invoking once again the relationship between Islam and terrorism. This is problematic because despite countless proclamations made by Western leaders, including by former US president George Bush and former Canadian prime minister Jean Chrétien immediately after the attacks, that Islam was not responsible for the events of September 11, the rise of Islamophobia and the fear of a backlash against Muslim minorities living in the West have become only too real. That is why US president Obama "chooses his words with particular care when he addresses the volatile connections between religion and terrorism [and avoids] labeling acts of brutal violence by Al-Qaeda, the so-called Islamic State and their allies as 'Muslim' terrorism or describing their ideology as 'Islamic' or 'jihadist'" (Shane 2015).

In terms of efforts to ban the veil, the focus has been on the banning of the burqa and the niqab because, as the most concealing of veils, many observers from feminists to conservative politicians reject that women actually choose to wear these garments. Because these are the types of veils that are symbolic of gender inequality, they should be banned in order to ensure individual liberty. Most observers accept that there is a difference between these face-concealing veils and the hijab. The wearing of the hijab, the type most worn by Muslim women in the West, has been accepted as a matter of choice. That is why as then prime minister Harper voiced his opposition to the niqab, he condemned the action of a Quebec court judge who had refused to hear a woman's case unless the woman removed her hijab (Rukavina 2015). Unlike the hijab, the burqa and the niqab are seen as examples of cultural male domination, imported from a fundamentalist interpretation of Islam and associated with the Salafist movement in Saudi Arabia. At first glance, why all feminists do not support banning these face-concealing veils makes little sense, except perhaps out of fear of agreeing with conservatives. As Egyptian-born, Muslim-American feminist Mona Eltahawy (2010) has argued:

> A bizarre political correctness [in defence of the niqab and the burka] has tied the tongues of those who would normally rally to defend women's rights but who are now instead sacrificing those very rights in the name of fighting an increasingly powerful right wing.... I detest the niqab and the burka for their erasure of women and for dangerously equating piety with that disappearance—the less of you I can see, the closer you must be to God. I defend a woman's right to cover her hair if she chooses but the face is central to human interaction and so the ideologues who promote its covering are simply misogynists.

Canadian conservative columnist Barbara Kay (2014) states similarly the oppressive nature of the niqab and burqa: "Face cover is anti-social, anti-equality and anti-community in the larger sense of the word. It is associated with oppressive, misogynistic regimes. It is not clothing and is not worn; it is a mask and is, so to speak, 'borne.'"

As asserted by then president Sarkozy, who was the leader of the conservative Union for a Popular Movement before taking the French presidency, the burqa is "a problem of liberty and women's dignity [and] a sign of subservience and debasement." It is not surprising that France under his watch was the first state to pass legislation banning the wearing of burqas and niqabs in all public places. France already had a law in place, passed in 2004, that banned headscarves in public schools by prohibiting the wearing of "conspicuous religious symbols" in state-funded schools. This 2004 law does not distinguish between different types of Muslim veils; is applicable to other religions (so, for example, students are also prohibited from wearing Jewish skullcaps or large Christian crosses); and applies only to public elementary and high schools (so it does not cover private schools or post-secondary educational institutions, nor does it cover public places). The veil ban that came into effect in April 2011 applies to all public places (so any place outside of a woman's private home), imposing a €150 fine and instruction in citizenship for women wearing face-concealing veils; and for anyone found forcing a woman to cover her face (for example, her husband), the penalty is even greater: a fine of €30,000 (Rustici 2011). The differential in fines stems from the perspective that a woman wearing a burqa or a niqab must necessarily be oppressed, and thus a greater punishment is meted out to the "oppressor." Belgium and Italy have followed suit in banning veils worn in public, and other European countries are considering similar bans. As highlighted by Andreassen and Lettinga (2012) in their examination of eight European states, including France and Belgium, the oppression of women is the primary reason given for the veil bans, and many feminists throughout Europe support the banning of veils. However, as they argue further, European "feminists who tried to put Muslim women's equality and self-determination on the agenda saw their feminist claims being hijacked by conservative and populist right-wing politicians who used it as a vehicle to curtail immigration and to exclude (non-liberal) Muslim minorities from the national community" (Andreassen and Lettinga 2012, 23). As Jocelyne Cesari (2005) asserts, the post-9/11 era has resulted not only in the targeting of Muslims in the West, but also in the legitimation of deeply held anti-Islamic public claims that were, particularly in Europe, once mainly the purview of far-right elements in society.

Yet, only a handful of states and smaller jurisdictions in Europe have actually banned the burqa and niqab. As Rosenberger and Sauer (2012) have observed about the veil debates in Europe, despite "the occurrence of fierce public contentions over the various meanings of the headscarf, it is surprising that policymakers in only a few nation states decided on restrictive headscarf regulations ... [where] prohibitive regulations are limited to specific social sites, namely state institutions, and to specific groups of covered women, e.g., pupils, teachers or public servants" (1). The United States and Canada have not passed any legislation banning veils but in 2011, the Canadian federal government placed a specific ban on face coverings, such as niqabs, for individuals swearing their oath of citizenship. Echoing European arguments about the oppression of women, then Conservative citizenship and immigration minister Jason Kenney stated:

> [The religious obligation to wear a veil] is a cultural tradition, which I think reflects a certain view about women that we don't accept in Canada. We want women to be full and equal members of Canadian society and certainly when they're taking the citizenship oath, that's the

right place to start. (quoted in Payton 2011)

This was the ministerial directive overturned by a federal judge that, as stated in the introduction, led then prime minister Harper to enter the fray on debates on the Muslim veil. Interestingly, when Harper announced that the federal government was appealing the judge's ruling, he was at an event in the province of Quebec. Not only have Quebecers overwhelmingly supported the niqab ban during citizenship ceremonies compared to the rest of the country—one poll placed Quebec public support at 87 percent, whereas overall nationwide support was 67 percent (Vincent 2015)—but successive provincial governments in Quebec have stood alone in proposing veil bans through the years.

The most overreaching legislative ban was proposed by the Parti Québécois government under then premier Pauline Marois, the province's first female premier. It would have banned Quebec provincial government employees from wearing veils of any type (so not just burqas or niqabs) as part of their job requirement. Introduced in fall 2013 in the Quebec National Assembly as Bill 60, the Quebec Charter of Values (2013)—or its full title, the Charter Affirming the Values of State Secularism and Religious Neutrality and of Equality between Women and Men, and Providing a Framework for Accommodation Requests—met with a great deal of controversy. Contained in the wording of the full title were arguably the three principal reasons why the then minority government under Marois proposed the Charter of Values:

1. To preserve secularism in Quebec (the legislation was purportedly directed to all religions, such as Judaism, Christianity, and Sikhism, so not just Islam);
2. To end "female oppression and submission" (the position of the Quebec government was similar to that of many European governments in seeing veils as oppressive); and
3. To clarify accommodation requests (such requests would be limited; for example, recipients of government services would have to have their faces uncovered).

The proposed legislation would have applied to all government employees and it would have banned them from wearing "overt and conspicuous" religious symbols, such as veils, kippahs, turbans, and "large crosses." The argument was made that because provincial government employees represent the state, and the state is secular, which means that it must be neutral (i.e., not showing partiality for any particular religion), then government employees should not be wearing religious symbols. However, the Bouchard-Taylor Commission, established by the previous Liberal government under Jean Charest in 2007 to look at the reasonable accommodation of minorities, stated in its 2008 report that this logic is problematic. "It is inconsistent, according to the [Bouchard-Taylor] Report, to assume that people who publicly display religious symbols are less impartial than individuals who, although they have religious affiliations, do not display them publicly" (Eberle 2013). Moreover, not only would small crosses have been allowed (after all, these would not be overt and conspicuous), but the crucifix in the National Assembly, the large cross on top of Mount Royal in Montreal, Christmas trees in public institutions, and opening prayers at municipal meetings would have also been allowed because, according to Bill 60, these reflected "the emblematic and toponymic elements of Quebec's cultural heritage that testify to its history" (Quebec Charter of Values 2013).

The criticisms levied against the proposed Charter of Values were varied and compelling. For example, many argued that it would have violated the freedom of religion found in both the Canadian Charter of Rights and Freedoms and the Quebec Charter of Human Rights and Freedoms (the Quebec Charter would have been amended by the proposed legislation to prevent challenges). Others criticized that it would have perpetuated an environment of intolerance and hostility toward immigrants and minorities (these sorts of critiques were not new in Quebec; they also arose in response to Herouxville's infamous "code of conduct" in 2007 as well as to demands that women had to have their faces uncovered when they voted in provincial elections or received government services). Others pointed out that it demonstrated the division between feminists, privileging white women's voices, particularly given Janette Bertrand, a well-known Quebec television personality, published a letter co-signed by 20 other women in three Quebec newspapers on October 15, 2013, supporting the Charter. Moreover, the Charter of Values was seen as a political ploy by the Parti Québécois not only to distract voters from real problems, such as the economy, but also to further its separatist agenda by building a "national" identity.

However, believing that the proposed Charter of Values had widespread support throughout the province, Premier Marois called for an election to take place on April 7, 2014, with the expectation of turning her minority government into a majority. Instead, the Parti Québécois suffered a dramatic defeat at the hands of the Quebec Liberal Party, which formed a majority government under Premier Philippe Couillard. Marois lost her own seat in the provincial election and resigned from the leadership of the Parti Québécois. After the election, reports surfaced that the Marois government had not consulted its justice ministry for a legal opinion on whether the Charter of Values was constitutional, and indeed because challenges to the law would have been imminent, had clearly acted irresponsibly if the Charter of Values had come into effect (Macpherson 2014). Although the Charter was defeated along with the Parti Québécois, the provincial Liberal government under Premier Couillard tabled Bill 62—what it calls a neutrality bill—in the National Assembly in June 2015. Similar to Bill 94 introduced by a previous Liberal minority government under then premier Jean Charest in 2010, the proposed provincial legislation bans face-concealing veils in the giving and receiving of provincial government services. The majority government under Couillard can easily pass the bill. Less than two weeks after the Quebec government tabled its bill, the federal government under then prime minister Harper introduced legislation on June 19, 2015, to ban the niqab in citizenship ceremonies, thus seeking to enshrine in law what was a ministerial directive struck down in court. Introduced "exactly one hour and 15 minutes before the House of Commons rose for the last time before the [fall] election," Bill C-75—the Oath of Citizenship Act—was an example of "wedge politics" where, particularly in Quebec, support for such legislative bans "pits logic against emotions—and can win elections" (Fitz-Morris 2015). Given the unpopularity of the Harper government going into the October 19, 2015, federal election, the Conservatives appeared to be using every measure, no matter how problematic, to gain support. Although the niqab ban did become an issue during the 78-day fall election campaign, and New Democratic Party leader Thomas Mulcair conceded that his stance on opposing the ban likely cost his party votes, particularly in Quebec, the emergence of a majority Liberal government under Justin Trudeau underscored the importance of the Liberal leader's speech on March 9, 2015, condemning the niqab ban from the very beginning. Entitled "Canadian Liberty and the Politics of Fear," and identified by Trudeau in a *Huffington Post* interview during the fall election as the speech of which he is most proud, he stated unequivocally:

> For me, it is basic truth that prime ministers of liberal democracies ought not to be in the business of telling women what they can and cannot wear on their head during public ceremonies—least of all, this liberal democracy. Cloaking an argument about what women can wear

> in the language of feminism has to be the most innovative perversion of liberty that conservatives have invented in a while. It is, of course, not the first time the most illiberal of ends has been packaged in the language of liberation.... But what's even worse than what they're saying is what they really mean. We all know what is going on here. It is nothing less than an attempt to play on people's fears and foster prejudice, directly toward the Muslim faith. (Trudeau 2015)

In all these cases, from the legislation passed in France and other European states, to the number of legislative attempts in Quebec, Trudeau arguably identifies the problem for many feminists, which is that veil bans cannot be easily disentangled from anti-immigrant and anti-Muslim sentiments that exist in Western society, sentiments that have become more prevalent in the post-9/11 era because of the association of Islam with terrorism. Indeed, because the burqa and niqab are associated with more conservative forms of Islam, the veil has also become a symbol of religious extremism, which has made it a security risk that needs to be addressed. In October 2014, in the face of the growing strength of the Islamic State (also referred to as ISIS and ISIL) in Iraq and Syria and its apparent success in radicalizing Muslims in the West, Australian lawmakers considered banning all individuals with "facial coverings" from the public galleries in Parliament due to security concerns, relegating these individuals to a separate glass-enclosed section usually reserved for children. Clearly directed at women who wear burqas or niqabs, which created an immediate public backlash against the discriminatory treatment of Muslim women who wanted to view their country's lawmakers at work, then Australian prime minister Tony Abbott quickly backtracked. As Australia's human rights commissioner Tim Wilson pointed out, not only was there no justification for such a ban from a security perspective, but there was also the irony that "if there was a danger, then why would we sit people with children?" (quoted in Massola 2014). Unlike in the immediate aftermath of 9/11, many members of the Western public, as in Australia, have been less willing to support measures that violate individual rights undertaken by their governments in the name of security because these measures have led in many ways to religious and racial profiling due to the association of Islam with terrorism. That is why, among many reasons including problematic aspects of the Harper government's Anti-Terrorism Act 2015 (Bill C-51) related to the further securitization of the state, there were widespread protests against the bill throughout Canada. Seeing the veiling of Muslim women as a security risk, however, is nothing new. As Nussbaum (2012) points out, "what inspires fear and mistrust in Europe and, to some extent, in the United States [and, it makes sense to add, Canada and Australia] is not covering per se, but Muslim covering" (107). The wording of the French ban is instructive in this regard. It "is worded to trip safely through legal minefields: The words 'women', 'Muslim' and 'veil' are not even mentioned" (Rustici 2011). Nussbaum (2012) points out that instead the law prohibits "wearing attire designed to hide the face," but with a "long list of exceptions," namely "if the attire is prescribed or authorized by legislative or regulatory dispensation, if it is justified for reasons of health or professional motives, or if it is adopted in the context of athletic practices, festivals, or artistic or traditional performance" (133). In other words, the French law makes an exception for all face-concealing attire *except* the burqa and niqab.

Nussbaum's (2012) analysis goes further. In exploring why veil bans do not constitute reasonable limits in a liberal democratic society, she also explores feminist concerns about the oppression of Muslim women. She looks in particular at two concerns: first, the burqa is a symbol of male domination that objectifies women, and second, the burqa is evidence of coercion or violence in women's lives. Nussbaum points out that symbols of male dominance that objectify women are found everywhere in liberal democratic societies, from the easy availability of harmful pornographic material to women's decisions to undergo plastic surgery, but these practices are not banned. As Nussbaum states, "the way to deal with sexism, in this case as in all, is by persuasion and example, not by removing liberty" (116). In terms of the second argument, Nussbaum states that domestic violence is also everywhere in liberal democratic societies and it is not a uniquely Muslim problem. All forms of violence in the home are illegal, and in terms of "coercive pressure," all families make demands of their members and the government does not step in because "intervention would [only] be justified … in cases in which the behaviour constitutes a gross risk to bodily health and safety" (124). In other words, women's oppression is nothing new in Western societies. To single out the veiling of Muslim women only adds to the fear of backlash toward Muslim minority communities in the post-9/11 environment.

The cross-cultural nature of women's oppression is encapsulated in a thought-provoking drawing, entitled "Cruel Culture," by a New Zealand cartoonist, Malcolm Evans, that has been circulating on the web since it was first published in a number of New Zealand newspapers in January 2011. The cartoon depicts a white, blond-haired woman wearing a bikini, and with sunglasses on, she is staring at a woman wearing a niqab, who, in turn, is staring at her. As she looks at the other woman, the bikini-clad woman thinks: "Everything covered but her eyes. What a cruel male-dominated culture." In returning her look, the niqab-clad woman thinks: "Nothing covered but her eyes. What a cruel male-dominated culture."

Figure 3.2: "Cruel Culture"

Source: By permission of Malcolm Evans

The cartoon shows that the male gaze as a way of explaining the source of women's oppression transcends cultural boundaries. Because the focus remains on a woman's appearance in a male-dominated society, it matters little whether she is wearing a bikini or a niqab (or a burqa). What matters is how societal constructs dictate how women should look and how women, in turn, have internalized their oppression.

WOMEN'S DRESS, SEXUALITY, AND SOCIAL HARMONY

The analogy, however, between the bikini and the niqab invites further examination because the veil has signified not only the oppression of women but also their sexual repression. In the aftermath of then Australian prime minister Abbott's attempt in October 2014 to ban women wearing burqas and niqabs from the public galleries in Parliament, Mariam

Veiszadeh, an Australian lawyer, community advocate, and former refugee born in Kabul, Afghanistan, started a social media campaign in Australia to encourage non-Muslim women to take and share pictures wearing a hijab in order to show solidarity with Muslim women (Whiting 2014). Interestingly, the criticisms levied against the campaign were directed to what was described as the inappropriate, if not offensive, posting of sexy-looking selfies of Australian women in hijabs because "liberal attitudes that give rise to drinking, clubbing, bikinis, blowjobs and Slutwalks [cannot be reconciled with] the traditions that give rise to the hijab and niqab" (Lehmann 2014). The argument here is that the veiling of Muslim women is about modesty, and thus rooted in conservative traditions, so sexually liberated women donning the headscarf were making a mockery of the Muslim faith. This conservative argument, however, brings out concerns that the veil is an affront to sexual liberation. After all, women's dress in the West has evolved alongside sexual freedoms, "beginning with Coco Chanel, who believed women should share the same liberties as men and replaced restrictive corsets and long skirts with jersey dresses, knits and pants [so that] instructing a woman to cover up to preserve sexual modesty and prevent lustful thoughts is viewed as archaic and misogynistic" (Kingston 2012).

Muslim women are veiled, then, because of the need to hide as opposed to celebrate the female body. Because "Muslims are positioned as a threat to feminist achievements of (bodily) self-determination and equality," they are positioned even more as being fundamentally different from the West (Andreassen and Lettinga 2012, 20). Given the lesser positions accorded to both women and sexual minorities in some Muslim-majority states, like Iran, Afghanistan, or Saudi Arabia, where Islam is the official religion, the "new version of the 'clash of civilizations' ... is not about democracy but gender equality and sexual [liberalization] ... [and] the construction of Muslims as *essentially different* from liberal Western subjects and of their culture as *inherently* sexist and homophobic" (Bilge 2010, 10). Given large-scale immigration from Muslim-majority countries to the West, this problematic view has permeated immigration policies. For example, this is the reasoning behind the Netherlands deciding that potential immigrants would have to go through "integration tests that included compulsory viewing of a film of Dutch culture featuring a topless sunbathing woman and gay men kissing" (23). This would be the "test" if Muslim immigrants could overcome their difference and assimilate into Dutch society.

The Western idea of veiling as indicative of repressed sexuality, however, is a "reversal of earlier historical depictions of non-Western sexuality [because] 'Oriental' cultures have traditionally been the repository of Western sexual fantasy" (Mottier 2008, 119). For example, the work of Sir Richard Burton, the 19th-century British explorer who translated *Arabian Nights* and the *Kama Sutra*, brought out the idea of the exotic, erotic other. Harems, in particular, were seen as sites for sex. Why has there been a change in Western thinking? It is because sexual liberation has become the marker for the West, leading to Western conceptions of the veil as sexual repression and a rejection of the beauty of the female body. At the same time, harking on this difference between the West and Islam has led others to argue that the veil can be seen as an act of resistance and, in that way, challenges rather than exemplifies oppression. Grounded in post-colonial feminist critiques of Western hegemony, "the veil becomes a symbol of contest, as well as a marker of self-authored difference and authenticity," where veiled women are standing up against Western imperialism, global capitalism, and post-9/11 Islamophobia and "[liberating] themselves from the oppressive beauty culture of the West and the objectifying male gaze" (Bilge 2010, 20). As Zunera Ishaq (2015), the Pakistani-born woman from Toronto who challenged the 2011 ministerial directive that would have forced her to take off her niqab while giving her oath of citizenship, has stated: "I like how [the niqab] makes me feel: like people have to look beyond what I look like to get to know me. That I don't have to worry about my physical appearance and can concentrate on my inner self. That it empowers me in this regard."

However, as discussed in Chapter 2, the feminine body-as-object in the West is problematic for Western feminists. The taming and controlling of the female body has led to the pathologizing of fat, creating an unattainable thin body ideal, which has led to women's self-loathing and body shame. Internalizing their own oppression due to self-objectification, women are led to believe that they need to succumb to a "beauty myth" perpetuated in Western society. However, Kathy Davis (1991) has argued that women in the West are not simply "cultural dupes" when they focus on their bodies, particularly because many women say that looking or feeling beautiful is something that they do for themselves. According to Catherine Hakim (2010), many women who focus on their appearance and wear more provocative clothing, such as bikinis, low-cut blouses, form-fitting dresses, thongs, or stilettos, are simply building their "erotic capital." Whether women are choosing to dress the way that they do or internalizing their own oppression (i.e., false consciousness) has been a key question. Although as discussed in the previous chapter, the body-as-object can be transcended by the body-as-process, instilling body confidence, and women who live healthy, active lifestyles or do regular exercise might choose to wear a bikini, not because they fit a thin body ideal, but because they are less self-conscious and feel body confident, feminists have been divided on women's dress and sexuality. Many women in the West have chosen to resist what they see as the objectification of women's bodies and have refused to succumb to societal constructs of feminine beauty and dress, so rejecting "the oppressive beauty culture of the West and the objectifying male gaze" (Bilge 2010, 20) ties, rather than divides, many Western and Muslim women.

As Bakht (2012) notes, there has not been a great deal of research done on why Muslim women wear the niqab, but there have been studies on why women wear the hijab. According to these studies, women's reasons vary from expressing their religious identity, to resisting sexism and racism, to maintaining a modest form of dress, to making a fashion statement. As stated earlier, women who wear the hijab are not the targets of veil bans. Although Bakht argues that research on the hijab is instructive for understanding women's reasons for wearing the niqab, there is a difference between the two types of veils. The niqab (like the burqa) is face-concealing, and although women like Ishaq may choose to wear it, it is a "mask," as Barbara Kay (2014) has argued, one that closes a woman off from social interaction. There is a great deal to be learned from body language and body cues when individuals interact with others. One of the arguments made by the French government in defending its burqa ban law when it was challenged in the European Court of Human Rights was the necessity for transparency and social harmony. Handing down its decision in July 2014, the European Court accepted the French argument that the government's goal was to encourage citizens to "live together." The Belgian government, which has a similar ban, participated in arguing the case, and its representative stated plainly that the law is "about social communication, the right to interact with someone by looking them in the face and about not disappearing under a piece of clothing" (Willsher 2014).

However, as Nussbaum (2012) points out, why is it that the onus is placed on the individual wearing the burqa or niqab to make others feel comfortable? "People often have difficulty talking to people who look odd, and there's an unfortunate tendency to blame this difficulty on the person who looks odd rather than on oneself" (Nussbaum 2012, 112). Drawing on how society has historically stigmatized individuals with facial deformities or people with disabilities, Nussbaum notes that individuals have learned to interact socially with people who may make them initially uncomfortable, so singling out women who wear the burqa or niqab unfairly targets Muslim women. It is important to understand, according to Nussbaum, that "the faculty with which people search for life's ultimate meaning—frequently called 'conscience'—is a very important part of people, closely related to their dignity [so that] ... to violate conscience is to conduct an assault on human dignity" (65). Burqa bans "are not compatible with the idea of equal respect for conscience from which [a principle of equal liberty] springs" (105) because underpinning these arguments is the privileging of the majority over the minority without sound or defensible reasoning for violating the rights of the minority. Nussbaum admits that her contentions are "historically more American than European" because Europeans have preferred assimilationist strategies, specifically of religious minorities, and "have not been as eager as Americans to develop legal regimes that insist on fairness to minorities in matters where majorities make law, and even on some degree of accommodation for minority practices" (60). That might explain why both the United States and Canada (with the exception of Quebec, which, some argue, is more like France) have not moved to legislate veil bans.

At the same time, just because the United States and Canada have not passed legislation does not mean that anti-Muslim sentiments do not exist. The uneasiness with Muslim-minority communities is evident throughout the West. This is not surprising to observers who are familiar with historical representations of Islam in the West. For example, according to Jocelyne Cesari (2005), "it is striking how the idea of Islam as an international 'risk factor' current since the 1980s, is bolstered by centuries-old representations of Islam … [and the] same fixed ideas of Islam as an inherently violent and fanatical religion are continually re-invoked and readjusted to fit changes in international and domestic situations" (39). Cesari points out that this thinking regarding Islam was characteristic of European governments in dealing with their Muslim minorities long before 9/11, and that in the American case there was at least a distinction made between Islam as manifested in the Muslim or Arab world and Muslims who had immigrated to the West. This all changed in 2001. In the post-9/11 era, there has been a "convergence of European and American political discourse" (38). The ease by which this happened can arguably be traced to the relationship between liberalism and secularism.

LIBERALISM AND SECULARISM

Progress, as pointed out in Chapter 1, is an important component of a feminist liberal framework. However, the development of the modern liberal democratic state proceeding concomitantly with the advancement toward secularism has been uncritically accepted in the West, particularly by scholars in the humanities and social sciences (Berger 1999, 10). The proposition that "modernization necessarily leads to a decline of religion, both in society and in the minds of individuals" is the root of secularism (2). Irrespective of whether individuals are religious or not, the argument here is that everyone accepts that religion will inevitably recede to the background as societies modernize. Progressive-minded individuals see the decline of religion as a sign of progress, whereas religiously orthodox or conservative individuals see themselves as having to either reject modernity or adapt themselves to what is perceived as inevitable (3). In other words, secularism is seen as a moving force that cannot be stopped as societies modernize and progress. For some Muslim-majority states, like Turkey and Egypt, the forced unveiling of women in public was part of their modernization efforts to separate Islam from the state.

For many feminists, the progress toward secularism has been a welcome one because many of the world's religions, and in particular the three monotheistic faiths, namely Judaism, Christianity, and Islam, are seen as patriarchal institutions that have perpetuated the second-class treatment of women. It is commonly accepted that Western liberal democratic states rooted in Judeo-Christian traditions have progressed beyond religious dominance in public life because the separation of Church and State has properly placed religion in the private sphere. Liberal democratic states protect freedom of religion and conscience, and therefore protect the rights of individual believers, but they do not promote or protect any particular set of individual beliefs, and thus have done away with religious laws such as blasphemy. Many Western feminists identify themselves as either atheists or secularists, and if they subscribe to ideas and beliefs, it is often framed in terms of spirituality or alternative belief systems. The sacred texts of the three Abrahamic faiths, namely the Torah, the Bible, and the Quran, are themselves implicated in preaching the subordination of women so that it is not merely religious practices but also religious texts that undermine women's rights. As Bronwyn Winter (2001, 12) argues, "all monotheistic texts [are] oppressive to women, even if the occasional verse or liberal interpretation thereof may offer women some protection against disinheritance or male violence." In that way, regardless of the culture in which they are practised, all religions are arguably problematic for women. That is why Pope Francis excommunicated an Australian priest who advocated for women to be ordained into the priesthood (Stuart 2013); ultra-Orthodox Jewish men flying from New York to Tel-Aviv refused to sit next to women on a plane (Blumberg 2014); and a York University male student in Toronto asked not to be forced to interact with female students in his class (Grayson 2014).

Given the development of the modern liberal, secular state, Bruce Lincoln (2002) argues that what dominates Western society is a "minimalist" vision of the place of religion in social life (59). According to Lincoln, minimalists contend that however important religion might be to oneself, one's family, or one's religious community, religion and the state should be governed by different people, rules, and principles. Each must leave the other alone, except in very rare circumstances, such as when religious communities infringe on the civil or human rights of their members. Closely associated with this minimalist sensibility is what is referred to as the secularization hypothesis, which scholars trace to the work of August Comte, Emile Durkheim, Max Weber, Karl Marx, and Sigmund Freud, who together reflected the emerging conviction that religion—especially in its "maximalist" form in which it pervaded all aspects of a believer's life as well as the whole society and the state (Lincoln 2002, 59)—not only *would* eventually shrink in the face of the development of complex, rationalized, and increasingly differentiated democracies, but *ought* to do so to allow for the full flowering of individual autonomy and reason so celebrated during and after the Enlightenment. This normative position accounts for why liberal thinkers accept uncritically that religion must recede into the background.

However, as Elizabeth Hurd (2008) has argued, secularism, virtually unacknowledged in political science, is "a form of political authority in its own right, and its consequences [need to be] evaluated" (1). She presents two variants of what she calls "political secularism," which provides insight to how the West regards religion. The first variant, laicism, which has its origins in the French term *laïcité*, stems from a "separationist' narrative in which religion is outside of politics, "rul[ing] out in advance the linkages between religion and spheres of power and authority such as law, science, and politics within states" and "positing itself as public, neutral, and value-free, while assigning religion the role of its private, affective, and value-laden counterpart" (36–37). The second variant, Judeo-Christian secularism, stems from a more "accommodationist" perspective where the Judeo-Christian tradition is seen as the root of Western political order and democratic political institutions. Whereas "in the laicist account of secularization, the [Judeo-]Christian identity of the West was superseded, radically transformed, and for all practical purposes rendered irrelevant," this second type sees that identity as central to the emergence of the modern liberal democratic, secular state (39–40). According to Hurd, both of these variants have contributed to the "consolidation of modern national identities as secular and democratic," and particularly in the case of French and American national identities, that consolidation has been in opposition to Islam. As Hurd argues, "laicist assumptions contribute to depictions of Islam as a surmountable though formidable stumbling block to the rationalization and democratization of societies, whereas Judeo-Christian secularist assumptions lead to more ominous conclusions in which Islam is portrayed as a potential threat to the cultural, moral, and religious foundations of Western civilization that must be successfully defused" (47).

Hurd's arguments are compelling. She reveals how political secularism, with its laicist and Judeo-Christian secularist variants, has been characteristic of virtually every liberal democratic state. In other words, Hurd draws attention to the extent to which Western ideas of secularism are embedded in the construction of Islam as the "other," so that even before 9/11, there was already a predisposition in the West not only to capitalize on differences between the West and Islam, but also to see Islam as a threat. The idea of Judeo-Christianity as the norm in the West and Islam as its contradistinction points arguably to another system of dominance that contravenes the universal ideals of equality, freedom, and justice in liberal thinking. In addition to sexism, heterosexism, racism, classism, and ableism, it is perhaps important to acknowledge "righteous secularism"—the term Hurd (2008, 34–35) used—as another system of dominance that undermines equality between individuals, thus accounting for why Muslim women in the West may be specifically disadvantaged because of their faith. The veiling of women in the West is not about cultural differences between the West and Islam, but about systems of dominance that undermine individual autonomy. That does not mean that Muslim women are reduced to religion alone in terms of their identity because individuals are differently situated in the West, but that secularism is not simply a marker of difference but also one of power.

Understanding this may also help secular feminists in taking religion seriously. Taking the position, as Bronwyn Winter (2001) does, that all monotheistic texts, such as the Quran, are oppressive of women undermines individual efforts to reconcile issues of faith and gender equality. Faith is a central part of the identities of many women in Muslim-majority countries throughout the world and Muslim-minority communities in the West. Particularly in the West, a woman's Muslim identity may be more properly seen as about theology (i.e., Islamic ideas as found in the Quran) than it is about religion (i.e., Islamic cultural practices as found in differing parts of the world). In that way, this may speak more to Nussbaum's articulation of conscience as "the faculty with which people search for life's meaning" (2012, 65). Many Islamic feminists have sought to reinterpret sacred texts in ways that challenge patriarchal practices in their communities, and in expressing their religious piety as Muslims, some of them wear a veil, even a face-concealing one.

RECOMMENDED FILMS, VIDEO CLIPS, AND WEBSITES

"Behind the Veil." 2015. Episode of *Fifth Estate*, CBC (Canada). Original broadcast date: April 3, 2015. www.cbc.ca/fifth/episodes/2014-2015/behind-the-veil.

I Wasn't Always Dressed Like This. 2013. Documentary directed by Betty Martins (United Kingdom). www.d-aep.org/portfolio/i-wasn%C2%B4t-always-dressed-like-this/.

Me and the Mosque. 2005. Documentary directed by Zarqa Nawaz (Canada). www.nfb.ca/film/me_and_mosque.

Veiled Voices. 2009. Documentary directed by Brigid Maher (United States). www.veiledvoices.com/.

Women of Islam: Veiling and Seclusion. 2004. Documentary directed by Farheen Umar (United States). www.womenofislam.net/.

ADDITIONAL READINGS

Ardizzoni, Michela. 2004. "Unveiling the Veil." *Women's Studies* 33, no. 5: 629–49.

Barlow, Rebecca, and Shahram Akbarzadeh. 2006. "Women's Rights in the Muslim World." *Third World Quarterly* 27, no. 8: 1481–94.

Cady, Linell E., and Tracy Fessenden. 2013. *Religion, the Secular, and the Politics of Sexual Difference*. New York: Columbia University Press.

Deveaux, Monique. 2013. "Regimes of Accommodation, Hierarchies of Rights." In *Revealing Democracy: Secularism and Religion in Liberal Democratic States*, edited by Chantal Maille, Greg M. Nielsen, and Daniel Salee, 77–94. Brussels: Peter Lang.

Farley, Margaret A. 2008. *A Framework for Christian Sexual Ethics*. London: Continuum International Publishing Group.

Fernandez, Sonya. 2009. "The Crusade over the Bodies of Women." *Patterns of Prejudice* 43, no. 3–4: 269–86.

Fox, Jonathan. 2012. *Religion, Politics, Society, and the State*. New York: Oxford University Press.

Marcotte, Roxane. 2010. "Muslim Women in Canada: Autonomy and Empowerment." *Journal of Muslim Minority Affairs* 30, no. 3 (September): 357–73.

Moghissi, Haideh, ed. 2006. *Muslim Diaspora: Gender, Culture, and Identity*. London: Routledge.

Nussbaum, Martha. 2012. *The New Religious Intolerance: Overcoming the Politics of Fear in an Anxious Age*. Cambridge: Harvard University Press.

Nynas, Peter, and Andrew Kam Tuck-Yip, eds. 2012. *Religion, Gender and Sexuality in Everyday Life*. Farnham, UK: Ashgate.

Chapter 4

FEMALE GENITAL MUTILATION/CUTTING

INTRODUCTION

In 2010, the American Academy of Pediatrics (AAP) issued, and then quickly reversed, a policy statement on a "ritual nick" for the genital cutting of girls in the United States. Whereas the AAP's first statement, issued in April 2010, was a detailed consideration of female genital mutilation/cutting (FGM/C), making note of pediatricians' "respect for parental decision-making" in the case of male circumcision due to their acknowledgement of "the legitimacy of including cultural, religious, and ethnic traditions when making the choice of whether to surgically alter a male infant's genitals" (AAP 2010a, 1092), its reversal a month later was terse, found under "AAP Publications Reaffirmed and Retired" where the earlier statement was simply listed as "Retired May 2010" (AAP 2010b, 177). The AAP's first statement generated a global outcry of opposition, ranging from influential women's rights groups in the United States, such as Equality Now, to respected international organizations, such as the World Health Organization. Taina Bien-Aimé, a prominent voice in the fight against FGM/C, was then executive director of Equality Now. Currently the executive director of the Coalition Against the Trafficking of Women, she stated at the time:

> Perpetuating any form of FGM, however seemingly innocuous, is denying girls their fundamental right to bodily integrity—and failing to recognize FGM as part of a system of violence and discrimination against them. One can't violate just a little less or discriminate a little less. The AAP's suggestions are the equivalent of advising doctors to agree to bind three toes instead of a girl's whole foot, or supporting child marriage at age 13 instead of 8. (quoted in Harris 2010)

Like many newspapers throughout the United States and Canada, an editorial in the *Globe and Mail* (2010) echoed Bien-Aimé's uncompromising stance, stating that "condoning this ritual, even in a mild form, is the wrong message to send, [adding that] in the U.K., the U.S. and Canada, female genital mutilation is illegal." The editorial goes on to say:

> There is no reason for western, liberal democracies to tolerate this cultural practice. It is a form of violence and discrimination against women. The procedure is not comparable to male circumcision because the clitoris is cut, the inner labia is cut and the opening of the vagina sewn together to ensure chastity, so the motivation is to control a woman's sexuality.

The term *female genital mutilation* was coined by US feminist and global activist Fran P. Hosken, whose landmark 1979 publication, entitled *The Hosken Report: Genital and Sexual Mutilation of Females*, placed FGM/C on the international agenda (Johnsdotter and Essen 2010, 30; Johnsdotter 2012, 98–99). Hosken was key in influencing public opinion in the West, and set the stage for subsequent international resolutions and national legislation banning FGM/C. She explicitly rejected the use of *female circumcision* because the term downplayed the gravity of the harm to girls and women. FGM/C is not comparable to male circumcision where the procedure simply entails the removal of the foreskin (prepuce) from the penis. Indeed, Nussbaum (1999) compares clitoridectomy, one type of FGM/C, to "the amputation of the penis" and infibulation, another type, to "'the removal of the entire penis, its roots of soft tissue, and part of the scrotal skin'" (119). Many African feminists have been at the forefront in bringing out the horrific nature of the practice, often using the voices of young and defenceless victims:

> It took five people to hold me down, and I was only eight. All the neighbours had gathered and were shouting advice to the Olola [a revered elderly of the community] and jeering at me for lacking courage. In the struggle, the Olola cut the wrong section, which has left me permanently damaged. It was a nightmare that remains with me today. (Akintunde 2010, 193)

Akintunde calls FGM/C "a socio-cultural gang-up against womanhood," and like Nussbaum, demands that it be universally condemned and outlawed. Condemnation in the West has gone well beyond academia to include high-profile voices, such as Somali-born supermodel Waris Dire, who, at five years old, was forced to undergo FGM/C. Dire went public with her ordeal in a 1997 interview with *Marie Claire* magazine, was appointed as a UN special ambassador from 1997 to 2003, and established her Desert Flower Foundation in 2002, named after her 1998 autobiography. In 2013, she was recognized with the Woman of the Year award in the United Kingdom for her campaigning efforts against FGM/C (Saner 2013). Although some activists—such as Ghanaian-born Efua Dorkenoo, who founded FORWARD (The Foundation for Women's Health, Research, and Development), a British non-governmental organization battling FGM/C—loathed the use of the term "female genital *cutting*" because it does not capture the mutilation that is being done (Bien-Aimé 2014), most non-governmental organizations prefer to use it. Out of respect for girls and women who have undergone FGM/C, female genital *mutilation* "is considered to be too offensive and possibly counter-productive to preventive work" (Johnsdotter and Essen 2010, 30). This text uses a combination of the terms *female genital mutilation/cutting* because it is the term used by many international organizations working on this issue. As UNICEF (2013) points out, using *mutilation* brings the necessary attention to the issue that this is about the violation of the rights of girls and women, but *cutting* highlights "the importance of employing respectful terminology when working with practising communities" (7).

The global consensus today against FGM/C is remarkable given that for decades cultural relativists have used Western-led efforts to eradicate FGM/C as a prime example of cultural imperialism. The term *female genital mutilation* was not adopted by the World Health Organization (WHO) until 1991, when it recommended that the United Nations adopt the term after the Inter-African Committee on Traditional Practices Affecting the Health of Women and Children adopted it in 1990. With WHO in the lead, the initial focus of international efforts was on the harmful consequences of the procedure, from the more immediate harms of severe pain, shock, bleeding, bacterial infections, and open sores, to more long-term consequences, such as bladder and urinary tract infections, cysts, infertility, complications during childbirth, surgeries, and even death. However, this proved to be counterproductive "because the focus on health may have inadvertently promoted the 'medicalization' of the practice, meaning that it is carried out by medical professionals" (UNICEF 2013, 8). For example, in Egypt, where there is a very high incidence of FGM/C, the procedure has been performed primarily by the medical community. That is why it was important that at the 1993 Vienna World Conference on Human Rights, FGM/C was recognized as a form of violence against women (VAW) and, in turn, violence against women was seen as a human rights violation (UNICEF 2013, 8). The premise that women's rights are human rights has become an important rallying cry for the global women's movement, and violence against women is a violation of human rights. In December 2003, the UN General Assembly passed the Declaration on the Elimination of Violence Against Women, defining VAW as "any act of gender-based violence that results in, or is likely to result in, physical, sexual or psychological harm or suffering to women, including threats of such acts, coercion or arbitrary deprivation of liberty, whether occurring in public or in private life." As then US First Lady Hillary Rodham Clinton so memorably stated at the UN Fourth World Conference on Women in Beijing in September 1995: "If there is one message that echoes forth from this conference, let it be that human rights are women's rights and women's rights are human rights once and for all."

The idea of human rights establishes rights inherently in the individual (i.e., by virtue of being human), signalling its universal applicability regardless of the individual's national, cultural, religious, or ethnic identity. Three years after the establishment of the United Nations in 1945, the General Assembly had adopted the Universal Declaration of Human Rights (UDHR) and it remains a guidepost for many who believe in the universality of human rights. At the very outset, the UDHR proclaims in its preamble that the "recognition of the inherent dignity and of the equal and inalienable rights of all members of the human family is the foundation of freedom, justice and peace in the world." According to Article 25 of the UDHR, "everyone has the right to a standard of living adequate for health and well-being" (United Nations 1948). Along with seeing FGM/C as a form of violence against women, this statement in the UDHR "has been used to argue that FGM/C also violates the right to health and bodily integrity" (UNICEF 2013, 8), and this is a crucial capability in Nussbaum's model. However, cultural relativists contend that rights are culturally specific and that the imposition of universal human rights standards is actually a form of cultural imperialism. The West, they argue, has been particularly guilty of this form of imperialism because "the 'truths' of human rights are disguised forms of power, part of a complex system of global political manipulation" (Langlois 2009, 19), and a prime rationale used by the West to declare "truths" and impose its views on others is the promotion of women's rights.

Nussbaum (1999) is unequivocal and trenchant in her critique of the cultural relativist position. She argues that there are "cultural universals," so that invoking culture as a defence to violate women's rights is not only wrong-headed but also unethical. She points out that FGM/C is a cultural practice that is not religiously justified and done often by force on very young girls in dangerous and unsanitary conditions within many societies characterized by high illiteracy and male domination. FGM/C is grounded in beliefs that it will preserve a woman's virginity, curb her promiscuity, eliminate any proclivity for homosexuality, and enhance her chastity and marriageability (Akintunde 2010). These are the sorts of beliefs about women's sexuality that rest on the valorization of the heterosexual conjugal bond. Akintunde outlines some of the most problematic superstitions given for the existence (and persistence) of the practice: "if the head of a baby boy touches the clitoris, it will die; If an uncircumcised mother delivers a baby girl, she [the mother] will die.... A woman should be infibulated and the vagina sutured to ensure that she does not run after men when her husband is away" (200). Nussbaum (1999) argues that although gendered practices and continuing inequalities persist in the West, which, according to cultural relativists, should prevent Westerners from preaching to others, cultural relativists suffer from "moral narcissism" and "moral obtuseness and parochialism" (122). As she states clearly about her position:

> It is better to risk being consigned by critics to the 'hell' reserved for alleged Westernizers and imperialists—however unjustified such criticism would in fact be—than to stand around in the vestibule waiting for a time when everyone will like what we are going to say. And what we are going to say is this: that there are universal obligations to protect human functioning and its dignity, and that the dignity of women is equal to that of men. If that involves assault on many local traditions, both Western and non-Western, so much the better, because any tradition that denies these things is unjust. (30)

Almost a quarter of a century after the World Health Organization adopted the term *Female Genital Mutilation*, it is widely recognized that women and men in affected communities must be part of international and national efforts to eradicate FGM/C (UNFPA-UNICEF 2013; UNICEF 2013). Seeking social justice for girls and women is a universal obligation, but implementing change must be culturally sensitive and culturally appropriate. Invoking a universal obligation is not about imposing a universal solution. Female genital mutilation/cutting rests on the problematic control of women's sexuality, and the harmful practices of clitoridectomy, excision, and infibulation performed on girls must be eradicated. What global efforts have been made to end FGM/C, and does ending the practice change attitudes regarding women's sexuality? How has criminalizing FGM/C in the West opened up questions about women's choices regarding their bodies, particularly in light of female genital cosmetic surgery becoming more popular in the West? What does focusing on consent mean for male circumcision, a practice that, if performed, is largely uncritically accepted in Western society? These are the questions that will be addressed in this chapter. Although concerted efforts to end FGM/C are largely found in the region covering from the Atlantic coast to the Horn of Africa, where

FGM/C is prevalent, this practice is also found in many Western countries, including the United States and Canada, given increasing immigration from this region. It has become evident that, as progress has been made, it has become difficult "to draw an unambiguous line between acceptable and condemnable practices" of FGM/C so that academics and practitioners, such as the AAP, who do not outright condemn FGM/C, particularly in the West, are seen as "morally suspect" (Johnsdotter 2012, 91–92). This chapter explores the assumptions made by the AAP in considering the "ritual nick" and why those assumptions may be instructive in the understanding of culture. In the reconciliation of cultural practices and gender equality, it is clear that a woman's right to sexual pleasure is a necessary component of human flourishing and not merely a Western cultural ideal.

GLOBAL EFFORTS AND CHANGING ATTITUDES

On December 20, 2012, the UN General Assembly adopted a resolution by consensus banning female genital mutilation/cutting. Entitled "Intensifying global efforts for the elimination of female genital mutilations" (although not commonly used, the UN's use of the plural is deliberate, likely to capture the diversity of cultural practices), the resolution recognized "that female genital mutilations are an irreparable, irreversible abuse that impacts negatively on the human rights of women and girls, affecting about 100 million to 140 million women and girls worldwide, and that each year an estimated further 3 million girls are at risk of being subjected to the practice throughout the world," but that "despite the increase in national, regional and international efforts and the focus on the abandonment of female genital mutilations, the practice continues to exist in all regions of the world." The resolution directed member states to do more to eradicate what had become a globally accepted harmful practice directed at girls, often at a very young age, and certainly before any recognized age of consent. Former Egyptian minister of family and population Moushira Khattab, who was a key figure in banning FGM/C in Egypt, a country where over 91 percent of women and girls have been cut, asserted that the passage of the 2012 resolution "[marked] a historic day in the global fight against violence and discrimination against women and girls," pointing out that the initiative for the ban stemmed from African states in the UN, which, along with Western states with immigrant communities, "[were] under a legal obligation to protect their citizens from a savage crime perpetrated in cold blood against innocent girls" (Khattab 2013).

In understanding FGM/C, both the general definition and four-type classification of FGM/C by the World Health Organization have become widely accepted by intergovernmental, governmental, and non-governmental organizations, as well as by academics, activists, and journalists. In 2008 WHO was joined by nine other UN agencies, namely the Office of the United Nations High Commissioner for Human Rights, the Joint United Nations Programme on HIV/AIDS, the United Nations Development Programme, the United Nations Economic Commission for Africa, the United Nations Educational, Scientific and Cultural Organization, the United Nations Population Fund (UNFPA), the United Nations High Commissioner for Refugees, the United Nations Children's Fund (UNICEF), and the United Nations Development Fund for Women—now part of UN Women, the United Nations Entity for Gender Equality and the Empowerment of Women, which was created in July 2010 as part of the UN reform agenda—and they all jointly released a document entitled *Eliminating Female Genital Mutilation: An Interagency Statement* (WHO 2008). This 2008 report has been crucial to global efforts to ban FGM/C, including the largest global program initiated in 2007, the UNFPA-UNICEF Joint Programme on Female Genital Mutilation/Cutting, which has implemented a "culturally sensitive human rights-based approach" to end FGM/C in 17 African countries (UNFPA-UNICEF 2013). The necessity to continue and fund this global program, currently in its second phase (2014–17), is specifically mentioned in the historic UN General Assembly resolution banning FGM/C, which was passed in December 2012.

More recently, UNICEF (2013) has released a comprehensive, statistical overview of the practice of FGM/C in the 29 countries in Africa and the Middle East where FGM/C is concentrated. An impressive report, it is the first study that has included data from all 29 countries identified (the accepted list of 28 has grown to 29 with the inclusion of Iraq; it also now puts the figures to 125 million girls and women who have been subjected to FGM/C because of more accurate statistics, as opposed to the 140 million often cited in earlier publications). The report uses the WHO definition: FGM/C "refers to all procedures involving partial or total removal of the female external genitalia, or other injury to the female genital organs for non-medical reasons" (UNICEF 2013, 6). However, the UNICEF report goes beyond simply reiterating the WHO four-type classification, bringing out how more nuanced understandings of the four types of FGM/C have evolved through the years. Below are edited excerpts from UNICEF's (2013, 7) description of the

WHO typology, but presented in table form and supplemented with drawings from the American Academy of Pediatrics (AAP 2010a). The AAP encourages the use of their drawings for educational purposes, particularly useful for those unfamiliar with FGM/C.

Table 4.1: Classification of Female Genital Mutilation/Cutting

Type I (clitoridectomy)	Partial or total removal of the clitoris and/or the prepuce. Also referred to as *clitoridectomy*, and by practising communities as *sunna*, which is Arabic for *tradition* or *duty*. **Normal female genital anatomy** 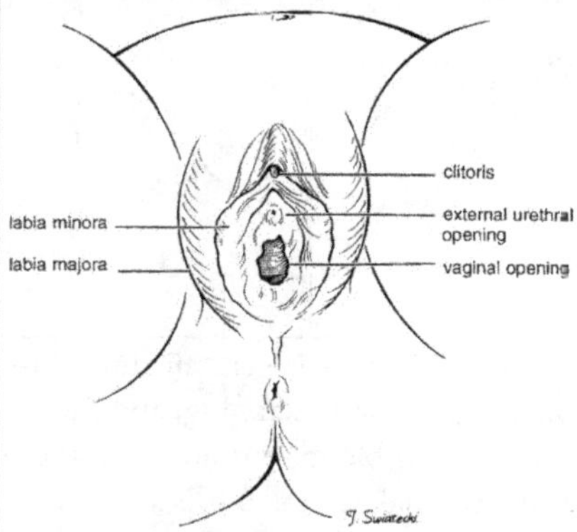 **Type 1** 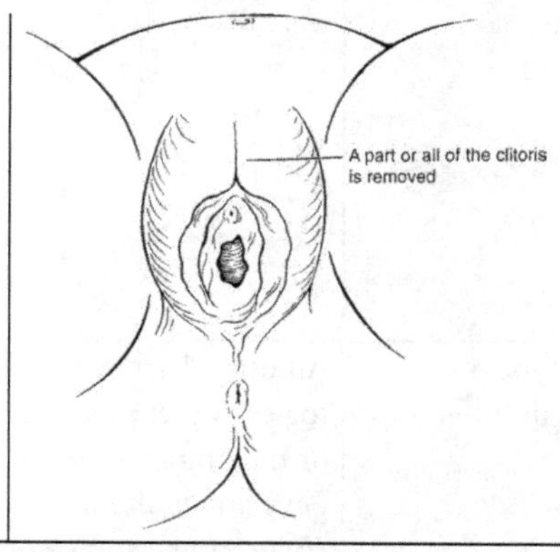
Type 2 (excision)	Partial or total removal of the clitoris and labia minora, with or without excision of the labia majora. The 2007 WHO definition recognizes that there is considerable variability in this form or degree of cutting. Often referred to as *excision* in English, but in French, *excision* generally refers to all forms of FGM/C. **Normal female genital anatomy** 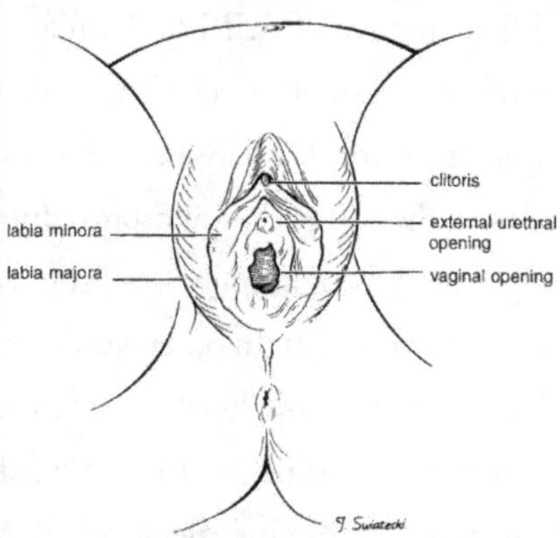 **Type 2** 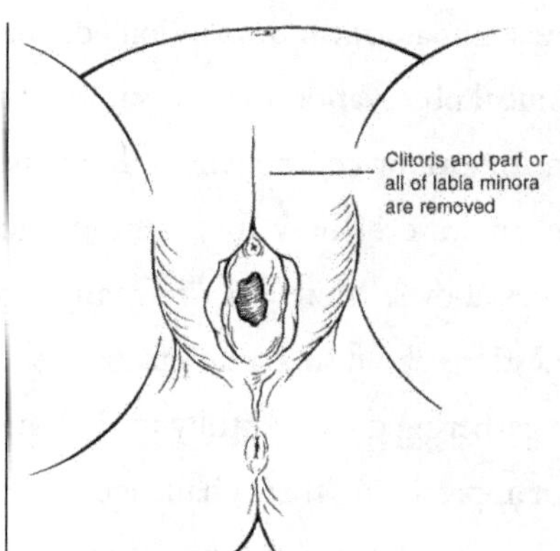

<table>
<tr><td>Type 3
(infibulation)</td><td>Narrowing of the vaginal orifice by cutting and bringing together the labia minora and/or the labia majora to create a type of seal, with or without excision of the clitoris. In most instances, the cut edges of the labia are stitched together, which is referred to as infibulation, resulting in near complete covering of the urethra and the vaginal orifice, which must be reopened for sexual intercourse and childbirth, a procedure known as defibulation. This may be followed by reinfibulation.
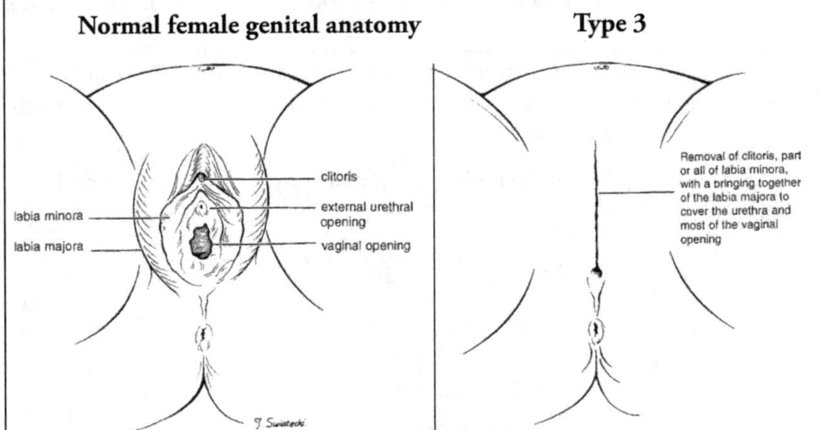
</td></tr>
<tr><td>Type 4
(all others)</td><td>All other harmful procedures to the female genitalia for non-medical purposes, for example: pricking, piercing, incising, scraping, and cauterization. Pricking or nicking involves cutting to draw blood, but no removal of tissue and no permanent alteration of the external genitalia. It is sometimes called symbolic circumcision; some communities have described it as a traditional form of FGM/C. It has been proposed as an alternative to more severe forms of cutting in both African and other countries where FGM/C is performed.</td></tr>
</table>

Sources: UNICEF 2013; AAP 2010a

The UNICEF report goes on to say that although the WHO typology may provide "a precise anatomical description" of the different types of FGM/C, "it may be more useful in clinical observation than in surveys that rely on self-reports" (7). These self-reports constitute an important component of how changes in practices are assessed, but many women may be unaware of how they were cut (and thus how their specific procedures align with the types above). Moreover, "in many settings it may be culturally inappropriate to ask detailed questions about such matters, or to show illustrations" (7). In other words, there are challenges to gathering data and fully understanding the impacts of global efforts to eradicate FGM/C, but appreciating these challenges only adds to the usefulness of the UNICEF report.

The report divides the 29 countries in terms of the prevalence of FGM/C among girls aged 15 to 49, ranging from very high prevalence, where more than 80 percent of girls and women have been subject to FGM/C, to very low prevalence, where less than 10 percent have been cut. Although infibulation, the most severe form (Type 3), was particularly evident in Somalia, Djibouti, and Eritrea (where the prevalence rates are 98 percent, 93 percent, and 89 percent respectively, all very high), it was also significantly found in Senegal (where the rate is 26 percent, moderately low) and Niger (where the rate is 2 percent, very low) (UNICEF 2013, 27, 45). The prevalence rate in a country does not dictate the severity of the cut done to girls and women, but there is a correlation between girls and women who support the continuation of the practice and countries with high and very high prevalence rates (53). The UNICEF report states that FGM/C should be eradicated instead of "advocating for milder forms of the practice" because, given that anti-FGM/C programs have been implemented in the communities studied, "the type of cutting has changed little across generations … [suggesting] that pursuing the elimination of FGM/C by moving towards a progressive reduction in the degree of cutting does not hold much promise" (118). International efforts should be directed to abandoning the practice instead of addressing the severity of the cut, and what should be done is "to raise the status of girls and women in the society" (118).

How this is to be done is a real challenge for many societies and communities practising FGM/C. In her study of Bibo-Dioulasso, Burkina Faso (a country with a 76 percent prevalence rate according to the UNICEF report), where there have been national campaigns against FGM/C since 1996, when the practice became a criminal offence, Elena Jirovsky (2010) found that although both women and men expressed opposition to FGM/C "using arguments they had got from the [anti-FGM/C] campaigns or their peers," they nevertheless adhered to beliefs about the need to control women's sexuality (88). Listening to fears such as "[women] would not be able to control their sexual needs, would be unfaithful to their partners and would probably get sexually transmitted infections … [because] women having more than one partner was a common explanation in this community for the problem of HIV," Jirovsky found that the national campaigns may have helped women and men to understand the harms caused by FGM/C, but these campaigns did not necessarily get at the underlying attitudes regarding gender inequalities. As she states about her findings: "people may stop the practice for various reasons, but opinions about women and representations of women's sexuality would remain" (89). In other words, although it might be assumed that opposing FGM/C is a result of changing attitudes, it may simply be that other factors are at play, such as fear of governmental reprisal. According to the UNICEF report, legal and social norms (along with moral norms) dictate individual behaviour. Legal norms are enacted by government whereas social norms are enacted by social groups (17). Although UNICEF recognizes the significance of changing legal norms, throughout the report the focus is on the importance of changing social norms. The report argues that it is the fear of social disapproval resulting in shame, stigma, exclusion, and even ridicule that prevents any one individual or family from abandoning the practice of FGM/C on their own (19), and that "when legal norms run counter to social norms, moral values or religious beliefs, legislative reform may have a limited effect on changing attitudes and practices" (89).

CRIMINALIZING FGM/C

Changing legal norms, then, needs to be placed in context of changing social norms. Laws prohibiting FGM/C have been enacted not only in 24 of the 29 countries in Africa and the Middle East where the practice is concentrated, but also in a number of Western countries, including the United States and Canada. According to UNICEF (2013), 59 countries have adopted specific legislation outlawing FGM, and 26 of them are in Africa and the Middle East, although South Africa and Zambia are not among the 29 countries identified where FGM/C is prevalent (8). Of the 29 countries, only five—Cameroon, Gambia, Liberia, Mali, and Sierra Leone—have not passed laws. Sweden was the first Western country to pass a law in 1982, strengthening the law in 1998 to change the terminology from prohibiting "female circumcision" to "female genital mutilation" and to impose greater penalties. In September 1996, the United States Congress outlawed FGM as part of the Illegal Immigration Reform and Immigrant Responsibility Act of 1996; and in May 1997, the Canadian federal government amended the Criminal Code and included the practice of FGM as aggravated assault under section 268(3). Table 4.2 shows a number of states that have passed laws against FGM/C, including the specific 24 countries in Africa and the Middle East where FGM/C is concentrated.

Laws alone will not result in the eradication of FGM/C, and the observations of the UNICEF report that laws tend to be ineffective unless they are "accompanied by measures to influence cultural traditions and expectations" (8–9) are no less applicable to Western states with immigrant populations than the countries in Africa and the Middle East, which are of UNICEF's primary concern. Moreover, women are largely the conveyors of the practice, and as the UNICEF report states, the chances of a girl being cut increase when her mother supports the continuation of the practice (115). Although FGM/C is about the control of women's sexuality, it is not primarily about men directly oppressing women, and so that as a form of violence against women, it must necessarily be treated as a systemic problem, not an individual one or even one that can be resolved within families. Not only does the practice speak more to societal norms, and expectations to conform being followed by mothers in cutting their daughters, but UNICEF has found that there is often very little discussion between wives and husbands regarding the cutting of their daughters. Moreover, "girls and women tend to consistently underestimate the share of boys and men who want FGM/C to end" (117–18). Enforcing laws, then, end up being applied against women who themselves would not have consented to being subject to the procedure, thus victimizing them further. This is highly problematic given that laws are constructed, particularly in Western countries such as Sweden, the United Kingdom, and Australia, so that a girl or woman regardless of age *cannot* consent to being cut in any way, namely that any type of the modification of the vagina for non-medical purposes is a crime. Given the extraterritoriality of laws that allow governments to prosecute those who perpetrate a crime even if the crime was not committed within the country itself, mothers, grandmothers, aunties, and other women in a community who themselves have been cut can be further victimized under the law. Meant to address "vacation cutting," where girls living particularly in the West are taken to their countries of origin for the procedure (Turkewitz 2014), this can further target mothers who believe that what they are doing is the best for their daughters.

More problematically, laws against FGM/C in the West end up reviving concerns about Western privilege and the extent to which representations of immigrant (mainly racialized) women as oppressed are juxtaposed to Western (mainly white) women who exercise agency. The number and types of cosmetic surgical procedures available in the West have dramatically expanded in the last few decades, and alongside more commonly known types, such as breast augmentation, liposuction, tummy tucks, and butt lifts, are emerging a set of procedures referred to as female genital cosmetic surgery (FGCS). Encompassing what Marge Berer (2010, 5) refers to as "a mind-boggling list of procedures," such as "labia reduction, labiaplasty (also called *nynfopastia* in Brazil), genitoplasty, pulling the labia to make them longer, filling or replenishing of the labia majora, female genital reshaping, intimate surgery (translated from the Brazilian *cirurgia intima*), vaginal narrowing or tightening (e.g., after vaginal delivery or [for] increased pleasure for men), vaginal rejuvenation, hymen reconstruction, hymen repair (for restoration of virginity), clitoral lift, clitoral hood reduction, [and] clitoral repositioning [parentheses in original]," FGCS is becoming more commonplace in the West. Indeed, its increasing popularity has led the Society of Obstetricians and Gynecologists of Canada to release a statement expressing its "great concern" about the "proliferation of non-medically indicated surgery to the genital area" and to "[call] on physicians to refrain from advertising the services or suggesting they boost sexual satisfaction" (Blackwell 2014). Given that laws against female genital mutilation/cutting state that any type of the modification of the vagina for non-medical purposes is a crime, why wouldn't FGCS be covered? "How can it be that extensive genital modifications, including reduction of labial and clitoral tissue, are considered acceptable and perfectly legal in many European countries, while those same societies have legislation making female genital cutting illegal, and the World Health Organization bans even the 'pricking' of the female genitals?" (Johnsdotter and Essen 2010, 29). In other words, in terms of genital modifications, how can there be one set of rules for Western women and another for non-Western (namely, African immigrant) women?

Table 4.2: Selection of States That Have Specifically Criminalized FGM

Criminal Legislation/Decree (year enacted) * Later dates reflect amendments to the original law, or new laws	
Africa and the Middle East	
Benin (2003)	Iraq, Kurdistan region (2011)
Burkina Faso (1996)	Kenya (2001, 2011*)
Central African Republic (1966, 1996*)	Mauritania (2005)
Chad (2003)	Niger (2003)
Côte d'Ivoire (1998)	Nigeria, some states (1999–2006)
Djibouti (1995, 2009*)	Senegal (1999)
Egypt (2008)	Somalia (2012)
Eritrea (2007)	Sudan, some states (2008–9)
Ethiopia (2004)	Togo (1998)
Ghana (1994, 2007*)	Uganda (2010)
Guinea (1965, 2000*)	United Republic of Tanzania (1998)
Guinea-Bissau (2011)	Yemen (2001)
Western States	
Australia (All states and territories, including amendments 1994–2013*)	New Zealand (1995)
Belgium (2000)	Norway (1995)
Canada (1997)	Spain (2003)
Cyprus (2003)	Sweden (1982, 1998*)
Denmark (2003)	United Kingdom (1985, 2003)
Italy (2005)	United States, federal law (1996), 21 of 50 states (1994–2013)

Sources: Center for Reproductive Rights (www.reproductiverights.org/document/female-genital-mutilation-fgm-legal-prohibitions-worldwide); UNICEF 2013

Although the reasoning of many European countries fits with the protection of women's rights (i.e., just because a girl reaches the age of consent does not mean that her rights are not being violated), such laws as constructed would have to apply to all women. For some feminists who see women turning to cosmetic surgery as another manifestation of oppressive beauty practices fuelled by male-dominated understandings in society, victimizing Western women in the same vein as FGM/C, the application of the law to cover FGCS makes sense. However, because this was not the original intent of anti-FGM/C laws (in the United States the 1996 law was even enacted as part of immigration legislation), this has led to ambiguity in enforcement. To address the ambiguity is why in March 2015, the Home Affairs Committee of the British Parliament recommended that the British law be amended to explicitly cover FGCS. However, not only is cosmetic surgery widely regarded as a choice for women, but this may also belittle the gravity of harm being done to girls and women subject to FGM/C. Moreover, the law does not apply to men, so men are seen as able to make choices, but women are not. These are the sorts of responses that, not surprisingly, have been made to the National Health Service in the United Kingdom, which, in the interest of protecting women who have been cut, has classified vaginal piercings, such as clitoris rings, as FGM/C (Nelson 2015). Arguably, the problem for many European countries as well as Australia is that laws against FGM/C apply to all women regardless of age, unlike the legislation in both the United States and Canada, which applies only to girls under the age of consent. Although this means that, under the law in the United States and Canada, a woman can consent to FGM/C, there is no differentiation between Western and non-Western women in terms of choosing genital modifications. Whether it is a matter of choice or false consciousness is a matter of debate, but the question applies to both and, in that way, representations of women as the oppressed African immigrant and the liberated Westerner are not being perpetuated. Seeing the debate in this way shows that education, rather than legislation, is likely the best way to move forward in addressing both female genital mutilation/cutting and female genital cosmetic surgery. The question of whether individual women who are differently situated in terms of race, ethnicity, class, sexual orientation, able-bodiedness, or country of origin exercise agency or choice leads to considerations about their capabilities and whether progress has been made. This, then, invites further inquiry regarding the accommodation of traditional cultural practices in a liberal democratic society.

CULTURE AND TRADITION

According to the UNICEF (2013) report, one of the reasons likely accounting for a greater percentage of girls and women against FGM/C in low-prevalence countries is that they interact with others who do not practise FGM/C (76). As an example, in cases where religious belief is given as a prime rationale for the practice, exposure to a broader community of faith may lead to abandonment of the practice. That seems to account for changes in attitudes among the Mandinga and Somali immigrant communities in Europe, which, according to UNICEF, were exposed to other Muslim communities that did not practice FGM/C (70). Similarly, the Muslim Council of Britain, established in 1997 and the largest Muslim umbrella organization in the United Kingdom, is working with FORWARD, the British non-governmental organization battling FGM/C mentioned earlier, to reach out to mosques and other Muslim community organizations throughout the United Kingdom. Developing a resource flyer specifically stating that FGM/C is "Non-Islamic, against the teachings of Islam and brings Islam into disrepute," the Muslim Council of Britain (2014) has recognized that in the post-9/11 environment, the practice of FGM/C, like veiling, has been used by anti-Muslim voices to argue that Islam oppresses women. FGM/C is practised by Muslims, Christians, and non-religious societies in Africa; it is a cultural practice, not one dictated by religious edict.

Is FGM/C, however, a cultural practice that should not be accommodated in a liberal democratic society because it is a tradition rooted in the control of women's sexuality? Lisa Wade (2011) argues that the answer depends on whether the model of culture is reified or dynamic. A reified model of culture sees culture as unchanging with "nonambiguous boundaries and nonoverlapping memberships" where "powerful groups often characterize themselves as culture-less" and lesser others as "culture-bound" (521). According to Wade, this model often serves as "the basis for denigration of non-Western societies" where non-Western women "are believed to be incapable of liberating themselves" so they must be liberated by others, usually Westerners (522). In contrast, a dynamic model of culture sees culture as changing where "women in different cultural contexts can use their own cultural tools to empower themselves," recognizing that the culture is not immutably patriarchal and that women have agency to create change (522). In examining a 1996 case where physicians in a Seattle hospital offered to provide a "ritual nick" for a group of Somali parents who wanted to have their daughters cut, Wade argues that the physicians subscribed to a dynamic model of culture, whereas their opponents subscribed to a reified model. The physicians saw the ritual nick "as a significant departure from infibulation and, therefore, a meaningful cultural change enacted thoughtfully by a self-conscious community" (527). Their opponents saw it "as a continuation instead of an interruption of [Somali] cultural practices" that rested on the control of women's sexuality (529). In the end, because the outcry was based on the rejection of any type of FGM/C, even one that would cause no harm whatsoever (but it would fall under Type 4 in the typology of the World Health Organization), physicians withdrew consideration of offering a ritual nick, and as Wade recognizes, these same arguments would play out again in 2010, when the American Academy of Pediatrics briefly considered it. Although Wade sees the reified model as leading to "cross-cultural antagonism" and "zero tolerance," making feminism and multiculturalism fundamentally incompatible (532), she does not regard the dynamic model as a panacea. She expresses concern that the dynamic model romanticizes cultural change, which may "trivialize social justice concerns" (533) because it may simply be that although a culture can change, it may not have changed enough. In that way, laws that express zero tolerance for FGM/C may make sense, but only for girls under the age of consent.

This, however, brings up the question that if liberal democratic societies, like the United States and Canada, have zero tolerance for the cutting of girls' genitals, why do they tolerate the cutting of boys' genitals? As Johnsdotter (2012) points out, "A child protection perspective is often lost in the zeal to protect *all* African women" (108). There are those who argue that no genitals (female, male, or intersex) should be cut before the age of consent (Earp 2014). All children, regardless of gender, should not have their genitals mutilated, and that is what is lost when the sole focus is FGM/C. At the same time, there are those who argue that male circumcision is primarily symbolic, that it causes no harm (and some argue that it actually provides health benefits), that it is not rooted in the control of men's sexuality, and therefore that it is a cultural ritual that can be accommodated within a liberal democratic society. These are the reasons why scholars, like Nussbaum (1999), reject making equivalencies between FGM/C and male circumcision. Yet, these are the very same reasons why the physicians in the Seattle hospital defended a ritual nick for the cutting of girls. They argued that there are "connections between Somali and American culture" and that "Somalis were not incomprehensibly 'traditional,' they were like Jewish Americans who also followed a tradition of medically unnecessary genital cutting because of its symbolic meaning" (Wade 2011, 528). Meanings of traditions do change, but the physicians likely downplayed the extent to which the nick still represented control of women's sexuality.

Seeing progress is an important component of a feminist liberal perspective. Meanings of traditions do change because cultures are dynamic, so that a traditional practice need not be eradicated if its original meaning and intent have lost social force. In the contemporary Western context, specifically in Anglo-American countries like Canada and the United States, this is the sort of reasoning pointed out in Chapter 2 as to why a married woman should have the choice of whether to adopt her husband's surname, instead of this practice being prohibited, as in the Quebec Civil Code. Although this traditional practice is rooted in the legal practice of coverture, which mandated that a married woman did not have a separate legal status or existence from her husband, women who choose to change their names upon marriage these days do not see their identities being subsumed to their husbands. More importantly, Western society as a whole does not regard the practice as such because most people see it simply as a matter of choice. As discussed in Chapter 2, that is why a heterosexual woman who identifies herself as a feminist adopts her husband's name. Although there are still those who argue that the practice perpetuates male dominance, the original meaning and intent of the practice has lost social force to the point that it is compelling to talk about women *choosing* to take their husband's name. At the very least, it is certainly not about the control of women's legal existence, which, historically, required a married woman to adopt her husband's name.

In the case of FGM/C, it may be that a parent's choice to modify a daughter's genitals will no longer be symbolic of the control of her sexuality, so that a "ritual nick" (just like marital naming practices in the West) is simply about a historic tradition. Based on a dynamic model of culture, a "ritual nick," unlike the harmful practices of clitoridectomy, excision, and infibulation, can be accommodated in a liberal democratic society, thus questioning zero tolerance for any type of FGM/C. It may still be debatable whether it should continue, particularly in light of children's rights, which informs current debates about male circumcision, but it will no longer be primarily about women's rights. That said, there are those who argue that the focus on FGM/C is a reflection of the sex-obsessed nature of the West, where sexuality has taken centre stage, and that other societies are not as concerned about sex. The argument here is that the West simply projects what it considers important, and given the global power structure, imposes it on other societies, accounting for why Western feminists—beginning with US feminist Fran Hosken, who coined the term *female genital mutilation*—have made it a priority. This line of argument is extremely problematic given the centrality of women's sexual freedoms. The need for sexual pleasure is not a Western cultural determination, but a universal one. Nussbaum (1999, 126) highlights that arguments made by feminists like Yael Tamir, an Israeli academic and former politician, who "[denigrate] the importance of sexual pleasure as an element in human flourishing," are fundamentally flawed. As discussed in Chapter 1, Nussbaum's capabilities model differentiates between capability and functioning. Women should have the capability—the ability to choose—to have sexual pleasure in their lives, and it is not up to others to remove that capability when they are too young and too defenceless to prevent it. Just as she makes the distinction between starving and fasting, Nussbaum differentiates between FGM/C and celibacy to highlight the distinction between capability and functioning.

RECOMMENDED FILMS, VIDEO/AUDIO CLIPS, AND WEBSITES

Africa Rising. 2009. Documentary directed by Paula Heredia (United States). www.equalitynow.org/africarising.

The Cut: A Documentary. 2009. Directed by Linda May Kallestein (Norway). www.thecutdocumentary.org/.

The Cutting Tradition. 2009. Documentary directed by John Howarth and Nancy Durrell McKenna (United Kingdom). www.cultureunplugged.com/documentary/watch-online/play/52827/The-Cutting-Tradition. See also: www.safehands.org/media/films/.

Desert Flower. 2009. Film directed by Sherry Hormann (Germany). www.desertflower-movie.com/. See also Desert Flower Foundation: www.desertflowerfoundation.org/.

The Perfect Vagina. 2008. Presented by Lisa Rogers, Channel 4 (United Kingdom). Original broadcast date: August 17, 2008. www.topdocumentaryfilms.com/perfect-vagina/.

"Plastic Surgery below the Belt?" 2014. *The Current*, CBC Radio (Canada). Original broadcast date: April 2, 2014. www.cbc.ca/player/Radio/The+Current/ID/2446133132/.

ADDITIONAL READINGS

Braun, Virginia. 2009. "'The Women Are Doing It for Themselves.' The Rhetoric of Choice and Agency around Female Genital 'Cosmetic Surgery.'" *Australian Feminist Studies* 24, no. 60: 233–49.

———. 2010. "Female Genital Cosmetic Surgery: A Critical Review of Current Knowledge and Contemporary Debates." *Journal of Women's Health* 19, no. 7: 1393–1407.

Dustin, M. 2010. "Female Genital Mutilation/Cutting in the UK: Challenging the Inconsistencies." *European Journal of Women's Studies* 17, no. 1: 7–23.

Heyes, Cressida J., and Meredith Jones, eds. 2009. *Cosmetic Surgery: A Feminist Primer*. Farnham, UK: Ashgate.

Mottin-Sylla, Marie-Hélène, and Joëlle Palmieri. 2011. *Confronting Female Genital Mutilation: The Role of Youth and ICTs in Changing Africa*. Translated by Mamsaït Jagne. Ottawa: IDRC, Pambazuka Press, ENDA. www.intact-network.net/intact/cp/files/1319371534_132757.pdf.

Nyangweso, Mary. 2014. *Female Genital Cutting in Industrialized Countries: Mutilation or Cultural Tradition?* Santa Barbara, CA: Praeger.

Wade, Lisa. 2009. "Defining Gendered Oppression in U.S. Newspapers: The Strategic Value of 'Female Genital Mutilation.'" *Gender and Society* 23, no. 3 (June): 293–314.

Chapter 5
RAPE AND SEXUAL VIOLENCE

INTRODUCTION

Posted as a 20-second video clip on Instagram, it was the university chant that dominated Canadian news headlines at the start of the 2013–14 academic year. Students at Saint Mary's University (SMU) in Halifax were captured clapping and cheering "SMU boys, we like them young" on September 2, 2013, during frosh week. The students, both men and women, proceeded to chant in unison what "young" meant:

> Y is for your sister
> O is for oh so tight
> U is for underage
> N is for no consent
> G is for grab that ass.

The troubling cheer was led by about 80 student leaders as part of first-year orientation activities for 300 to 400 other students, and it went viral, grabbing national and international media attention. Saint Mary's, however, was not unique; students on the opposite coast were also reported a few days later making the same chant. At the University of British Columbia (UBC) in Vancouver, UBC students also "like[d] them young," but the "G" in their acronym stood for "go to jail," indicating an apparent awareness that what they were cheering about was a criminal act. In Canada, the act is called sexual assault, commonly known as rape, so that it would seem that the students—both men and women—were chanting about the sexual assault or rape of minors, specifically girls. How could this happen in institutions of higher learning, where students are taught to think critically about the world around them, specifically about the words that they use? Condemnation came quickly, apologies were expressed, and promises were made. A council or task force was established by each university to recommend changes. The Report from the President's Council (Saint Mary's University 2013), entitled "Promoting a Culture of Safety, Respect, and Consent at Saint Mary's University and Beyond," was released on December 15, 2013, and the report outlining recommendations of the UBC President's Task Force on Gender-Based Violence and Aboriginal Stereotypes (University of British Columbia 2014), entitled "Transforming UBC and Developing a Culture of Equality and Accountability: Confronting Rape Culture and Colonialist Violence," was released on March 28, 2014. Both reports pointed to the university as a microcosm of the larger society where "sexualized violence" persists (Saint Mary's University 2013, 24) or, more broadly, "systemic violence," which points to how "sexual and gender-based violence … [is] tied to systemic issues of intersectional violence where women, Indigenous Peoples, people of colour, and sexual and gender minority populations are often the target" (University of British Columbia 2014, 2).

As discussed in the last chapter, violence against women (VAW) is a violation of human rights, and sexual violence is a form of violence against women. *Sexual violence* and SMU's term *sexualized violence* are often used interchangeably, and although UBC's term *systemic violence* points to the importance of intersectional violence, bringing out how women (and men) are differentially situated in terms of class, race, ethnicity, sexual orientation, and other markers of identity, it is clear that women (as a whole) and men (as a whole) experience violence differently throughout the world because of the persistence of gender inequalities. The World Health Organization (WHO 2002) has defined sexual violence as "any sexual act, attempt to obtain a sexual act, unwanted sexual comments or advances, or acts to traffic, or otherwise directed, against a person's sexuality using coercion, by any person regardless of their relationship to the victim, in any setting, including but not limited to home and work" (149–50). WHO has further clarified that sexual violence consists of "acts that range from verbal harassment to forced penetration, and an array of types of coercion, from social pressure and intimidation to physical force" (WHO 2012). Although sexual violence can be broadly understood to include forced prostitution and sex trafficking, as well as unwanted sexual advances or sexual harassment, sexual abuse of children or mentally or physically disabled people, forced marriage or cohabitation, denial of right to use contraception or to adopt other measures to protect against sexually transmitted diseases, and forced abortion, it is also used to understand rape, and the focus of this chapter is on rape as an example of sexual violence. Moreover, the current attention on attitudes about, and the presence of, rape on university campuses makes this an even more pressing, relevant issue for society. According to the 1993 UN Declaration on the Elimination of Violence against Women, the three principal areas where women have experienced violence are in the home, in the community, and at the hands of the state. This is why, in seeing how women have been subject to sexual violence, it makes sense to look at marital rape (in the home), rape by strangers or acquaintances (in the community, which includes the university), and systematic rape as a weapon of war (at the hands of the state) (United Nations General Assembly 1994).

Although widely evident historically in the raping and pillaging of conquering armies, the contemporary use of rape as a weapon of war has been seen most notably in the former Yugoslavia, Rwanda, Sierra Leone, the Darfur region in Sudan, the Democratic Republic of the Congo, and, more recently, in Libya and Syria. Wherever conflict has occurred, armies and militias have seemed ready and willing to employ rape against the female population of their enemies. The work of the International Criminal Tribunal from the former Yugoslavia and the International Criminal Tribunal for Rwanda in the 1990s brought to the forefront the widespread practice of rape during conflicts. Established by the United Nations, these two ad-hoc tribunals recognized rape as an international crime that was later codified by the International Criminal Court when it came into being in 2002. According to Mark Ellis (2006/2007), the recognition of rape as an international crime is not one that stands on its own, unlike in domestic laws. Rather, rape is a subsection of three recognized crimes in international law, namely as a crime of genocide, as a crime against humanity, and as a war crime. First, rape as a crime of genocide establishes that rape is an instrument of destruction, leading to "ethnic cleansing" or the destruction of a cultural or national group. This is evident in the use of gang rape, sexual torture, psychological torture, rape camps, and forced impregnation, and all these acts are subject to international prosecution. Second, rape as a crime against humanity brings out that the murder, extermination, enslavement, deportation, and other inhumane acts committed against a civilian population, specifically directed against women, before or during war, or persecutions based on political, religious, or racial grounds whether or not domestic law has been violated, are all prosecutable. Third, rape as a war crime establishes that rape is no longer a trophy of war, and that the systematic, planned use of rape as a war tactic is subject to prosecution. The latter is important because the burden of proof for a war crime is lower than for other international crimes.

The point that Ellis (2006/2007) makes is that the "brutality and systematic consistency of the sexual violence perpetrated [against women]" has finally been recognized in the international arena (225), and that although rape is a subsection of another crime, it nevertheless "draws attention to the heinous nature of the crime" and "aligning rape with the crimes that have been universally recognized as among the worst acts of [hu]mankind demonstrates that rape is equally grave" (247). Prosecutions of wartime rape have been difficult despite the significance of international legal changes, and the attention paid to the issue by the United Nations Security Council beginning with the landmark passage of UNSC Resolution (UNSCR) 1325, entitled "Women, Peace and Security," in 2000, which signified for the first time that the Security Council recognized gender-based violence and the differential impact of war and conflict on women, followed by UNSCR 1820 in 2008, which specifically focused on rape and sexual violence as a matter of international peace and security. In June 2014, British Foreign Secretary William Hague and actress Angelina Jolie, acting as the special envoy for the UN High Commissioner for Refugees, co-chaired the Global Summit to End Sexual Violence in Conflict in London in order to bring high-profile attention to the issue. In her opening comments in the summit, Jolie stated: "Warzone rape is a crime that thrives on silence and denial. The stigma harms survivors, it causes feelings of shame and worthlessness. It feeds ignorance, such as the notion that rape has anything to do with normal sexual impulses" (as quoted in Johnson 2014).

Yet, even in the domestic context despite decades of rape law reforms in countries like Canada and the United States, understandings of rape remain contested in the popular imagination. In large part, this is because of the continuing saliency of rape myths. From arguments focusing on men's uncontrollable sexual urges, to women provoking the rape, to false reporting of rapes by women who "changed their minds," to, more recently, widespread media stories of female perpetrators in positions of authority and underage male victims, understandings of rape end up boiling down to sex. For example, think about the kinds of reactions to news reports when a female teacher (particularly a young, "hot" one) has had sex with an underage male student. Despite what appears to be a double standard, arguments will be made that this situation is not comparable to a male teacher having sex with an underage female student. In that case, the teacher is taking advantage of the student, exploiting his position of power to force her to have sex, while the female teacher–male student scenario simply cannot be seen as coercion: What teenage boy would not want to have sex with an older woman who can offer him the kind of sexual experience and sexual knowledge that he can only fantasize about? The fact that the underage male student cannot give consent to his teacher under the law is simply irrelevant to the arguments made. These understandings about male sexuality, which undermine the importance of consent, are perpetuated further by beliefs about "legitimate rape." This became prominent during the 2012 American election season when Rep. Todd Akin, who was running for the US Senate seat for Missouri, infamously stated that women do not get pregnant from what he called "legitimate rape" because, as he stated, "the female body has ways to try to shut that whole thing down." Although Akin's comments were made in the context of debates over abortion, his beliefs reflect the kind of biological determinism about both male and female sexuality that perpetuates rape myths.

This chapter points out that the persistence of rape myths accounts for the underreporting of rape despite over three decades of legal reform in Canada and the United States. Rape is sexual violence where there is always an absence of consent. Why is this understanding so contested? Is it because of the practice of BDSM (bondage, discipline, sadism, masochism), which has been in the news given the popularity of *Fifty Shades of Grey*, a book about rough sex that has sold over 100 million copies worldwide and has been turned into a box office hit? Is it because there is a lack of understanding of the significance of the shift in language in criminal law, as evident in Canada and in many states in the United States, from rape to sexual assault? What do rape myths tell us about society today? Is there a rape culture in Canada and the United States? These are the kinds of questions that will be addressed in this chapter. Understanding consent has become increasingly important in the efforts to address campus rape in Canada and the United States, and, as pointed out in this chapter, instituting "affirmative consent" is the way to deal with sexual assault cases, where the burden of proof is shifted to the accused as opposed to the complainant. The reason why is clear. Not only have rape survivors undergone a traumatic event in their lives, often left with lifelong scars and pain, but their sexual freedoms have also been fundamentally violated, which, if it takes away their capability for sexual pleasure, undermines individual autonomy and sexual justice.

BDSM AND CONSENT

Focusing on rape as sexual violence is important because it is a turn of phrase of commonly held views historically of rape as violent sex. The targeting of women in conflict situations worldwide, specifically in the use of rape as a weapon of war, clearly centres on the use of violence, but central to understanding rape in the community and the university is the absence of consent, accounting for why the SMU and UBC chants were so problematic, where violence may not even be present. There is a difference between sexual violence and sexual practices that involve the infliction of pain, and although the difference centres on consent, the law does not recognize consent if it leads to bodily harm. This issue about the law, though, is more about societal attitudes regarding sex in terms of erotic feelings and desires than it is about gender. There are sexual practices, exemplified in BDSM, where consenting adults indulge in what those in the mainstream would see as kinky, fringe, or rough sex. As Margot Weiss (2011) explains, those who practise BDSM are composed of "a diverse community of aficionados of bondage, domination/submission, pain or sensation play, power exchange, leathersex, role-playing and fetishes" (vii). Fantasies around dominance and submission can be highly erotic despite the compelling arguments of radical feminists that these fantasies are products of patriarchal societies where women are socialized into eroticizing submission and learn to find satisfaction in being dominated. Sex-positive or sex-radical feminists highlight that there are both women and men who want to dominate and be dominated, and BDSM is a way for them to express their sexual freedoms and desires. Inflicting and receiving pain is an important element of BDSM practice, and although it carries risk, it is "generally no more risky than football, rock climbing, or other sports" (Weiss 2011, 285). Although the law in Canada and the United States does not prevent consenting adults from indulging in a wide array of sexual practices, individuals cannot consent to their own assault or any kind of bodily harm.

In October 2014, Jian Ghomeshi, a popular Canadian Broadcasting Corporation (CBC) radio personality with a Canadian and American following, was fired from his radio show, *Q*. He immediately wrote a Facebook post directed to thousands of his followers and revealed that, in his defence, his sexual preference for rough sex was the reason for his dismissal by the CBC. Ghomeshi (2014) stated that although "[his] tastes in the bedroom may not be palatable to some folks [and] they may be strange, enticing, weird, abnormal, or outright offensive to others," he engaged in consensual sexual activity with women, "using safe words and regularly check[ing] in with each other about [each of their] comfort levels." However, right after Ghomeshi posted his statement, the *Toronto Star* published an investigative report that the newspaper had been putting together for a number of months. In the report, three women accused Ghomeshi of "physically attack[ing] them on dates without consent, [alleging that] he struck them with a closed fist or open hand; bit them; choked them until they almost passed out; covered their nose and mouth so that they had difficulty breathing; and that they were verbally abused during and after sex" (Donovan and Brown 2014).

The Ghomeshi story dominated news headlines in Canada as well as the United States, but not in the way that the radio host might have hoped by being the first to speak about his desire for rough sex, explaining why he was fired from the CBC. As more and more women came forward with allegations of assault, it became apparent that Ghomeshi had a pattern of abusive behaviour. According to Brenda Cossman (2014), even if Ghomeshi's account of the events was accurate and he had "engaged in rough sex, very rough sex with consenting partners, [a]ccording to the law, if it was rough enough to cause bodily harm, then he has still committed assault, regardless of consent." Cossman adds that "BDSM sexuality still lives on the margins of legality in Canada" and "Ghomeshi's defense that the sex was consensual—even if it is true—is not the end of the story" because the issue in this case is bodily harm or assault, not consent.

This reasoning introduces issues around sexual practices that involve pain or bodily harm, and the extent to which court decisions reflect a particular interpretation of what constitutes proper sexual behaviour. The British Columbia Civil Liberties Association (2006) has argued:

> Boxing matches, ear-piercing, and tattooing are all considered risky, potentially painful activities to which one can … consent on the basis that they are seen to have social utility. On the other hand, sexual activities that involve the infliction of pain are criminalized. In these cases, the Courts appear to have taken it upon themselves to be the final arbiters of which activities serve a 'generally approved social purpose.'… Intuition suggests that if a person were accidentally injured in the course of 'normal' non-BDSM sexual contact, injuries sustained would not be subject to prosecution for assault providing the activity did not exceed the scope of the consent … It follows that it [is] not only the sexual aspect of BDSM, or the fact that it is socially unusual, that has led it to be singled out as unworthy of even the most basic protections of the law. Rather, it is the perception that the activity and the participants are sexually deviant. (7–8)

Sexual activities that involve pain or bodily harm to which individuals have consented invite questions about what individuals consider erotic or sexually arousing, and why it is that certain activities and individuals are considered "deviant," as opposed to "normal." These are the kinds of questions that arise in discussions of why such practices largely remain in the fringes of society.

However, rape is not violent sex; rape is sexual violence. Explicit force or infliction of pain may not even be used by the assailant, who may use other types of coercion or threat (or perhaps even none at all), but consent is always absent. The absence of consent was becoming more and more evident in Ghomeshi's case, and as BDSM activists argued, he was using his desire for rough sex to mask violent behaviour. The violence just made it easier to condemn his actions. Indeed, part of why the public tide turned against Ghomeshi so quickly was because women stated that they were physically hurt. The abuse was *obvious* because, as CBC stated in a memo to its employees, despite knowing for months about allegations against Ghomeshi, it was when executives saw "for the first time, graphic evidence that Jian had caused physical injury to a woman" that they fired him (*CBC News* 2014). If the allegations are true, Ghomeshi had committed sexual assault. In February 2016, facing four sexual assault charges and one count of overcoming resistance by choking, Ghomeshi's trial began in a Toronto courtroom (a sixth charge would be tried at a later date). Just days into the heavily covered trial, his defence attorney skillfully called into question the credibility of one of the complainants by showing inconsistencies in her statements to police (what lawyers call "whacking" the witness), including something as trivial as whether she wore hair extensions at the time of the event. This sort of berating courtroom tactic, unsurprising to advocates of rape survivors, is why so many victims do not report sexual assaults. According to Nicole Pietsch, Co-ordinator of the Ontario Coalition of Rape Crisis Centres: "What you'll see in this court case is a reflection of what survivors go through any time they go to court.... Any time I've ever accompanied survivors to court, they've faced a cross-examination that made them feel like they were telling a lie, that people didn't believe them, that they had messed up and they weren't being a good witness" (as quoted in Mehta 2016). Although Ghomeshi had allegedly used violence or force against the women, the use of force is not necessarily present in sexual assault. However, it is always non-consensual and largely gendered because, as scholars point out, the main predictor of being a victim is gender, i.e., being a woman (McKenzie and Rozee 2010). In understanding the difference between rape and sexual assault, we need to look at the reform of rape legislation.

LEGAL CHANGES AND RAPE MYTHS

Martha Nussbaum's (1999) descriptions of rape cases in the United States prior to legal changes brought about by the feminist movement are reminiscent of what she calls a "strange era" (141). It was an era where a woman who was raped had to show that she explicitly resisted in the face of force or threat of force in order to demonstrate non-consent. Lying there and taking it would have meant that she wanted it, regardless of the likelihood of harm in demonstrating resistance. It was an era where, if a woman did not make a complaint immediately, it meant that she was lying, regardless of the trauma she experienced in being violated. It was an era where a woman's sexual history mattered and questions would arise on whether she was chaste enough to be raped. After all, the common belief was that a promiscuous woman, or a prostitute, because she was "sexually active with others [would obviously] 'do it' with anyone" (141). It was an era where "no" meant "yes" because a woman was seen as "playing games" or "playing hard to get." According to Nussbaum, this was an era where false beliefs about sexual desires and sexual behaviour not only affected social policies and court judgments, but also shaped the desires and preferences of women, deforming their preferences. "Women who had been raped, however violent and non-consensual the incident, felt shamed and sullied and frequently did not even consider turning to the law for help" (Nussbaum 1999, 141). Women blamed themselves, feeling guilty about their own sexual desires, as if consenting to sex meant consenting to abuse, harm, and violence.

Nussbaum then goes on to point out that rape law has changed, as evident in the United States and Canada, and that "this is an area in which feminist critique has transformed and continues to transform law" (142). Under English common law, rape was defined, in the words of Sir William Blackstone in the 18th century, as "the carnal knowledge of a woman forcibly and against her will" (which until January 1, 2013, was largely the definition used by the Federal Bureau of Investigation in the collection of national crime statistics). This definition pointed to three central elements in rape: intercourse, force, and non-consent; and the woman, as understood, was not the wife of the assailant because there was spousal immunity in rape (see Lyon 2004). This definition would set in legislation the parameters of gender (women cannot rape and men cannot be victimized); sexual orientation (same-sex victimization was excluded); marital status (a man could not rape his wife); violence (it is not rape if force was not used); and the sexual act (anal, oral, and other penetrative and non-penetrative sexual acts were excluded). In particular, the parameter of the sexual act was a clear indication at the time that "women's sexuality was defined by men's sexuality in that the requirement of vaginal penetration was the only standard with which a woman's body could be sexually violated in rape" (Tang 1998, 259).

Rape law falls under state jurisdiction in the United States, whereas it falls under federal jurisdiction in Canada. The influence of the women's rights movement in both countries led to significant legal changes. By the end of the 1970s, all 50 states in the United States had enacted some form of rape law reform, with Michigan being the first to pass a comprehensive criminal sexual assault law in 1974 (Bachman and Paternoster 1993). In 1983 Canada's Criminal Code was amended, replacing the crimes of rape and indecent assault with a three-level categorization of sexual assault. Generally speaking, laws were reformed in three primary ways: first, to use gender-neutral language (recognizing that men can also be victimized); second, to prevent examination of a victim's sexual history (pointing to the importance of rape shield legislation); and third, to eliminate the evidentiary requirements of (1) corroboration (which required that the victim have additional evidence that the rape occurred), (2) resistance (which required that the victim show that she resisted her attacker), and (3) fresh complaint (which required that the victim report the rape immediately). Laws were also changed to take away spousal immunity and recognize marital rape. The reforms eliminated the parameters of gender, sexual orientation, marital status, violence, and the sexual act, thus recognizing that men can be raped (and women can be perpetrators); that rape can occur in same-sex situations (indeed when men are raped, they are likely victimized by other men); that rape can occur within marriage (further protecting women in their private lives); that violence or use of force is not always present in rape (although different wording is often then used); and that rape is not confined to sexual intercourse (leading many jurisdictions to replace the single crime of rape with a broader understanding of sexual violation). In particular, as Nussbaum highlights, the elimination of the marital exemption in rape law has been a significant step forward because it not only "discards the legal fiction that man and wife are 'one person,'" which historically has meant that women were the property of men, but also shows that domestic violence is multi-faceted and includes marital rape. Indeed, "the prevalence of intimate partner rape may be even higher than previously estimated if we consider that battered women are particularly susceptible to being raped by their partner," as evidenced by clinical studies that show "between one third and one half of battered women report being sexually assaulted by their partner at least one time during their relationship" (Bergen and Bukovec 2006, 1375).

In Canada and in most states in the United States, the word *rape* has been expunged from law. The reasons why vary, but for many feminists the term was problematic, from the stigma of the word unduly attached to victims, to its association with sexual activity as opposed to violent crime (before the 1983 reforms in Canada, rape was an offence against public morals as opposed to crimes against the person), to its narrow focus on sexual, specifically vaginal, penetration for abuse to occur. *Sexual assault* is a broader term that can encompass all non-consensual sexual touching. The following table illustrates the three levels of sexual assault in the Canadian Criminal Code.

Table 5.1: Sexual Assault in Canada

Definition	Categories
An assault committed in circumstances of a sexual nature such that the sexual integrity of the victim is violated. This term is used to refer to all incidents of unwanted sexual activity, including sexual attacks and sexual touching.	**Level 1—Sexual assault (Criminal Code s.271):** Sexual assault that involves minor physical injuries or no injuries to the victim.
	Level 2—Sexual assault with a weapon, threats to a third party, or causing bodily harm (Criminal Code s.272): Sexual assault that involves a weapon, threats, or causing bodily harm to the victim.
	Level 3—Aggravated sexual assault (Criminal Code s.272): Sexual assault that results in wounding, maiming, disfiguring, or endangering the life of the victim.

Source: Statistics Canada, 2008.

In the United States, most states, like New Jersey, have replaced *rape* with *sexual assault*, as in Canada, but there is a greater variety of terms used in the United States to capture different levels of offences against an individual's sexual integrity. The word *rape* is still found in the legislation of 24 states, with some states, such as Pennsylvania, stating that the use of force is what distinguishes rape from sexual assault. Other states, such as South Carolina and Florida, use neither *rape* nor *sexual assault*, preferring to use terms such as *criminal sexual conduct* or *sexual battery* in their laws (Bazelon 2014; Palmer 2011). Despite the differences in terminology, the point of rape legislative reform was not only to focus on victims, eliminating the legal barriers in the reporting and the prosecuting of rape, but also to change societal attitudes because rape has been "inextricably connected to the degradation and commodification of women and their sexuality" (Plaxton 2014). As *Globe and Mail* journalist Kirk Makin (2013) stated recently: "The idea was to change culture, not just laws, to acknowledge that *sex crimes* are not about sex, but acts of physical and psychological violence, and to make it clear that victims should not be blamed but emboldened to seek redress" (italics added; see below).

Yet, despite over three decades after reform of rape law in Canada with the passage of Bill C-127 in 1983, rapes remain under-reported and conviction rates remain low; the same is true for the United States. One of the reasons for this, according to Shannon Sampert (2010), is the persistence of rape myths, which she finds in analyzing Canadian newspapers' coverage of sexual assault cases, beginning with journalists' widespread use of terms that include *sex*, such as *sex crime* (see Makin, quoted earlier, who perhaps should have simply used *rape* as a term), *unwanted sex*, or *underage sex* to describe rape. Rape myths are "prejudicial, stereotyped, or false beliefs about rape, rape victims, and rapists," a definition Sampert (304) takes from the work of Janice Du Mont and Deborah Parnis (1999). As Sampert argues, "legislative changes cannot work if the underlying societal beliefs continue to support myths and stereotypes about sexual violence" (302). She identifies a number of sexual assault (or rape, which is the term used here) myths in her analysis, and this chapter focuses on the four below.

> Myth #1: Rape is about uncontrollable male lust, not about violence.
> Myth #2: Innocent men are regularly accused of rape and women regularly lie about it.
> Myth #3: Men of good standing do not rape women.
> Myth #4: The rape was provoked by the victim.

The first myth speaks to problematic understandings about male sexuality, grounded in biological determinism. Not only does research into male sexuality undermine the idea of uncontrollable male sexual urges (given the social shaping or construction of male sexuality), but also, as Nussbaum (1999) points out, "arousal is no justification for the use of force" (141). A good example of this myth being propagated insidiously comes from high-profile anti-abortion advocates in the United States running for Senate seats in the 2012 elections. Abortion is a highly contested issue in the United States and, as discussed earlier, support for women's reproductive rights is one of the primary sites of the culture wars. Social conservatives, such as former Republican vice-presidential candidate Sarah Palin, have sought to define life as starting at conception (this is what conservatives see as a "pro-life" position), to limit women's access to abortion services, and to curtail women's reproductive rights. According to the US National Right to Life Committee, pregnancies resulting from rape or incest are the "hard cases" because the group recognizes that the girl or woman has been victimized. However, many anti-abortion advocates, such as Palin, make no exception for these hard cases. If a pregnancy results from rape or incest, the girl or woman is expected to carry the pregnancy to term, which leads to doubly victimizing her. This continuing victimization of a girl or woman who has been raped is an unpalatable position to many in the public.

That is arguably why Rep. Todd Akin infamously stated that women do not get pregnant from what he called "legitimate rape" because if pregnancy resulted, it must not really have been rape. The reasoning for this, as Jacqueline Murray (2012) argues, is rooted in medieval thinking when it was believed that "a woman's body will experience different biological responses to intercourse depending on whether the sex act is consensual or coerced." Women become pregnant, it was believed, when they consent to sex and experience sexual pleasure. This sort of thinking is obviously unfounded, if not outright ridiculous to modern thinkers, but as Murray argues, there is a "flip side to these beliefs" and this is the notion of uncontrollable male sexual lust. This is based on biological determinism: just as a woman uncontrollably (in the words of Akin) "shut[s] that whole [pregnancy] thing down" when sex is forced, a man uncontrollably builds up lust, "perhaps even harming a man's body or health, unless he has sex." According to Sampert (2010), the idea of uncontrollable male sexual urges has been "the most powerful myth about rape" (305) and clearly reduces the act to one of sex as opposed to violence.

The second myth is that women regularly make false accusations and innocent men suffer. This myth is propagated in the media whenever a false accusation has been made, as if this is a regular pattern. One of the disturbing fallouts of any unfounded story, such as the account of an alleged gang rape at a University of Virginia fraternity party, published by *Rolling Stone* in November 2014, is that it fuels the myth that women regularly lie about being raped (Duhaime-Ross 2014). Although in its retraction *Rolling Stone* accepted responsibility for failed journalistic practices in publishing the story, the magazine nevertheless states:

> The editors and Erdely [the journalist who wrote the story] have concluded that their main fault was to be too accommodating of Jackie because she described herself as the survivor of a terrible sexual assault. Social scientists, psychologists and trauma specialists who support rape survivors have impressed upon journalists the need to respect the autonomy of victims, to avoid re-traumatizing them and to understand that rape survivors are as reliable in their testimony as other crime victims. (Coronel et al. 2015)

In other words, the journalist did not follow standard practices of reporting, editing, and fact-checking *out of respect* for the victim. Does this not also sound like victim-blaming? This is another myth that will be explored later. Moreover, out of fear of not being believed because of the myth that women regularly lie, many women who have been sexually assaulted do not report the crime. This is why the women who accused Jian Ghomeshi of sexual assault initially did not come forward. It is also the same reason given by the over 40 women who have accused Bill Cosby of rapes that occurred decades ago, but as captured in a powerful July 2015 cover of *New York* magazine, 35 of them ended their anonymity and together detailed their stories of assault (Malone and Demme 2015). In addition, because of how the Ghomeshi case unfolded, #BeenRapedNeverReported became a powerful hashtag on Twitter, leading *Huffington Post* to publish thousands of tweets of survivors to illustrate the extent to which women do not report sexual assaults out of fear of being blamed or disbelieved (Yeung 2014).

The third myth that men of good standing do not commit rape results in sympathy for the accused instead of the victim. A particularly egregious example of this was the reactions of CNN correspondents in March 2013 after a guilty verdict was handed down in the Steubenville rape case where two high school boys assaulted a 16-year-old girl. Poppy Harlow, the correspondent on the scene at the trial, made on-air statements such as the following: "These two young men—who had such promising futures, star football players, very good students—literally watched as they believed their life fell apart" (Makarechi 2013). This type of sympathy with the assailants, as opposed to the victim, led to outrage in the popular press and social media with demands that the network issue a formal apology. Another example was in 2009, when television host Whoopi Goldberg defended director Roman Polanski, who had pleaded guilty to assaulting a minor, but had stayed in exile in Europe for decades to avoid jail time in the United States. According to Goldberg, Polanski did not commit "rape rape" and was being unduly ostracized. After all, Polanski was an outstanding director and family man. As Sampert (2010) states, "the myth of the 'good man' accused of sexual assault works alongside the myth that men are falsely accused of sexual assault" (319). That was certainly the case with the public image of Bill Cosby, who played Dr. Cliff Huxtable, a lovable, upstanding father figure on his hit TV series, *The Cosby Show*, which ran from 1984 to 1992.

The fourth myth is that the rape was provoked by the victim. As discussed above, this is closely associated with concerns about false accusations. Victim-blaming is the foundation of the "strange era" discussed by Nussbaum in looking at rape cases prior to reform of rape legislation where the scrutiny and dissection of a victim's dress, behaviour, and sexual history was common in the courtroom, and it was largely the victim, not the assailant, who was put on trial. Although the legal changes have shifted to protecting the victim, ideas around a "perfect victim" have arisen. This has now led to the discrediting of sexual assault when the victim does not dress or act as expected (e.g., a victim providing a condom to her assailant out of fear of contracting a sexually transmitted disease), resulting in the myth that the victim somehow provoked the rape. Victim-blaming can also come in the form of "warnings" on how an individual can protect herself from sexual assault. This often singles out a woman's behaviour instead of targeting that of the assailant. According to Sampert (2010, 324), "these warnings feed the belief that women provoke their sexual assaults or are responsible for failing to prevent sexual assault." Addressing this myth is how "SlutWalks" began. Precipitated by a police officer's comments in 2011 to students at York University in Toronto that if women wanted to avoid being raped, they should stop dressing like "sluts," it has become a global movement symbolizing the fight against victim-blaming and slut-shaming.

The persistence of rape myths points to how changes in law alone are insufficient in changing attitudes about rape so that sexual assaults are reported, investigated, and prosecuted. At the same time, as a product of the women's rights movement from three to four decades ago, rape law reform is also tied to gender equality because rape, as a manifestation of the degradation of women and women's sexuality, is grounded in sexism. Rape law reform has not been simply about prosecuting rapists but also about confronting sexist attitudes: it has not simply been about changing laws but changing culture. As discussed in the last chapter, cultures are dynamic, and the sexism of the past is not the sexism of the present. An important aspect of a feminist liberal perspective is recognizing the progress that has been made in individual autonomy and sexual justice, particularly in Western societies like that of Canada and the United States. In that way, a crucial dimension of rape myths is that they are recognized as *myths*. Unlike 30 or 40 years ago during the "strange era" brought out by Nussbaum, women and men do not uncritically accept that rape is about sex or uncontrollable male lust, or that women regularly lie about rape, or that men of good standing do not rape, or that women act in ways to provoke rape. What is interesting about any example that can be given today of a rape myth being propagated is the response, usually immediately and often through the popular press and social media, to counteract the myth. This is evident in reactions to Todd Akin's comments on "legitimate rape," or to attempts to discredit the victims of Jian Ghomeshi or Bill Cosby, or to sympathetic coverage of the assailants in the Steubenville rape case, or to the police officer who advised female students to stop dressing like "sluts."

At the same time, the SMU and UBC rape chants exposed the extent to which sexist attitudes can become embedded in individual thinking so that chanting about rape can become normalized. The young women and men chanting had internalized sexist attitudes about rape, rape victims, and rapists to the point that many of them did not consciously realize that they were perpetuating rape myths. That is why it was crucial that universities responded immediately to address the issue. Despite the adoption of gender-neutral language, and the importance of recognizing the victimization of men, rape is a gendered phenomenon. Women overwhelmingly are the victims of rape. It is overwhelmingly women whose bodily integrity and sexual freedoms are violated so that being "sex-positive" after being raped is often merely an invitation for many women to relive the trauma and pain. It is in this context of recognizing that a victim's capability for sexual pleasure may be taken away that current debates on rape culture and "affirmative consent," two central issues in the efforts to address campus rape in Canada and the United States, should be examined.

RAPE CULTURE AND AFFIRMATIVE CONSENT

The rape chants at Saint Mary's University and the University of British Columbia in September 2013 were followed by two disturbing incidents at the University of Ottawa (UO) that became public in March 2014. One involved a Facebook conversation between five male students making sexually degrading and violent comments about the female president of their student organization, and the other involved an alleged sexual assault committed by members of the men's hockey team. The university president immediately suspended the hockey team until an investigation was completed and soon thereafter established a task force on respect and equality, chaired by Professor Caroline Andrew, a widely respected feminist scholar in political science, to address the larger problem of sexual violence in the university. In December 2014 another troubling incident became public, this time involving a group of male students at Dalhousie University's Faculty of Dentistry, who, as part of a Facebook group calling themselves "Class of DDS 2015 Gentlemen," were discovered making misogynistic comments about their female peers in the program, even dating back to 2011. A majority of the 2015 dentistry class composed of both women and men, including members of the Facebook group, agreed to participate in a restorative justice process, and an external task force was appointed to look into the incident and make recommendations. In January 2015 the University of Ottawa's Task Force on Respect and Equality released its report, entitled "Ending

Sexual Violence at the University of Ottawa," highlighting that its work was part of "a broader, ongoing discussion about rape culture on North American campuses," and making specific references to the rape chants at SMU and UBC and the incident at Dalhousie, as well as to the growing attention focused on campus sexual assault in the United States led by President Obama (University of Ottawa 2015, 5–6).

The SMU, UBC, and UO reports all identify a rape culture in Canada, accounting for why the incidents on their campuses occurred. As in the United States, this has spurred a great deal of debate. According to the UBC report, a rape culture is "a culture that has created an environment on campus or in society in general in which *rape and other forms of gender-based violence are normalized, tolerated or excused* [and it] includes jokes, legal jargon, laws, popular culture, words and imagery, that make violence against women (or those perceived to be women) and sexual coercion seem normal and victim based" (University of British Columbia 2014, 21; italics added). The UO report makes clear that "rape culture is deeply connected to other forms of oppression based on race, sexual orientation, gender identity, ability and class [and its] key characteristics include blaming victims, denying the pervasiveness of sexual assault and minimizing its negative effect" (University of Ottawa 2015, 6). The existence of a rape culture in Canada has been met with a great deal of derision. Not only do detractors argue that rape chants and Facebook posts are immature university students' harmless acts of banter, but they also contend that the number of sexual assault cases, like that allegedly committed by the UO men's hockey team, is overblown, resulting in what a *National Post* (2014) editorial calls a "moral panic" brought on by "alarming statistics" that are largely unsubstantiated.

Calling into question the findings of research on sexual assault has become a principal way for detractors in both Canada and the United States to discredit concerns about a rape culture. Emily Yoffe's "The College Rape Overcorrection," published online in *Slate* in December 2014, is a prime example of this. Yoffe (2014), looking at "the numbers," argues that "bad policy is being made on the back of problematic research" and proceeds to question the veracity of researchers' claims that, for example, one in five women in university will be sexually assaulted by the time they graduate. Hers is a compelling piece anchored in large part by the story of a male student unjustly treated after being accused of rape, but as Jennifer Baker (2015) points out, Yoffe has gained "avid support from anti-feminists and men's rights activists for defending the status quo on campuses, finally bringing some 'common sense' to the 'campus rape hysteria' … but she's not a researcher on campus rape."

Baker goes on to argue that Yoffe has both misunderstood and misrepresented key concepts and underlying premises of the research that she examines because it is in the interest of "Yoffe and her 'antifeminist' fans, who have made the issue of campus rape personal, a matter of their hunches about women being right." And their hunches about women—that their safety is not in jeopardy because there is no campus rape epidemic—means that the policies that they see as taking away men's rights are misguided.

Moreover, detractors bring out that one of the largest rape prevention organizations in the United States, RAINN (the Rape, Abuse and Incest National Network), has argued that rape culture is not the problem because rape is not caused by cultural factors but committed by individuals who consciously choose to do the crime. Canadian journalist Matt Gurney (2014) points out that, according to RAINN, potential victims need to be educated to increase their personal safety, applauding the organization for taking what has become a controversial stance because of accusations by what he calls "rape-culture activists" of victim-blaming. American journalist Caroline Kitchens (2014) also welcomes RAINN's stance because "by blaming rape culture, we implicate all men in a social atrocity, trivialize the experiences of survivors, and deflect blame from the rapists truly responsible for sexual violence." According to Kitchens, the "average guy" should not be vilified and therefore his rights should not be violated in the apparently misguided goal of protecting women. Although men are more likely to be victims of sexual assault than to be falsely accused of committing it (Kingkade 2014b), American detractors of rape culture are particularly concerned about false accusations in large part because of federally mandated changes to which universities must comply.

In looking at the debates about rape culture, the American and Canadian contexts differ because of the current political environment where President Obama and key legislators in Congress are championing changes to campus sexual assault policies. Although the US federal government does not have a constitutional mandate to preside over education, unlike in Canada where the provinces clearly exercise constitutional jurisdiction over educational matters, the US Department of Education wields a great deal of influence over post-secondary institutions, particularly over the enforcement of civil rights. Unlike Canada, which does not have a ministry of education at the federal level, the United States has passed laws governing educational matters, including what is referred to as "Title IX" of the Education Amendments of 1972. According to the United States Department of Justice (n.d.):

> Title IX is a comprehensive federal law that prohibits discrimination on the basis of sex in any federally funded education program or activity. The principal objective of Title IX is to avoid the use of federal money to support sex discrimination in education programs and to provide individual citizens effective protection against those practices.

Although this law was originally passed to ensure equality of access to school athletic programs by both women and men, it has expanded to include sexual harassment and sexual violence as forms of sex discrimination in universities. Key to why this happened was a civil suit launched in 1977 against Yale University for not addressing sexual harassment as part of Title IX enforcement. It was Catherine MacKinnon as a law student in Yale who wrote the rationale for why sexual harassment was a form of sex discrimination, thus falling under Title IX. On that basis years later, another student at Yale successfully sued the university in 2003 for failing to support her after she reported a sexual assault on campus, thus discriminating against her (Kingkade 2014a). It is this reasoning that has fuelled Title IX complaints against universities with the US Department of Education Office for Civil Rights. The number of complaints has grown significantly in two years from 17 cases in 2012 to 96 cases in 2014, and this growth has been due in large part to victims demanding justice through student-led and student-driven activist groups, such as End Rape on Campus and Know Your Title IX (Sneed 2015).

In launching the White House Task Force to Protect Students from Sexual Assault in January 2014, President Obama acknowledged the work of student activists in bringing attention to sexual assault on university campuses. In April 2014, the White House Task Force released its first report, entitled *Not Alone*, to ensure "sexual assault survivors that they are not alone [and that the federal government will] help schools live up to their obligation to protect students from sexual violence" (White House Task Force 2014, 2). The Obama administration also launched the "It's On Us" public awareness campaign in September 2014 to engage all students, particularly men, to help prevent sexual assault on campus. A year earlier, Obama had signed the Campus Sexual Violence Elimination (SaVE) Act, or Campus SaVE Act, as part of the Violence Against Women Reauthorization Act of 2013. Amending what is referred to as the Clery Act of 1990, named after Lehigh University student Jeanne Clery, who was brutally raped and murdered in her dorm room in 1986, the

Campus SaVE Act instills further requirements on universities: first, to increase transparency on the statistical collection and reports of sexual violence on campus; second, to adopt and publish procedures on victims' rights; third, to adopt and publish procedures on the adjudication of reports of sexual violence, including adopting "preponderance of evidence" as the standard of evidence (as opposed to "beyond a reasonable doubt" as in criminal trials); and fourth, to adopt and provide prevention and awareness programs on sexual violence (see Carter 2014). Because lack of compliance with this legislation can lead to universities losing funding from the federal government, universities have begun adopting "affirmative consent" as part of their policies and procedures on sexual assault, although states, such as California and New York, have passed or are considering passing laws to require universities in their states to adopt policies based on affirmative consent.

The focus on consent, as opposed to the use of violence or force in campus sexual assault cases, is illustrative of the fact that in an overwhelming number of sexual assault cases in both the United States and Canada, the victim knows her attacker. Often referred to as acquaintance rape (or date rape, although some see this term as sanitizing the act), this is the most common type of sexual assault committed both in the university and in the larger society where the victim is often not physically hurt except for the violation. Debunking a common misconception that rapes are overwhelmingly committed by strangers wielding weapons against victims in dark alleys, acquaintance rape is often difficult to prosecute, not only because there is often no physical evidence, but also because there is usually no one else in the room except for the victim and the assailant, leading to what many argue as a "she said–he said" scenario. In addition, just as with marital rape, there is often a general reluctance on the part of enforcement authorities to see sexual assault in cases of individuals who know each other unless there is physical evidence of harm (that is likely why marital rape tends to be more documented in studies of battered women). It is useful to remember that a central element of rape historically has been the use of force, accounting for why *rape* has been the appropriate term used as a weapon of war. War is clearly about violence and the use of force. It is more difficult when the focus is solely on consent because the role of coercion is not readily evident in the sexual act.

Defining consent as *affirmative consent* is a way to address this difficulty. Under California law passed in September 2014, *affirmative consent* is defined as the following:

> [It is] affirmative, conscious, and voluntary agreement to engage in sexual activity. It is the responsibility of each person involved in the sexual activity to ensure that he or she has the affirmative consent of the other or others to engage in the sexual activity. Lack of protest or resistance does not mean consent, nor does silence mean consent. Affirmative consent must be ongoing throughout a sexual activity and can be revoked at any time. The existence of a dating relationship between the persons involved, or the fact of past sexual relations between them, should never by itself be assumed to be an indicator of consent.

Universities in California are required to adopt this definition, but universities throughout the United States, regardless of whether the states in which they are located have adopted legislation, have adopted variants of this definition to comply with federal Title IX requirements. Key to this definition is that consent must be affirmative, conscious, voluntary, and ongoing. Consent must be *received* with every step of the sexual act, which means that the onus is placed on the individual accused to prove that he received consent as opposed to the victim to show that she did not give it. Instead of "No Means No," affirmative consent means "Yes Means Yes."

Affirmative consent policies in universities have become widely contentious in the United States, and opposition to them has come in two primary forms. First, it is seen as subverting due process because it favours the accuser over the accused. The argument made is that because the process is one-sided, men will be unable to defend themselves in false accusations by partners who simply changed their minds. Second, affirmative consent is seen as taking away the spontaneity of sex. The argument is that sex "in the real world" is not one where an individual stops at every step to confirm consent. Moreover, alcohol is often involved in university sexual liaisons, and the lines between "drunk sex" and sexual assault are not always clear. However, getting clarity is the point of affirmative consent. The onus is placed on the accused to prove that he received consent and the consumption of alcohol is not a mitigating factor. Saying that he was too drunk to understand if he received consent is not a defence. "The affirmative consent standard helps [to establish victim-centred policies and procedures in universities] by shifting the burden in disciplinary hearings from the complainant, who had to prove assault occurred, to the accused, who must show that he or she sought consent" (Grinberg 2014).

Part of the controversy over affirmative consent in the United States is because of the differences in how the 50 states define consent. Many states require that victims demonstrate that they did not give consent. Other states differentiate between voluntary or involuntary intoxication in determining the capacity to give consent, but the point is that it is up to the victim to demonstrate that consent was not given. In contrast, Canada already has an affirmative consent standard in law. "This came seven years after the sexual assault reforms of 1992, which, at their core, introduced the standard that 'reasonable steps' were taken [by the accused] to ensure the prospective sex partner really wanted to engage in sexual activity. Silence and lack of resistance do not equal consent" (Boesveld 2014). That is why the SMU report made it clear that students at Saint Mary's need to understand the law in Canada, where "sexual activity without consent is sexual assault," and that "consenting to one kind of sexual activity does not mean that consent is given to any other sexual activity or instance" (Saint Mary's University 2013, 26, 27).

Having affirmative consent in law does not necessarily lead to increased reporting by victims or higher conviction rates because, as discussed, Canada with its affirmative consent standard differs little from the United States. Despite decades of rape law reform, rape myths remain an impediment to victims coming forward and successful prosecutions (because police officers and judges also succumb to rape myths and, particularly in acquaintance rape cases, the victims often still end up being the ones on trial). Although rape myths are being challenged, sexual assaults are very real and they occur on campus. As James Hamblin (2014) points out, the problem with debating if rape culture exists is that "many writers who say rape culture does not exist seem to argue with a hyperbolic definition—that of a world of misandry so pervasive that women must live in fear of inevitable rape and men of inevitable blame." The problem is not that women and men are so divided that they live in fear of each other—that is not what rape culture is. Rather, it is in the normalization of rape that attitudes about rape, rape victims, and rapists, grounded in sexism, are perpetuated. That is how myths of women regularly making false accusations (i.e., she changed her mind) or provoking a rape (i.e., she really wanted it) end up as arguments against affirmative consent in universities because victim-blaming is sexist. Unlike in the United States, universities in Canada are not mandated by government to establish policies and procedures to address sexual assault. However, they have the opportunity to follow the lead of American universities in instituting affirmative consent in their policies. After all, it is also already the law in Canada.

Shifting the onus to the accused to prove that he received consent helps to end victim-blaming, and therefore begins to address sexist attitudes embedded in individual thinking. Universities, as centres for higher learning that foster critical thinking skills, are places where young people are taught how to live and act in the world. Many young men in university understand that when they engage in sex and their partner gets pregnant, there may be lifelong consequences beyond their control because the decision to continue or terminate the pregnancy rests solely with the woman. Similarly, many young men can also understand that when they engage in sex and they are unsure of consent due to alcohol or other factors, there may be consequences beyond their control. Just as there has been a shift from women being seen as solely responsible for pregnancies, there must also be a shift from women being perceived as sexual gatekeepers in society. Young men will learn to make judgments that go beyond the immediate moment to ensure that they have received affirmative consent. Being able to make good judgments may include limiting their alcohol consumption, or knowing that they may have to forego a potential sexual encounter if they choose not to do so. Having sex will not simply be seen as an act, but as a conversation. A male student once said that when he left for university, his father told him, "Always use a condom." Imagine the cultural change if his father also added, "Always get consent."

Sexuality is meant to be celebrated and sexual pleasure, as reiterated in the last chapter, is a crucial element in human flourishing. Jaclyn Friedman, an author, activist, and media commentator who has spoken at a number of university campuses, has long argued for a shift in thinking around sexual consent. In her 2008 co-edited work with Jessica Valenti, entitled *Yes Means Yes!: Visions of Female Sexual Power and a World Without Rape*, she asserts that a world of egalitarian sexual partners (i.e., where men treat women as collaborators and not conquests) and of celebrated female sexual pleasure (i.e., where men—and women—internalize that rape takes away women's capability) is a world without rape. This is the kind of transformation of intimacy that signals progress in individual autonomy and sexual justice.

RECOMMENDED FILMS, VIDEO CLIPS, AND WEBSITES

End Rape on Campus. www.endrapeoncampus.org/title-ix/.

The Hunting Ground. 2015. Directed by Kirby Dick and produced by Amy Ziering. www.thehuntinggroundfilm.com/.

Know Your IX: Empowering Students to Stop Sexual Violence. knowyourix.org/.

1 Is 2 Many. 2014. A 60-second clip by the White House. Published April 29, 2014. www.youtube.com/watch?v=xLdElcv5qqc. See also: www.whitehouse.gov/1is2many.

Signs. 2015. "Digital Archive on Consent." Currents: Feminist Key Concepts and Controversies. signsjournal.org/currents-affirmative-consent/#currentsdigitalarchive.

Spelling Lessons: A Spoken Word Response to the UBC and SMU Rape Chants (Trigger Warning). 2013. By Lucia Lorenzi. www.lucialorenzi.wordpress.com/tag/rape-chant/.

ADDITIONAL READINGS

Anderson, Letitia. 2010. "Politics by Other Means: When does Sexual Violence Threaten International Peace and Security?" *International Peacekeeping* 17, no. 2: 244–60.

Bennice, Jennifer, and Patricia Resick. 2003. "Marital Rape: History, Research, and Practice." *Trauma, Violence and Abuse* 4, no. 3 (July): 228–46.

Halley, Janet. 2015. "The Move to Affirmative Consent." *Signs*, Currents: Feminist Key Concepts and Controversies. signsjournal.org/currents-affirmative-consent/halley/.

Kirby, Paul. 2013. "Refusing to Be a Man?: Men's Responsibility for War Rape and the Problem of Social Structures in Feminist and Gender Theory." *Men and Masculinities* 16, no. 1: 93–114.

Lyon, Matthew. 2004. "No Means No: Withdrawal of Consent during Intercourse and the Continuing Evolution of the Definition of Rape." *Journal of Criminal Law and Criminology* 95, no. 1: 277–314.

Meger, Sara. 2010. "Rape of the Congo: Understanding Sexual Violence in the DRC." *Journal of Contemporary African Studies* 28, no. 2: 119–35.

Westmarland, Nicole, and Geetanjali Gangoli. 2012. *International Approaches to Rape.* Bristol: The Policy Press.

Chapter 6
PORNOGRAPHY

INTRODUCTION

The extent to which the pornography industry is a business like any other where online advertising and distribution of content have become crucial parts of the profit-making enterprise is evident in recent concerns about the dominance of Mindgeek. A multinational conglomerate founded in Canada and currently based in Luxembourg, Mindgeek is the world's largest provider of online pornography, attracting over 100 million viewers daily, becoming a huge user of bandwidth just like other video sites, such as Netflix, YouTube, and Twitch, and "[operating] nearly a hundred websites that in total consume more bandwidth than Twitter, Amazon, or Facebook" (Auerbach 2014). The concerns over Mindgeek stem from its ownership of 8 of the top 10 porn aggregator "tube sites," which include PornHub, YouPorn, and RedTube. Brought about by high-speed Internet, tube sites are "file-hosting sites that offer rivers of free streaming videos," and "the sheer ease of uploading content—anyone's content—onto a site and then drawing users to view it" results in widespread piracy, a phenomenon first evident in the music industry (Fayner 2010). Because of its ownership of tube sites, Mindgeek profits from advertising revenue generated by the sheer volume of free porn on its sites, derived in large measure from the mass online piracy of content produced by the professional porn industry (Auerbach 2014).

However, after the 2008 recession, Mindgeek expanded its control of the porn industry by moving into the production side. The company purchased production companies at bargain rates, and along with Hustler and Vivid, became one of the major players in the "traditional" porn filmmaking industry located in California's San Fernando Valley. Paradoxically, this has resulted in "industry workers [being placed] in the difficult situation of seeing their work pirated on sites owned by the same company that pays them" (2014). Mindgeek has very little competition in the distribution of pornography, and because it makes most of its profit from ads on its tube sites, the company has little incentive to protect the work of its content producers. This not only pushes down the wages of industry workers but also, like other media companies driven more by profit than creativity, devalues the artistry of making films.

According to anti-porn feminists, however, not only does pornography have little to do with artistic value, distinguishing it from erotica, but society should be concerned with not only its production but, more importantly, its consumption. They argue that pornographic images are shaping the attitudes and behaviours of a primarily male viewership with pernicious consequences for women as a whole. The harmful effects of the sexual representation of women have been at the heart of feminist opposition to pornography, yet watching or consuming pornography has become normalized in today's society. Pornography is ubiquitous in the digital age. Because of its widespread availability and accessibility on the web along with some assurance of anonymity, it can be viewed by anyone who has a computer. That is why parents install Internet filters to block their children's access; women end up monitoring the surfing habits of their male partners; and couples use it as a tool to spice up their sex lives, with some making their own porn movies to distribute online (thus not simply becoming consumers of pornography but also producers and actors). Indeed, not only has the suffix of *.xxx* been available for purchase and use alongside *.gov* and *.com* since 2011, but what was once a prominent site of the feminist sex wars has given way not to the call for the eradication of pornography because of the misogynistic portrayal of women, but to sex therapists offering advice to men on "what not to learn from pornography" (Zebroff 2012). In other words, although it is generally accepted that "porn is 'fantasy' and more often than not, a male-centric one," and "if you are learning how to have sex from porn, you may be getting misinformation, especially when it comes to pleasing a woman," it is simply a given that watching porn is normal behaviour, particularly for men (Zebroff 2012). That is why sex therapists will often list pointers on how to satisfy a woman for men who watch porn, so they will not be misled into thinking that pornography portrays women's sexual desires with any kind of accuracy.

Pornography is not illegal in Canada or the United States. However, there are strict laws against child pornography. In Canada, it is a criminal offence to make, print, publish, import, distribute, sell, or simply possess child pornography. The law was strengthened further in 2005 to remove claims of "artistic merit," and to include written material and audio formats (so not just pictures, videos, or other visual portrayals) where the "dominant characteristic" is the description for a sexual purpose of sexual activity involving a person under 18 years of age. These materials do not have to be explicitly pornographic; they can merely be implied. Critics have argued that the law is tantamount to censorship, including self-censorship for fear of being prosecuted, such as the 2006 decision by a small Saskatoon-based magazine not to publish an image of a popular Victorian-era painting, Sir John Everett Millais's 1879 *Cherry Ripe*, because of widespread covert pedophilia in Victorian society. The magazine was concerned that the painting of the young girl, because her look can be read as sexual coquettishness due to the period of when it was painted, would be considered child pornography. There are significant concerns about the overreach of the law, but because this is about the sexual exploitation of children, with all the emotional reactions that it engenders, any debate is quickly shut down and individuals, even one with sound conservative credentials such as University of Calgary political scientist Tom Flanagan, can be quickly vilified if questions are raised about the scope of the law. Flanagan, who was an adviser to Stephen Harper before the latter became prime minister, made a controversial remark in 2013 on the reach of Canada's child pornography law during a talk unrelated to the subject and quickly became a political pariah. He subsequently wrote a book, entitled *Persona Non Grata, The Death of Free Speech in the Internet Age*, detailing his experience (Flanagan 2014).

The focus of this chapter is adult pornography, and as discussed in Chapter 1, it has been one of the primary battlegrounds between radical feminist and sex-radical feminist groups. There are no laws against adult pornography in Canada and the United States; what is criminalized is obscenity. Because of the protection of the freedom of expression in liberal democratic societies, such as in Section 2 of the Canadian Charter of Rights and Freedoms and the First Amendment of the US Bill of Rights, what constitutes obscene or offensive material not only has depended on what is considered socially acceptable at any given time, but also has been weighed against individual freedoms. For example, D. H. Lawrence's *Lady Chatterley's Lover*, first published in 1928, was considered obscene in the United States and Canada and it was banned from publication until 1959 in the United States and 1960 in Canada. The kind of explicit sexual language in *Lady Chatterley's Lover* would not even merit a comment these days, except perhaps to show shock or disbelief that it was ever subject to censorship. Indeed, it has been widespread opposition to censorship and the centrality of freedom of speech and expression in democratic societies that has led to the lack of enforcement of obscenity laws in both Canada and the United States, although in 2005 the Bush administration did set up the Obscenity Prosecution Task Force in the Department of Justice, which the Obama administration quietly shut down in 2011.

This chapter begins with looking at terminology before delving into critiques of pornography and determinations of its harmful effects on women. What is the relationship between pornography, erotica, and obscenity? What has been the basis for a radical feminist critique of pornography? What does it mean to live in a porn culture, and how does contemporary anti-porn feminism analyze pornography's harmful effects on women? What is the difference between objectification and sexualization, and to what extent is it important not to conflate the two terms? How can the harmful effects of pornography be recognized, but not condemn all hard-core representations of sex, which, for some individuals, may be important to their sexual agency? What is "egalitarian pornography"? These are the questions that will be addressed in this chapter. The chapter ends with a discussion of feminist porn and points out that a sex-positive, anti-harm position not only recognizes the diversity of pornographies—and the term is deliberately used in plural form—but is also consistent with a feminist liberal perspective.

PORNOGRAPHY, EROTICA, AND OBSCENITY

As Beggan and Allison (2003, 302) point out, the definition of pornography as the "[presentation of] images of women that are objectifying, degrading, and dehumanizing" reflects a specific position that is not universally shared by feminists, accounting for the differences between the anti-pornography position of radical feminist groups and the pro-pornography position of sex-radical or sex-positive feminist groups. That is why Beggan and Allison prefer a simple dictionary definition: "the depiction of erotic behaviour ... intended to cause sexual excitement" because it "exclude[s] any judgment of morality" (302). Rosemary Tong (1989) brings out that anti-porn feminists (or, according to Tong, feminist anti-pornographers) differentiate between two types of sexually explicit material: "*erotica* (from the Greek *eros*, love or a creative principle) and thanatica (from the Greek *thanatos*, death or a destructive principle)" (113). Tong states that thanatica is pornography, thus setting the stage for differences between erotica and pornography.

> There are two crucial differences between them: (1) whereas erotic representations show sexual relationships between fully consenting, equal partners who identify emotionally with each other, thanatic representations show sexual relationships in which full consent, real equality, and emotional identification are absent; and (2) whereas erotica encourages both men and women to treat each other as full human persons, thanatica encourages men in particular to treat women as mere objects. (113)

Pornography and erotica both speak to the representation of women in sexually explicit material, but they are grounded in diverging understandings of the relationship between women and men. They may both lead to sexual stimulation or sexual arousal, but "pornography proposes a temporary 'fix' for our sexual frustrations; eroticism offers us something more elusive—an opportunity to experience sensuous delight of a higher order" (Seltzer 2011). It is this idea of a "higher order" that elevates erotica to the level of art, and in that way, illustrates more clearly how erotica differs from pornography. First, erotica is about aesthetics: it is, for example, about the beauty of the nude body or the sex act, and the sense of appreciation that such beauty elicits in those who view, read, or listen. It may arouse the viewer, the reader, or the listener, but only because his or her senses are heightened by the beauty he or she faces. Second, erotica is experienced openly and in "polite company." There is no shame in viewing, reading, or listening to depictions of nudity and sexual activity as art. Such examples include *Nudes* by Amedeo Modigliani or Robert Mapplethorpe, or Michelangelo's famous *David*. Third, erotica is about the realization of higher goals, leading individuals to think or act in ways that go beyond the portrayal in the artwork. Erotic art may prompt one to understand how sexual minorities, such as gays and lesbians, remain persecuted in contemporary society, or to learn how women have been portrayed through centuries as sexual objects. Finally, erotica is "fine art" rather than "commercial art," where "the work's monetary value [is] a secondary consideration" (i.e., the art may not even sell), unlike pornography, where it is "sex for sale" and the primary motive is profit (Seltzer 2011).

The distinction between erotica and pornography, however, is not always clear-cut. As A. W. Eaton (2007) notes, even scholars through the years have had difficulties in distinguishing works of art from works of pornography (676 n.3) so that one individual's view of erotica is pornography to another, and vice versa. In October 2014, a 73-year-old teacher was dismissed from a Montreal private school because some of her students discovered that she had acted four decades earlier in a number of films with explicit sex scenes. Although she defended her work as "art films" that were more properly seen as erotica, the school was "concerned about continuing to employ her, as it would compromise the school's values" (Gurney 2014). Although the teacher was eventually rehired, the reason for her initial dismissal was largely the same as that of a secretary in another Quebec high school who was fired in April 2011, but in this case, the secretary was moonlighting as a porn actress. These were hard-core pornographic films and she was fired because she, too, was seen as compromising the school's values. It did not matter that she was not in a position to influence young minds (she was, after all, not a teacher), or that she was very discreet in her day job and never advertised her other career (it was discovered by a male student in the school who saw one of her videos online), or that she had a young daughter to support and, like many single parents struggling to make ends meet, held down two jobs. The Quebec school board still dismissed her, and although school board officials acknowledged that she was not engaged in any illegal activity (that is why there was a settlement after she was fired), they still could not accept that a porn worker was in their midst. She has since become a full-time porn actress. The recency of the secretary's films reveals that if the teacher in the first case had been acting in "art films" four months or even four years earlier as opposed to four decades, she likely would also have not been rehired. Watching porn (or erotica) is regarded differently in society than "doing" porn, and a sex scene, whether it is tasteful or raunchy, is still a sex scene.

Similarly, what makes pornographic material obscene has not been readily apparent, and some radical feminist groups' use of obscenity law to abolish pornography has often placed them in the same company as social conservatives who want to censor all sexually explicit material. In Canada, obscenity is defined in Section 163(8) of the Criminal Code: "any publication a dominant characteristic of which is the undue exploitation of sex, or of sex and any one or more of the following subjects, namely, crime, horror, cruelty and violence, shall be deemed to be obscene." In 1992, the so-called *Butler* decision was handed down in which the courts established a different standard for obscenity, incorporating some understandings of harm in pornography based on inequality.

> [With the *Butler* decision] three standards had been developed to interpret "undue" according to the obscenity statute (mere "exploitation" of sex not being enough): (1) the community standards test, (2) the degradation and dehumanization test, and (3) the "internal necessities" test, providing an artistic defence for serious literary or political treatments. (Waltman 2010, 231)

Radical feminist groups saw it as a promising development in Canada because it recognized harm in terms of degradation and dehumanization as opposed to the so-called three-prong *Miller* test in the United States, where the focus was on "appeals to prurient interests" and "sexual conduct in a patently offensive way" in order to consider material obscene. However, according to Waltman (2010), the *Butler* ruling yielded few prosecutions of pornography based on harmful effects on women (although, problematically, it was used against LGBTQ retailers to censor their materials), and Canada differed little from the United States in its approach to obscenity enforcement, specifically in terms of harm to women.

In both Canada and the United States "obscenity law has historically been about morals of appropriate public behaviour, purporting to counter dissolution of social structures by containing sexuality inside stable (heterosexual) structures ... [as well as repressing] women's reproductive and sexual autonomy by regulating birth control information, abortion, and 'dissident' sexual practices" (Waltman 2010, 222). In other words, obscenity law has been a tool to sustain the heterosexual conjugal bond, historically disempowering women. Because some radical feminists share with social conservatives the desire to censor hard-core pornography, they find themselves being part of a movement that has used obscenity law in ways that counter their feminist goals, from prohibiting the mailing of contraceptives and information on abortion to censoring sexually explicit material depicting same-sex relations or what they consider undesirable material as part of sex education in schools (Kaminer 1992). That is why from a legal perspective, Nicola Lacey (1993) cautions that using laws to target pornography "might be exploited by right-wing litigants to attack a wide-range of sexually explicit art and literature ... [and a] feminist conception of pornography, already moulded to fit a legal framework, could be further distorted in the interpretive process so as to push it towards a conservative conception inimical to the direction of feminist analysis" (107–8). In that way, pursuing legal means, or even legal reform, may not be the best way to deal with the harms of pornography.

THE OBJECTIFICATION OF WOMEN

According to radical feminism, pornography is inherently and irrevocably exploitative of women. Women have simply become instruments or objects of male sexual enjoyment and, in that way, sexual objectification is a problem for women rather than men. As Nussbaum (1999, 246) states, "pornography standardly portrays the will of women from a fictive viewpoint, expressing the thought that they *want* to be used as things for male pleasure." She agrees with a great deal of what radical feminists, such as Catherine MacKinnon and Andrea Dworkin, have asserted about the deleterious effects of pornography, and indeed she sees little difference between soft-core and hard-core pornography. Nussbaum states that even a publication like *Playboy* (which many have claimed to contain "tasteful" and "artistic" portrayals of women, unlike a hard-core publication like *Penthouse*) treats "sex [as] a commodity and women become very like cars, or suits, namely, expensive possessions that mark one's status in the world of men" (234). She goes further and points out that "in the *Playboy* world it is sexier, because more connected with status, to have a woman of achievement and talent than an unmarked [or unknown] woman, in a way that it is sexier to have a Mercedes than a Chevrolet.... For what *Playboy* repeatedly says to its reader is, Whoever this woman is and whatever she has achieved, for you she is cunt, all her pretensions vanish before your sexual power" (235). As discussed in Chapter 2, a woman is often judged by her appearance, focusing on her body-as-object, which has defined femininity, but the sexual objectification of women due to pornography goes beyond judgments of appearance and treats women as mere sexual objects to be possessed by men.

According to both Nussbaum (1999) and Laurie Shrage (2005), the arguments of philosopher Immanuel Kant inform radical feminist understandings about sexual objectification. This notion is used to illustrate the pernicious effects of pornography and heterosexual male desire shaped by patriarchy. Nussbaum points out that, according to Kant, sexual desire is a powerful force that results in the thing-like treatment of individuals (i.e., it objectifies them). She then lists "seven ways to treat a person as a thing": instrumentality, denial of autonomy, inertness, fungibility, violability, ownership, and denial of subjectivity (218), and three of these ways help to illustrate Kant's view of sexual desire. Essentially, two individuals are in such throes of pre-orgasmic ecstasy that: (1) each treats the other simply as a tool for one's pleasure (instrumentality); (2) each dictates to the other what to do in order to achieve satisfaction (denial of autonomy); and (3) each forgets about what the other wants, fixated simply on ensuring one's own satisfaction (denial of subjectivity). Kant's view is that "in a typical sex act both parties eagerly desire both to be objectifiers and to be objects" (Nussbaum 1999, 224), and that humans degrade themselves to the level of animals when they indulge their sexual appetites, objectifying and dehumanizing others and themselves.

Shrage (2005) contends that Kant's sexual philosophy needs to be placed in context because he condemned all sexual activity outside of marriage (e.g., premarital sex, extramarital sex, masturbation, paid sex, homosexuality). Sexual activity within marriage was tolerable only because of the necessity of the procreation of the human race. As Shrage highlights from Kant's biographers, the philosopher was monastic and lived his life devoid of any sexual activity. The danger for radical feminists in drawing from Kant's view of sexual objectification is that their arguments against pornography end up being grounded in an anti-sex stance. That is why Nussbaum (1999) critiques Kant's perspective and asserts that there is a difference between objectionable and benign use of objectification. In a context of mutuality and equality between sexual partners where the intention is a reciprocal consent to the "surrender of individuation and a certain sort of porousness of boundaries that border on violability," objectification is benign (232). In other words, when sex is not grounded in systems of dominance and individuals are autonomous, the eagerness of both partners to be objectifiers and objects to reach orgasmic ecstasy is to be celebrated. This is the kind of sexual autonomy that is the foundation of Giddens's transformation of intimacy. Moreover, even until that sexual autonomy is fully realized, specifically for women, women should nevertheless embrace their sexual selves. As Nussbaum argues:

> [Although] social hierarchy is at the root of the deformation of desire [as articulated by radical feminists such as Catherine MacKinnon] … the deformation is more complicated than this, working not only through pornography but also through puritanism and the repression of the female erotic experience.... A certain sort of objectifying attention to bodily parts is an important element in correcting the deformation and promoting genuine erotic equality. (239)

In recognizing the harms of pornography, it is important not to undermine women's sexual agency.

PORN CULTURE

With the advent of the digital age, contemporary anti-porn feminists argue that we now live in a "porn culture" because Western society has been so inculcated with hard-core pornography by a primarily online industry driven by sheer profit that it continues to find newer and differing ways to degrade and dehumanize women, the most offensive being the development of "gonzo porn." According to Gail Dines (2006), one of the more prominent contemporary feminist voices against pornography:

> By far the biggest moneymaker for the industry, [gonzo] pornography makes no attempt at a story line, but is just scene after scene of violent penetration, in which the woman's body is literally stretched to its limit. One of the newer marketing ploys in gonzo is called ATM (ass to mouth), where the male performer anally penetrates a woman and then sticks his penis into her mouth, often joking about her having to eat shit.

Even sex-radical feminists have found the development of gonzo porn highly problematic. Gonzo porn was initially about moving away from "high production values, elaborate sets and costumes, or contrived storylines," and as Tristan Taormino (2013) argues, although she has "always been a fan of gonzo as a genre," it has become more extreme in the last decade (257).

> [Gonzo porn] had become all about rough sex, multiple impalements (how many things can we fit into how many orifices simultaneously?), gaping assholes, and circuslike stunts. It was as degrading and offensive as any antiporn feminist's worst nightmare. (Taormino 2013, 257)

Widespread piracy of online content has meant that this kind of pornography is free, available, and accessible with a click of a mouse. Dines's analysis is predicated on how porn has defined culture, and one of her primary concerns is the extent to which this porn culture has shaped the sexual understandings of both young men and women who, having grown up in the digital age, have been unrelentingly exposed to the objectification of women's bodies and the depiction of women as sex objects who exist strictly for men's pleasure. "This is not your father's *Playboy*" is one of Dines's favourite phrases in order to capture the impacts of technology, not only on the content of pornography, but also on its widespread availability, accessibility, and promise of anonymity because "users [can] buy and consume porn in private, without embarrassing trips to seedy stores or video rental shops" (Dines 2010, 48). She argues that "porn, rather than being an aberration, actually cements and consolidates [young men's] ideas about sexuality" (87) so that they "don't want to think of their girlfriends in the same way that they think of porn women, but they find it increasingly difficult to separate the two" (92).

For young women, according to Dines, they do not even have to watch porn "because images, representations, and messages of porn are now delivered to women via pop culture" in the form of "hypersexualized celebrities," such as Paris Hilton and Britney Spears (100, 103–4). Women have internalized their oppression such that they see it as empowering not only to wear "the accoutrements of hypersexuality—high heels, tight clothes, and so on—but also [to have] a body that adheres to an extremely strict standard [because they] need to look like [they] spend hours in the gym ... [which] is never good enough" (109–10). Dines's focus on "porn culture" as opposed to simply pornography means that the harms are so widespread in society that individuals do not need to watch pornography to be subject to its harms; just by living in today's society is harmful. Porn culture becomes pop culture; porn ideals become body ideals; and sexual objectification becomes what is understood as women's sexuality. Women simply become sex objects for the pleasure of men, and men are being "trained by the porn culture to see sex as disconnected from intimacy [so that] users develop an orientation to sex that is instrumental rather than emotional" (92). As Dines argues:

> Pornland is indeed paradise for men, as it is sex with no strings attached. And for women it is business as usual: men defining our sexuality in ways that serve them, not us. Only now this sexuality is sold to us as empowering. (119)

As Smith and Attwood (2013) point out, the current anti-pornography campaigning as exemplified by Dines's work is particularly concerned about the sexuality of youth. Unlike the radical feminism of the 1980s during the feminist sex wars, contemporary anti-porn feminism focuses on "the widespread accessibility of the Internet and its ability to bring 'outlier' sexual interests to the attention of naturally inquisitive but innocent children" and the extent to which this "has developed outside the knowledge of 'ordinary' adults and needs urgent redress" (43). Simply put, adults are simply unaware not only of the pornographic content on the web to which their children are exposed, but also of the extent to which their children's sexual understandings are being shaped by pornography. Young people are in danger because young men are being made to believe that "porn sex" is sex, and young women are being sexually objectified and internalizing their own objectification. That is why young women believe that they want "the accoutrements of hypersexuality." These are similar sorts of arguments made by the Saint Mary's University President's Council's report in pointing to "hypersexualization" as part of the cultural context of the troubling rape chant done by students. Hypersexualization, according to the report, "includes the cultural and marketing messages that our value as individuals comes from our sex appeal and behaviour, the sexual objectification of people (women in particular), the blurring of lines between adult and child sexuality, the mainstreaming of pornography and the exploitation of sex and sexuality for marketing purposes" (Saint Mary's University 2013, 19). Sexualization (or "hypersexualization" to demonstrate an even greater problem) and objectification have become the same thing. "Porn sex" is contrasted with "healthy sex," where "healthy sexuality" largely translates to a particular understanding of loving, caring, empathetic sex so that "a proper purpose for sex is assumed and there is no consideration of the variety of sexual practices that people engage in, diverse understandings of what sex is, or the multifarious reasons why people have sex" (Smith and Attwood 2013, 51). There is, in other words, an apparent disciplining of sexual behaviour in equating sexualization with objectification. These terms are often used interchangeably but whereas objectification is about harm, sexualization is arguably a process resulting from the sexual revolution in the West, which has led to greater sexual freedoms for women and sexual minorities.

That is why the *Report of the APA Task Force on the Sexualization of Girls* released by the American Psychological Association (APA) in 2007 has been met with criticism. The APA report lists four conditions of sexualization where only one condition needs to be present for sexualization to occur.

> (1) A person's value comes only from his or her sexual appeal or behavior, to the exclusion of other characteristics; (2) a person is held to a standard that equates physical attractiveness (narrowly defined) with being sexy; (3) a person is sexually objectified—that is, made into a thing for others'

> sexual use, rather than seen as a person with the capacity for independent action and decision making; and/or (4) sexuality is inappropriately imposed upon a person. (American Psychological Association 2007, 1)

As Lerum and Dworkin (2009) contend, the APA report is problematic because it disregards evidence that does not conform to its central premise that sexualization is harmful to women and girls, and does not bring in literature from critical feminism or sexuality studies that would ask different questions.

> Under what conditions might sexualization contain agency and resistance? Can desire play any role in sexualization? If one self-constitutes as an object of desire through sexiness, is this a sign of oppression? Under what conditions would this *not* be a sign of oppression? (Lerum and Dworkin 2009, 258)

By seeing sexualization as a product of the sexual revolution in the West, progress is highlighted. Reminiscent of arguments made in Chapter 2 regarding the politics of the body, Lerum and Dworkin contend that "women have now stretched beyond thin, passive sexualized ideals to include a broader range of strong, empowered, and muscular body ideals than ever before" (254). They add further that "the global story of women becoming more publicly sexual is not a simple story of oppression, as it developed in part as a result of women moving from economic dependency and domesticity to economic and sexual independence" (260).

Moreover, like Dines, the APA also discusses "healthy sexuality," which "fosters intimacy, bonding, and shared pleasure, and involves mutual respect between consenting partners," and this, the APA argues, stands in contrast to sexualization (American Psychological Association 2007, 1). Once again "healthy sex," specifically because it requires a partner, appears to be invoked to create parameters around sexuality. One of the misconceptions of Giddens's transformation of intimacy is that he equates sexuality with intimacy (see, for example, Smith and Attwood 2013, 51) when in fact his argument rests on "plastic sexuality," a term he uses to illustrate the extent to which sex has become pliable, diverse, and individual (i.e., outside of societal dictates). The freeing from sexual norms, particularly for women, has led to choices that, as part of an individual's self-development, she or he may choose to pursue an intimate relationship that reflects confluent rather than romantic love, but she or he may not make that choice. Sex does not have to be loving and caring; and an individual does not need a partner to enjoy sex because she can pleasure herself. This freeing from sexual norms is part of sexualization. Lerum and Dworkin (2009, 257) contend that "it is possible to both embrace sexual power as a goal while also critiquing sexual objectification." The question in looking at pornography is: How can harms be recognized without condemning all hard-core representations of sex, which may be important to sexual agency?

THE "HARM HYPOTHESIS" AND EGALITARIAN PORNOGRAPHY

Eaton (2007) points out anti-porn feminism has lost ground because it has been perceived as too extreme and unable to offer clear and compelling evidence about the harm to women caused by pornography. "Antiporn feminism has been extensively critiqued for its lack of theoretical rigor, shaky evidence base, and failure to distinguish its position from highly conservative views of sexuality and gender" (Smith and Attwood 2013, 47). As a philosopher, Eaton wants to think through the kinds of objections that can be reasonably raised against pornography while also embracing hard-core sexual representations as part of sexual pleasure. That is why she offers a "sensible conception of causation" based on a "harm hypothesis" in order to show that pornography shapes the attitudes and conduct of its audience in ways that harm women, but this is characteristic of *inegalitarian* pornography (677). She argues that there is also *egalitarian* pornography, which can help shape desires that are equally respectful of women and men (693). She defines inegalitarian pornography as sexually explicit representations of women that eroticize relations (namely, acts, scenarios, or postures) that characterize the subordination of women (676). She also points out that although other forms of representation are harmful to women, such as advertisements, movies, television, and music videos, pornography is especially harmful because it couches strong inegalitarian messages in an intensely eroticizing format (683). Inegalitarian pornography fuses pleasure with subordination, so that eroticization makes gender inequality appealing to both men and women. This, as noted earlier, is the sexualization of dominance and submission rooted in radical feminist thinking. Women end up collaborating in their own oppression because they internalize their subordination to men and this is what gives them sexual pleasure.

Eaton's "harm hypothesis" is based on three central elements. First, she argues that her hypothesis is based on a probabilistic, not a deterministic, conception of the causation of pornography's harm to women. It is not the case that if a man is a consumer of pornography, he will inevitably be abusive to women whether subtly or overtly. Eaton dismisses direct causation between pornography and harm to women. Indeed, it is this kind of direct causation that has led to the labelling of anti-porn feminism as extreme because it is simply not sustainable in terms of being able to provide irrefutable evidence. Instead of a direct causation, such as: "If *x*, then *y*" (pornography causes direct harm to women), Eaton offers the following probabilistic conception:

> *x* is a cause of *y* if and only if [pornography is a cause of harm if and only if]
> (i) *x* occurs earlier than *y* [pornography occurs earlier than harm] and
> (ii) the probability of the occurrence of *y* is greater, given the occurrence of *x*, than the probability of the occurrence of *y* given not-*x* [the probability of harm is greater with exposure to pornography than not being exposed]. (696)

In this probabilistic conception, pornography can be a cause of harm to women even if not every consumer of pornography behaves in ways that are harmful to women as long as the consumption of pornography as a whole increases the probability of harm to women. According to Eaton, the harm hypothesis is concerned not about the harm caused to women engaged in pornography but about third-party harms, i.e., effects on all other women. She discusses two stages of cause and effect in order to capture how harms to individual women (e.g., from those whose bodies are subject to looks to those whose rape cases are unfairly judged) can evolve to group harms where women as a group are diminished and a woman becomes a potential target of harm just because she is a woman.

Second, Eaton argues that her hypothesis posits that pornography is but one component in a multi-faceted, multi-factorial view of causality regarding gender inequality. She states that it is completely misguided to hold pornography single-handedly responsible for sexual assault or rape (and thus she finds no grounding for the radical feminist view that "pornography is the theory; rape is the practice") or for gender inequality in society. Rather, Eaton asserts that exposure to pornography is a salient risk factor for a variety of harms to women. She points to using epidemiology as a method for researchers to help identify risk factors for those who analyze pornography for harmful effects.

Third, the harm hypothesis is focused on post-production harms, namely those harms to women that are caused by the distribution and consumption of pornography, not those that occur during production (i.e., the process of making pornography).

The harms to women are focused on the consequences of actions of men consuming pornography, which can include women being objectified, harassed, and assaulted. The focus is not on the exploitation of, or harm to, women who work in the porn industry. They may be harmed, but that is not the point of the harm hypothesis.

However, Shrage (2005) exposes what she calls "the fallacies of antiporn feminism," not only to highlight the importance of protecting and empowering porn workers, but also to illustrate that the relationship between the porn consumer and the porn performer is economic, not social or personal. She asserts that there is a need to locate instrumental use (i.e., bodily intimacy between strangers) on market relationships rather than sexual desire. In that way, there would be less focus on how the sexual content of pornography impacts consumers and more on how processes of production and marketing impact porn workers. Moreover, according to Shrage, the dehumanization of women is caused by desexualizing them, i.e., by denying their erotic desirability or desires based on sexist or prudish values, so feminists should not mistake sexualizing women for sexually objectifying or degrading them. In other words, Shrage places the sexual agency of women at the forefront of discussions on pornography.

That is why Eaton sees the importance of distinguishing between egalitarian and inegalitarian pornography. She does not see the sexualization of women as necessarily objectifying them, but she does see that certain sexual representations in pornography may be harmful to women. In her response to Eaton's harm hypothesis, Shrage (2008) outlines the difficulties that anti-porn feminists have always had of *proving* harm. She argues that because "our best science cannot reliably tell us that inegalitarian porn harms women any more than our best science can tell us that religious instruction produces well disciplined children," trying to save anti-porn feminism only justifies research that in the past has resulted in censorship and other problematic forms of state regulation (Shrage 2008). However, in her response Eaton (2008) argues that "Shrage is opposed to the very notion that representations can have harmful effects," which is characteristic of the sex-radical position on pornography, and in that way, rejects that sexist representations can ever deform preferences. At the same time, Eaton (2008) agrees that the violent harmful effects of pornography have not been compellingly proven, so state intervention, such as censorship, is unjustified, which provides even more reason to work toward alternative representations. She quotes Annie Sprinkle, who is famous for saying, "The answer to bad porn is not no porn, but better porn!" Eaton (2008) then outlines some of the features of egalitarian pornography. Her criteria are in the table below, and although she does not similarly outline a criterion for inegalitarian pornography, the table shows what the main characteristics might look like, given her criteria for egalitarian pornography. In addition, Eaton (2008) states that inegalitarian pornography is primarily heterosexual, so that is reflected in the characteristics outlined below.

Table 6.1: Characteristics of Egalitarian and Inegalitarian Pornography

Egalitarian pornography (*Source:* Eaton 2008)	**Inegalitarian pornography**
Caters equally to female audiences	Caters primarily to male audiences
Accurately represents women's sexual pleasure and gives at least equal time to acts that women genuinely enjoy	Exaggerates women's sexual pleasure in order to present women as "sex starved" or to emphasize the sexual prowess of men
Foregrounds women's sexual pleasure rather than subordinates it to men's	Focuses primarily on men's sexual pleasure by limiting (equal) foreplay and ending the scene with men's orgasm (the "cum shot")
Represents women in attractive roles and postures without resorting to dominatrix stereotypes	Represents women in subordinate, fragile, or unsuspecting roles
Offers a variety of female body types, including many realistic portrayals of women's bodies without fetishizing them	Offers female body types that primarily fit into a narrowly defined body ideal (this would include slim women, perhaps with enhanced breasts and shaved genitals, who work on preparing their bodies to be seen by men)
Refrains from showing women desiring or enjoying their own degradation unless this is equally matched by men doing the same (this would mean no facial ejaculation scenes unless a gender-symmetrical counterpart were developed)	Routinely shows women apparently desiring their own degradation by showing them in various positions solely designed to emphasize the view of their orifices, depicting them with multiple partners, often with multiple penetrations, enjoying the infliction of pain, or speaking or being spoken to in vulgar, degrading ways
Represents bisexuality of both sexes or none at all	Restricts bisexuality to that of women, even when multiple men are present in the scene
Defies sexist clichés and stereotypes	Routinely propagates sexist clichés and stereotypes
Limits violence to explicitly consensual activities	Presents violent or painful acts without the explicit consent of the women, particularly where the scene depicts first-time encounters between the partners where no previous pattern of consent could exist, or where the violence or pain is severe or extended

FEMINIST PORN

A prime example of egalitarian pornography is an alternative and arguably subversive form of pornography referred to as feminist porn. Feminist porn is "both an established and emerging genre of pornography [and it] uses sexually explicit imagery to contest and complicate dominant representations of gender, sexuality, race, ethnicity, class, ability, age, body type, and other identity markers" (Penley et al. 2013, 9). Stemming from the feminist sex wars of the 1980s and developing out of genres of pornography known as women's porn, couples porn, and lesbian porn, feminist porn validates a female viewership of pornography. Indeed, the fact that women are consumers, too, is what led Carlyle Jensen, the owner of Good for Her, a sex-toy shop in Toronto, to stock her shelves with feminist porn films because "her customers wanted to see pornography, just not the mainstream stuff they found to be fake, robotic, emotionally vapid, and visually repetitive, and perhaps demeaning to women, [but rather] they wanted something they could feel good about watching" (Nasaw 2014). Jensen, along with store manager Chanelle Gallant and other staffers at Good for Her, established the Feminist Porn Awards (FPAs) in 2006 in order to recognize and promote outstanding feminist porn films (Penley at al. 2013, 12; Nasaw 2014). Celebrating its 10th year in 2015 and held annually in Toronto, the Feminist Porn Awards recognizes agency, diversity, and authenticity, focusing on women's involvement in production and judging films based on quality, inclusiveness, uniqueness, and hotness (which, according to its website, means "bodies are well-lit, framed and shot to perfection, desire radiates off the screen, and all parties involved appear enthusiastic [with] plenty of orgasms"). As Eaton (2008) points out, "egalitarian porn should include lots of sexually explicit, hot and lusty, lewd and raunchy representations that encourage masturbation or other sexual activity."

Although feminist pornographers are independent artists, they are also part of the mainstream adult industry, being funded and distributed by large companies, such as Vivid Entertainment. They "have adapted different strategies for subverting dominant pornographic norms and tropes" by either "[rejecting] nearly all elements of a typical adult film, from structure to aesthetics, [or] tweak[ing] the standard formula (from 'foreplay' to 'cum shot') to reposition and prioritize female sexual agency" (Penley at al. 2013, 6). Feminist porn is also about the empowerment of performers who decide if, how, and with whom they have sex. Tristan Taormino (2013), an award-winning, well-known feminist pornographer, discusses how as a producer and director she ensures a "fair and ethical process and a positive working environment" for performers where they set their own pay rates; choose their sexual partners in any given scene; decide if they want partners to have more recent STI-testing than the industry standard of 30 days; elect to use condoms, gloves, or dental dams; and generally be a collaborator in the making of the film (260). As Taormino states, "I value them as human beings, as sex workers, as performers, and I value the work they do. I hope they internalize this value and I raise the expectations for what a work experience can be" (263).

Feminist porn is built on "women's porn," and the experiences of Candida Royalle, one of the pioneers of this genre, serve as a reminder that alternative forms of porn are not a panacea. Royalle, a porn star in the 1970s, created Femme Productions in 1984 with the goal of creating pornography from a woman's perspective, which meant subverting conventions in the industry from eliminating the customary "money shot," where the man's ejaculation is evident to "prove" that the sex is real, to avoiding the ubiquitous lesbian and group sex scenes, to showing the complexity and variety of the sexual desire of women and thus undermining the usual trope of the "view of women as highly sexual and readily orgasmic" (Beggan and Allison 2003, 309). Royalle (2013) has talked about the challenges that she faced in the porn industry making films, stating that she would have liked to "say that [her] greatest source of pride is the impact [her] work has had on the enormous adult industry, but … 'women's porn' became co-opted by mass media, stripped of its original intent, and regurgitated by the still male-dominated porn industry, which wallows in low-brow shock entertainment for the masses" (68). Moreover, as Royalle (2013) points out, feminist porn, like women's porn, has not attracted the heterosexual male viewer.

Feminist porn has grown and coalesced because of technological advancements that have changed the porn industry. Pre-recorded content in the form of films has also given way to the "cam business," which, because it happens in real time, is much more difficult to pirate. Referred to as a "digital-era peep show," this is composed of "cam models" who solicit credits or "tips" rather than subscriptions or pay-per-view through websites that "provide the platform and then collect and distribute the tips to the models" (Richtel 2013). There is also a relationship to free pre-recorded content because porn sites attempt to convert visitors to paying customers in cam rooms. Although "cam girls" are often the source of journalistic interest, the cam business has been more profitable for gay male performers. Gay porn has been an important source of outlet—and validation—for sexual minorities. The multiplicity of pornographies shows that there are both inegalitarian and egalitarian ways in which women can, and have been, represented in sexually explicit material. It is important to recognize, as Eaton does, that the pursuit of censorship or any state law or regulation is not the way to address inegalitarian pornography, not only because the harm to women has not been definitively proven but, more importantly, because anti-porn feminist efforts lead to collaboration with conservative voices. The proliferation of violent, degrading representations of women may be counteracted by validating egalitarian forms of pornography.

Indeed, if pornography has become part of the sex education of young people, particularly young men, then it is more the reason to recognize the importance of, and exposure to, egalitarian porn. Instead of treating porn as all bad, there should be a way to situate and educate ways in which sexually explicit material can be founded on equal respect for women and men (see Albury 2014; Hartley 2013). Moreover, the diversity of nude body types would counteract problematic body ideals that affect both young women and men. There should be ways, in keeping with a feminist liberal perspective, to enhance rather than demean sexual agency, being careful not to conflate objectification, which points to harmful effects of pornography, with sexualization, which recognizes the importance of sexual agency. As Clarissa Smith (2010) argues, what has been lost in the focus on "porn culture," "pornographication," and "pornification" is the subversive potential of sexualization because it not only acts "as a potentially transgressive force against the traditional boundaries of public and private" but also recognizes "the pluralizing of sexual cultures to include those … who had been specifically excluded from sexual self-definition" (104). It bears repeating that sexualization is about the validation of diverse sexual identities, sexual experiences, and sexual cultures. Egalitarian porn points to how this kind of validation may be accomplished throughout society.

RECOMMENDED FILMS, VIDEO CLIPS, AND WEBSITES

Candida Royalle, Erotic Film Pioneer. 2009. Uploaded on December 14, 2009. Age-restricted video. www.youtube.com/watch?v=Ui4iblOBc78.

Feminist Porn Awards. www.feministpornawards.com/.

Jessica Drake's Guide to Wicked Sex: Plus Size. 2014. Film directed by Jessica Drake. www.wickedb2b.com/movies/jessica-drakes-guide-to-wicked-sex-plus-size.

Pornland: How the Porn Industry Has Hijacked Our Sexuality. 2014. Film featuring Gail Dines. www.mediaed.org/cgi-bin/commerce.cgi?preadd=action&key=253.

Stop Porn Culture. www.stoppornculture.org/.

Tristan Taormino's Sex-Positive Salon. Age-restricted website. www.puckerup.com/.

ADDITIONAL READINGS

Attwood, Feona. 2007. "No Money Shot? Commerce, Pornography, and New Sex Taste Cultures." *Sexualities* 10, no. 4: 441–56.

Bale, Clare. 2011. "Raunch or Romance? Framing and Interpreting the Relationship between Sexualized Culture and Young People's Sexual Health." *Sex Education* 11, no. 3 (August): 303–13.

Reading, Anna. 2005. "Professing Porn or Obscene Browsing? On Proper Distance in the University Classroom." *Media, Culture and Society* 27, no. 1: 123–30.

Rosen, Jeffrey. 2004. "The End of Obscenity." *The New Atlantis* 6, (Summer): 75–82.

Smith, Clarissa. 2010. "Pornographication: A Discourse for All Seasons." *International Journal of Media and Cultural Politics* 6, no. 1: 103–8.

Smith, Clarissa, and Feona Attwood. 2011. "Lamenting Sexualization: Research, Rhetoric, and the Story of Young People's 'Sexualization' in the UK Home Office Review." *Sex Education* 11, no. 3 (August): 327–37.

Taormino, Tristan, Celine Parrenas Shimizu, Constance Penley, and Mireille Miller-Young, eds. 2013. *The Feminist Porn Book: The Politics of Producing Pleasure.* New York: The Feminist Press at the City University of New York.

Chapter 7
PROSTITUTION AND TRAFFICKING

INTRODUCTION

On December 20, 2013, the Supreme Court of Canada handed down a unanimous decision (9–0) striking down the three provisions criminalizing prostitution under Canada's Criminal Code, giving the government one year to enact new laws. Referred to as the *Bedford* case, the decision stemmed from an appeal to uphold an initial landmark ruling in September 2010 by Ontario Superior Court justice Susan Himel launched by Terri-Jean Bedford, Valerie Scott, and Amy Lebovitch, three sex workers who were plaintiffs in the case. Although prostitution had technically not been illegal in Canada, the government had criminalized activities around prostitution in three principal ways: first, the "communicating" provision, which banned solicitation in public places; second, the "bawdy house" provision, which made "owning, managing, leasing, occupying, or being found in a bawdy house" unlawful; and third, the "living off the avails" provision, which was meant to target third parties, such as pimps and procurers. In her decision, Justice Himel struck down all three provisions under Canada's Criminal Code because they violated Section 7—the right to life, liberty, and the security of the person—of the Canadian Charter of Rights and Freedoms. She accepted the plaintiffs' arguments that these provisions undermined their safety, placing them in greater harm out of fear of prosecution. For example, the sex workers argued that they could not screen potentially dangerous clients because of the "communicating" provision; nor could they work indoors where it is safer because of the "bawdy house" provision, or hire bodyguards for protection because of the "living off the avails" provision.

The federal and Ontario governments appealed Himel's decision, and in its March 2012 decision, the Ontario Court of Appeal agreed with two-thirds of Himel's ruling. The Appeal Court upheld Himel's ruling on declaring the "bawdy house" and "living off the avails" provisions as unconstitutional (with the proviso that "living off the avails" should remain criminalized "in circumstances of exploitation"), but declared that the "communicating" provision would remain in full force in order to protect communities from organized crime, drugs, noise, and unwanted solicitations. The split ruling resulted in appeals both by the federal and Ontario governments and by the three sex workers to the Supreme Court, with the federal and Ontario governments appealing to reverse the Himel ruling fully and the sex workers to uphold it entirely. Although the Supreme Court upheld the Himel ruling in full, it stated that it was up to the federal government to decide a new prostitution regime.

> Concluding that each of the challenged provisions violates the Charter does not mean that Parliament is precluded from imposing limits on where and how prostitution may be conducted, as long as it does so in a way that does not infringe the constitutional rights of prostitutes. The regulation of prostitution is a complex and delicate matter. It will be for Parliament, should it choose to do so, to devise a new approach, reflecting different elements of the existing regime. Considering all the interests at stake, the declaration of invalidity should be suspended for one year. (Supreme Court of Canada 2013)

On June 4, 2014, nearly six months after the Supreme Court's decision, then Conservative justice minister Peter MacKay introduced Bill C-36, entitled the Protection of Communities and Exploited Persons Act, in the House of Commons. MacKay argued that it was a "made-in-Canada" approach that would criminalize the buying of sexual services, but not the selling, arguing that prostitution is about exploitation. The government would recognize that prostitutes are victims (except, as it turns out, in certain circumstances as discussed at the end of this chapter), so they would not be charged with a crime; the targets would be the buyers and third parties, such as pimps and procurers, who exploit them. Opposition to the Conservative government's proposed new prostitution law came immediately from many quarters, among them sex workers, including Bedford, Scott, and Lebovitch, who originally launched the case and testified in front of both the House of the Commons and the Senate during the committee hearings on the bill. They argued that the proposed law would further harm sex workers and drive the trade underground. Moreover, the Liberal Party under Justin Trudeau, which won the October 2015 election, opposed the bill and voted against it, although, at the time of the vote a year earlier, it was the third party in Parliament composed only of 37 members. Opposition also came, perhaps surprisingly, from more right-wing commentators in the public media. Among the latter included Rob Breakenridge, a radio commentator in Calgary, who opposed the continuing criminalization of prostitution because pornography was not similarly criminalized. He argued that there was a "double standard" because if "the end result is a consenting adult using his or her body in a sexual way in order to earn a living," then "is pornography somehow acceptable because the other participant in the sexual act is also being compensated?" (Breakenridge 2014).

From a legal perspective, the differences between pornography and prostitution are rooted in that pornography, as discussed in the last chapter, has been protected under freedom of speech or expression. Pornography is about the *performance* of a sexual act as opposed to the sexual act itself. That is why the last chapter looked at third-party harms and the consequences of the consumption of (inegalitarian) pornography. Porn workers are paid to act whereas prostitutes are paid for sex. As Theresa Reed AKA Darklady (2006) explains:

> Ultimately, the primary difference between being a porn star and being a whore is the presence of a camera and its associated artistic realities. Having sex in a discrete [*sic*] room alone with a businessman is prostitution. Having sex in front of a digital camera with a gonzo porn director in order to create a product for mass distribution is pornography. (256)

To illustrate this, in March 2014 as the Conservative government was deciding on the kind of prostitution system that Canada would adopt, the Canadian Radio-Television and Telecommunications Commission (CRTC) reprimanded three pornography channels, not for broadcasting pornography, but for not meeting the minimum requirement for Canadian content (what is understood in the industry as "CanCon"). The CRTC is the government regulatory agency responsible for enforcing Canada's Broadcasting Act, which states that programming must reflect "Canadian attitudes, opinions, ideas, values, and artistic creativity." According to the CRTC, the three porn channels risked losing their licences if they did not meet the required 35 percent of porn that had to be Canadian-made (which they did and their licences were renewed). This example perhaps supports Reed's (2006) contention that prostitution should be seen as a form of artistic expression so it can have legal protection like pornography. Her primary point is that individuals should have the right "to select the economic alternative best suited to their individual circumstances without the worry of social stigma, threat of legal penalty, or incarceration" and therefore, like pornography, prostitution should not be criminalized (257). Taking a sex-radical or sex-positive feminist perspective, Reed (2006) sees prostitution as sex work that is a matter of choice. In contrast, a radical feminist perspective sees prostitution as sexual exploitation, and like pornography, prostitution is a manifestation of male control of women's sexuality where men's access to women's bodies is underpinned by the predominance of male violence (see Coy 2012 for more recent work by radical feminists on prostitution). Prostitution, like pornography, has been one of the primary battlegrounds in the feminist sex wars.

Given the strength of party discipline in Canada and with a majority of members in the House of Commons, the Conservative government passed Bill C-36, and the Protection of Communities and Exploited Persons Act became law on December 6, 2014. For those who had opposed the legislation, there was a sad irony that it was on the National Day of Remembrance and Action on Violence Against Women. Established in 1991 by the Parliament of Canada, the day marks the anniversary of the murders in 1989 of the 14 young women at l'École Polytechnique de Montréal who were targeted and killed because they were women. In contrast, supporters of the legislation saw the date as fitting. Standing up in the House of Commons on December 5, 2014, Joy Smith, Conservative member of Parliament (MP) and one of the most ardent supporters of the legislation, stated: "This is a historic moment for Canada. Under Bill C-36, Canada's laws will uphold the equality of women as human beings, not objects to be bought and sold. It will seek to end the violence against women that is inherent in prostitution and human trafficking, tomorrow and every day of the year."

Prior to the passage of Bill C-36, Canada and the United States had similar laws criminalizing prostitution. Although this chapter shows the differences that now exist between their prostitution systems, the problematic conflation between prostitution and trafficking, grounded in the idea that all women in prostitution are trafficked and therefore all are victimized, has dominated the discourse in both countries. Accordingly, it is not surprising that having to enact a new prostitution law, Canada would adopt the system that it did. However, by delegitimizing prostitution the Canadian government has continued to stigmatize sex workers, a stigma that lies at the heart of societal attitudes. This chapter begins by looking at the linkages between the heterosexual conjugal bond and attitudes about prostitution in the West. What does the "madonna/whore" dichotomy tell us about conceptions of women's sexuality, and how can this dichotomy be undermined with the transformation of intimacy? More practically, what are the different prostitution systems that exist, and what kind of system does Canada now have? Is prostitution about sex work or exploitation? How do the Canadian and American systems differ? What is the difference between prostitution and trafficking, and how has the anti-trafficking movement reinvigorated the abolitionist stance on prostitution? Why is it important that prostitution be disentangled from trafficking? These are the questions that will be addressed in this chapter. The view that all sex workers are victims has resulted in a problematic alliance between social conservatives and radical feminists. In Canada's case, this has resulted in the Conservative government of the time adopting a prostitution regime that further limits the choices of women, particularly poor women, by effectively outlawing prostitution through the criminalization of the buying of sex.

THE MADONNA/WHORE AND WOMEN'S SEXUALITY

Labelled ubiquitously as "the world's oldest profession," prostitution has not always been condemned by societies and seen as degrading for women (Shrage 1994). In particular, courtesans throughout history, such as the Greek *hetaira*, the Italian *cortigiana*, the Chinese *yiji*, the Korean *gisaeng*, the Indian *tawaif* and *ganika*, and the Japanese *tayu* and *oiran*, have been exalted in their cultures. Although courtesans were highly educated, creative and skilled in music and the arts, and often resembled the upper-class women of their time, they nevertheless engaged in, and were compensated for, sexual favours with male patrons (Gordon and Feldman 2006). The condemnation of prostitution can be traced to medieval Christianity in the Western world. Political power had shifted toward the Church, and the Christian ideals of virginity, sexual abstinence, and celibacy prevailed throughout society. Sexual desire was seen as an obstacle to spiritual salvation, and Christian ethics demanded that individuals overcome what St. Augustine, one of the founding fathers of Western Christianity, called the "corruptions of the flesh." Only procreative sex in marriage resting on monogamy and fidelity would be tolerated because of the need to propagate the human race (Mottier 2008, 18–24). These Christian ideals of virginity, monogamy, and fidelity still resonate in socially and religiously conservative circles throughout the world today. Heterosexual marital sex would be at the heart of sexual morality, therefore making premarital, extramarital, and same-sex sexual behaviour morally objectionable. This is the valorization of the heterosexual conjugal bond.

The strict association of sex with procreation, and women as bearers of children, is at the foundation of the "madonna" concept in controlling women's sexuality. Drawn from Christian ideals of the Virgin Mary, the mother of Jesus, the idea of the madonna represents the sexual purity of women as wives *because* they are mothers. Although medieval Christian dogma around the impurity of sexual desire was meant to curtail the sexual freedoms of both women and men, the birth of science in the modern era began to focus on biological differences between women and men, bringing out the idea of uncontrolled male sexual desires, which continues to resonate today. With the idea of the wife as a madonna, there would have to be a necessary outlet for the husband, and the prostitute would serve that purpose. The prostitute would represent the female sexual appetite, the "dangerous sexuality of women," making her "unacceptable in polite society" (Nussbaum 1999, 286). However, she would also become an "ally of marriage" because her unfettered sexuality as a "bad" woman, unlike that of the proper nature of the "good" wife, would ensure the fulfillment of male sexual desires. The madonna would be worshipped and the whore would be shunned, but both would be central to male control of women's sexuality. The idea that men would turn to prostitutes out of "respect" for their wives remains evident in societies today where sexual liberation, particularly for women, is not widely accepted (such as the Philippines; see Ralston and Keeble 2009).

Moreover, the madonna/whore would become entrenched in Western ideas of romantic love. As discussed in Chapter 1, Giddens (1992) argues that romantic love perpetuates the idealization of motherhood where it marks the meaning of femininity just as being a breadwinner defines masculinity. While women's sexuality is kept within the confines of marriage, men's sexuality is defined by "the division between unsullied and impure women" because, without women's sexual freedoms, men need to "[separate] the comfort of the domestic environment from the sexuality of the mistress or whore" (Giddens 1992, 59, 43). That is why women's sexual liberation in the West has been crucial: it has severed reproduction from sexual intercourse and freed women to pursue their sexual pleasures in the way that men have. Women's sexuality is no longer confined by marriage and motherhood, allowing for the transformation of intimacy and the development of confluent love where intimacy is sought as part of self-development. Not only is there an ongoing reassessment of the relationship by individuals who choose to stay, but there is also no expectation of sexual exclusivity because monogamy, like the continuation of the relationship, is negotiated between the two partners based on their individual sense of self. Although confluent love "has no specific connection to heterosexuality," and Giddens points out that same-sex couples are more exemplary of confluent love, women's sexual liberation has the potential to undermine the madonna/whore dichotomy. As Giddens (1992) argues: "Confluent love develops as an ideal in a society where almost everyone has a chance to become sexually accomplished; and it presumes the disappearance of the schism between 'respectable' women and those who in some way lie outside the pale of orthodox social life" (63). Because the emergence of confluent love challenges the valorization of the heterosexual conjugal bond, the redefinition of women's sexuality would allow for greater acceptance of prostitution.

The problem, of course, is that the transformation of intimacy has not been realized in large part, as discussed in Chapter 2, by the uncritical acceptance of male aggression, specifically expressed in the uncontrolled male sexual appetite, illustrating the commonality in approach between social conservatives and radical feminists. As pointed out, "the feminist case against male violence [has been] turned into a defence of conservative forms" (Weeks 1985, 42). Under the guise of exalting women, conservatives are able to perpetuate traditional ideas around marriage, motherhood, and monogamy, which arguably removes women's agency, and in that way perpetuates the victimization of women central to radical feminist thinking. The example of the political sex scandal of former New York governor Eliot Spitzer helps to illustrate this.

In March 2008, Spitzer resigned from his position as governor after being investigated for prostitution-related charges. Spitzer, referred to as "Client 9," was a frequent patron of a high-end agency for prostitution where women were paid thousands of dollars for a one-night liaison. Spitzer was discovered by federal authorities because he was transferring large sums of money to offshore companies operating as fronts for the agency referred to as the "Emperors Club VIP." Spitzer's actions were seen as particularly noteworthy, not only because he prosecuted several prostitution rings as New York's attorney-general before becoming governor, thus earning him the nickname Eliot "Ness" Spitzer, but also because when he publicly announced his resignation as governor on March 12, 2008, his wife, Silda Wall Spitzer, was (literally) standing by his side. Acting as "the good wife," she remained married to her philandering husband, which was taken as an indication that even the most successful women—Silda Spitzer was a Harvard Law School graduate—can be victimized, and the reason that she did not immediately leave him was obviously because she could not. Why else would she put herself through such public humiliation if she had a choice?

Such an argument rests on ideas of romantic love, which valorizes the heterosexual conjugal bond; what if Silda Spitzer stayed with her husband because she assessed the relationship as in keeping with her continuing self-development, so it was more reflective of confluent love? She became less publicly visible after Eliot Spitzer resigned, and in 2013 when he ran in the Democratic primaries for the position of New York City comptroller as a way to redeem himself politically (he lost), she did not campaign with him. They announced their intention to divorce in December 2013, and in April 2014 Silda Spitzer was awarded a $7.5 million divorce settlement in addition to ownership of the couple's Fifth Avenue apartment, an annual payment of $240,000, and other monetary arrangements (Larson 2014). Instead of having been a victim, it can be argued that she exercised agency in choosing to stay with her husband, which, given the privileges of her race and class, speaks more to her individual autonomy. This is the same sort of argument made in Chapter 2 about Hillary Clinton's decision to stay with the former president after the Lewinsky scandal.

Moreover, the valorization of the heterosexual conjugal bond fosters the stigmatization of prostitution and its continuing criminalization. Eliot Spitzer was condemned not only for committing infidelity but also for paying for sex. Since the sexual revolution, casual sex as expressed in free love, one-night stands, hook-ups, booty calls, and friends with benefits has become part of the Western landscape, yet the idea of paying for sex remains outside of the legal norm in some countries, including Canada and the United States (with the exception of Nevada), although not in others, such as the Netherlands and New Zealand. In July 2013, a member of the Legislative Assembly of Alberta was arrested for solicitation of prostitution while attending a legislative conference in St. Paul, Minnesota. Mike Allen, the representative for Fort McMurray–Wood Buffalo in the provincial assembly and part of the governing provincial Progressive Conservative Party, resigned from the government caucus shortly after his arrest. Divorced with three grown children and apparently lonely after ending a serious relationship months earlier, Allen solicited an undercover female police officer from an online ad, and for $200, paid to have a threesome in a St. Paul motel room with whom he believed would be two female prostitutes. He was single, agreed to wear a condom, and appeared to be non-abusive and non-violent. Days after Allen's arrest, then Alberta premier Alison Redford would not even say his name because she was so disgusted by his behaviour. In July 2014, Allen was readmitted to his party's caucus after having pleaded guilty the previous December to a misdemeanor to solicit prostitution and paid $500 in addition to court costs (McDermott 2014). Had Allen's conference been in rural Nevada instead of Minnesota, or in the Netherlands or New Zealand instead of the United States, the legal outcome could have been different.

PROSTITUTION SYSTEMS: SEX WORK OR EXPLOITATION?

Sex work, as Christine Overall (1992, 709) states, can be broadly defined to encompass any sex act or service that involves an exchange of money, and thus would include a wide array of work from the phone sex industry to strip clubs to pornography to prostitution. For this chapter, the term *sex work* is used only in reference to prostitution in order to bring out differing positions on whether prostitution is work that can be chosen by women, or sexual exploitation. At the same time, from a historical perspective there was a shift beginning in the 1970s from seeing prostitutes in the international context as fallen women to sex workers because of a burgeoning economic approach focusing on prostitution as a global market. Given the growth of international migration due to differences in wealth and prosperity between countries, "it was only a small step to define prostitution as *sex work* and to argue it was an economic strategy women used to escape poverty and improve their position" (Outshoorn 2011, 129). In contrast, the use of the term *prostituted women*, as opposed to *sex workers*, has become part of the nomenclature of those who see global prostitution as sexual exploitation where the term is "thought to have originated among anti-prostitution activists in the Philippines as a way of conveying women's lack of choice in entering and remaining in systems of prostitution" (Tyler 2012, 87n1).

Prostitution as a matter of choice is perhaps best exemplified by the high-end escort identified by federal authorities in their investigation of former New York governor Eliot Spitzer. Earning thousands of dollars for a single night's liaison, Ashley Dupre was young, attractive, and until Spitzer was discovered, discreet. Her work would likely never have gone public if not for the investigation of her high-profile client because it represents the "hidden world of indoor prostitution in venues such as bars, brothels, massage parlors, tanning salons, or in services provided by escort agencies [like that of Dupre's] or independent call girls" (Weitzer 2007, 29). Although the exact numbers are not known, most scholars accept that the overwhelming majority of women in prostitution work indoors. Dupre went on to pose for *Playboy*, become a columnist and cooking contestant, give birth to her first child in November 2012, and marry the child's father in October 2013 in Paris (Garvey et al. 2013). Not only did Dupre (who now goes by Ashley Earle after taking her husband's surname) go into and leave prostitution of her own accord, but because she practised her craft indoors, she likely would not have been described as a prostitute had she been seen in public as she went to meet Spitzer.

The kind of prostitute to which most Americans and Canadians have been exposed is the street-based worker in what is referred to as outdoor prostitution. What makes the indoor/outdoor distinction important is the extent to which members of a community are aware of prostitution occurring in their midst. The street-based worker hanging out on street corners is highly visible to any particular community, which often causes complaints to the police, who, in turn, search for and harass the woman to get her off the streets. She likely has a pimp who may be largely responsible for putting her in a drug-induced state, thus increasing her vulnerability; she likely has experienced beatings by johns and has been abused as a child; she likely has been jailed or fined because her activities are illegal; and she likely has no place to go but back on the streets. Her situation is likely a clear case of victimization, but radical feminists who want to abolish prostitution (also referred to as *abolitionist feminists* in this context) do not distinguish between the high-end escort and the victimized street-based worker because prostitution, they argue, is fundamentally about the sexual exploitation of women.

The victimization of street-based workers is not merely an abstract concept to most Canadians. Considered by many to be the worst serial killer in Canadian history, Robert Pickton, a pig farmer from Port Coquitlam, BC, targeted and murdered sex workers from Vancouver's Downtown Eastside for years before he was finally arrested in 2002. Convicted of six counts of second-degree murder and sentenced to life in prison in 2007, he once bragged to an undercover officer that he killed as many as 49 women. An inquiry in 2012 into police failure and delay in investigating the missing and murdered women found "systemic bias by the police," who treated the women as "throwaways" because "they were poor, they were addicted, vulnerable, [and] aboriginal" (*CBC News* 2012). Many were engaged in what is referred to as "survival sex," selling sex in the worst conditions due to poverty or addiction, or just for basic necessity to survive. The inquiry commissioner, Wally Oppal, a former BC attorney-general, entitled his report "Forsaken" because he argued that the missing and murdered women in the sex trade, the majority of whom were Aboriginal, were forsaken not only by the police but also by the society at large.

In June 2013, when the Supreme Court heard arguments from 12 intervenors into the *Bedford* case (an intervenor is a group [or individual] who is given legal standing in a case even though the group is not part of the litigation, i.e., neither plaintiff nor defendant), Aboriginal advocacy groups were rightly involved. They show how one's view of prostitution affects the kind of system or law that a state should adopt. The Native Women's Association of Canada was one of seven women's groups, which included the Canadian Association of Sexual Assault Centres, to make up the Women's Coalition for the Abolition of Prostitution, a coalition established specifically to intervene in the *Bedford* case. The Women's Coalition (2013) stated in its factum to the Supreme Court:

> Prostitution is a practice of sex inequality. Most of those prostituted are women and girls. Almost all buyers/johns are men. The buying and selling of women's bodies in prostitution is a global practice of sexual exploitation and male violence against women that normalizes the subordination of women in a sexualized form.

Given the harms of colonialism experienced by the Aboriginal community, and the number of Aboriginal women in the sex trade, the Women's Coalition argued that prostitution has only harmed and exploited Aboriginal women further. That is why the Coalition, along with the Evangelical Fellowship of Canada, another intervenor in the case, argued that Canada should adopt the Nordic, or Swedish, model where the buying of sex is criminalized but not the selling of sex, thus penalizing the customers or johns but not the prostituted women. Sweden passed its law in 1999 with Norway and Iceland following suit. The Nordic model is widely supported by many feminists, but decried by many sex workers because it rests on a conception that women in prostitution are always in situations of exploitation, and like victims of rape and domestic violence, they need protection. Many sex workers see the Nordic model as a moralistic and maternalistic view of prostitution.

In contrast, in its factum to the Supreme Court the Aboriginal Legal Services of Toronto (2013) indicated its support for decriminalizing prostitution, highlighting that the communicating provision that remained in force after the Ontario Court of Appeal's decision needed to be struck down. The group argued that "the impacts of colonialism have pushed many Aboriginal people to the most extreme margins of society, and it is at those margins that we find those engaged in street-based sex work and survival sex" (Aboriginal Legal Services of Toronto 2013). It pointed out that the argument that the communicating provision needed to be maintained in order to protect communities from organized crime, drugs, noise, and unwanted solicitations overlooked the real harms being done. Because the communicating provision precluded sex workers from negotiating openly with potential clients, they unnecessarily put themselves at risk. According to the group, "the vulnerability of these neighbourhoods to harms associated with street-based work cannot in any way be compared to the harms faced by sex workers and those engaged in survival sex. Inconvenience and discomfort are not the same as dealing with what are essentially life and death decisions on a daily basis" (Aboriginal Legal Services of Toronto 2013). The group argued that Canada should decriminalize prostitution in order to make the trade safer for sex workers, particularly Aboriginal women, many of whom were engaged in street-based work or survival sex.

Generally speaking, according to many scholars (for example, Outshoorn 2011, 130; Andrijasevic 2010, 2), there are three types of prostitution systems, namely, regulationist, prohibitionist, and abolitionist. Those who argue for a prohibitionist or an abolitionist system want to ban or eliminate prostitution, unlike those who advocate for a regulationist system because they see a role for the state in reducing the harms of prostitution. In recent years, many prostitution advocates, particularly sex workers, have subdivided the regulationist system to distinguish between legalization and decriminalization. The legalization of prostitution as in the Netherlands, which passed its law in 2000, involves the government licensing of brothels and prostitutes, and to many sex workers, it is equivalent to the state acting as a pimp. Legalization essentially treats prostitution as a unique sector of society that must be regulated and controlled.

In contrast, the decriminalization of prostitution, as in New Zealand, is based on the premise that prostitution can be treated like other sectors in society, and thus existing criminal and labour laws can be used to mitigate harms to sex workers (as with any worker), who would, in turn, be governed by existing health and safety workplace regulations. New Zealand passed its law in 2003. There is no licensing required for small owner-operated brothels (i.e., four or fewer prostitutes). Decriminalization is the kind of prostitution regime favoured by many sex workers and their advocates. Prior to the Supreme Court decision in December 2013, Canada had a hybrid of regulation and prohibition because although prostitution was technically legal, activities associated with it were criminalized. With the enactment of Bill C-36 in December 2014, Canada has adopted an abolitionist system. Table 7.1 shows the different types of prostitution systems.

Table 7.1: Types of Prostitution Systems

Type		Legislation	Example
Regulationist	Decriminalization	Repeal of laws against prostitution; prostitution regulated by existing labour and health safety standards	New Zealand, Australia (New South Wales)
	Legalization	Prostitution is regulated by government with prostitution-specific laws	Netherlands, Germany
Prohibitionist	Prohibition	Prostitution is banned and all aspects of prostitution are criminalized, i.e., buying, selling, and third parties (e.g., pimps)	United States (not including rural Nevada)
Abolitionist	Abolition (Nordic Model)	Prostitution is exploitation; buyers and third parties are criminalized while sellers are decriminalized	Sweden, Norway, Iceland, Canada

The United States has a prohibitionist system where prostitution is illegal in all 50 states (prostitution law falls under state, not federal, jurisdiction) with the exception of rural counties in Nevada with a population of less than 400,000. The state allows these counties to have licensed brothels whereas, ironically, prostitution remains illegal in the "sin city" of Las Vegas. Although prostitution laws first arose in both Canada and the United States around the turn of the 20th century, justified in both countries by concerns over social morality or social nuisance, there has been little change in the American context.

As Dannia Altemimei (2013) points out: "Unlike in Canada, there has been no push for liberalizing reforms. To the contrary, in recent times, there has been a resurgence of traditional morality in the United States, which has led to an outcry against relaxing the criminal laws on prostitution in most states" (626). Indeed, this resurgence has been fuelled by the anti-trafficking movement and the conflation of prostitution and trafficking.

TRAFFICKING: FREE OR FORCED MIGRATION FOR SEX?

The trafficking of women for sexual exploitation is an issue that first came into prominence nearly a century and a half ago with the fears around "white slavery." It was widely believed throughout the United States and Europe that white women and girls were being abducted, sold, and moved across national borders into sexual slavery. In 1904 the International Agreement for the Suppression of the "White Slave Traffic" was reached, followed by the 1910 International Convention for the Suppression of the White Slave Trade, which criminalized trafficking. Four years after the 1945 establishment of the United Nations (UN), the International Convention for the Suppression of the Traffic in Persons and of the Exploitation of the Prostitution of Others was approved by the General Assembly, superseding previous agreements and recognizing trafficked victims without regard to gender or race. Member states that were signatories to the 1949 convention were committed not only to eradicating trafficking but also to abolishing prostitution. Although neither Canada nor the United States ratified the international agreement, both states criminalized prostitution. The 1949 convention clearly linked the two issues. As stated in the preamble: "prostitution and the accompanying evil of the traffic in persons for the purpose of prostitution are incompatible with the dignity and worth of the human person and endanger the welfare of the individual, the family and the community."

What followed in the global context was what some scholars refer to as "decades of silence" on the trafficking issue (Bertone 2009). As Joyce Outshoorn (2005, 149) states: "There was little pressure on implementation [of the 1949 convention], as trafficking faded from the public eye and prostitution ceased to be a major political issue." Global feminist activism became more pronounced during the UN International Decade for Women (1976–85), culminating a decade later with the Fourth World Conference on Women in 1995. The Beijing Platform for Action, arising out of the 1995 conference, affirmed the Convention on the Elimination of All Forms of Discrimination against Women, the so-called women's bill of rights adopted by the General Assembly in 1979, and although the trafficking issue was raised under efforts to eradicate violence against women, feminist groups were divided on prostitution and no agreement on trafficking was reached until 2000.

Many scholars have argued that the divide between feminist groups on the trafficking issue rests on their positions on prostitution (Keeble and Ralston 2003; Outshoorn 2005; Bertone 2009; Foerster 2009; Weitzer 2010; MacKinnon 2011). On the one hand, there are those who see trafficking and prostitution as one and the same. Grounded in radical feminist thinking, all acts of prostitution are seen as the sexual exploitation of women where women's bodies are treated as commodities to be bought, sold, and trafficked (like any commodity traded by criminals, such as drugs and arms) without dignity or worth. Women can never voluntarily or freely choose to be a prostitute. Founded by US activist Kathleen Barry, who authored *Female Sexual Slavery* (1979), the Coalition Against Trafficking in Women takes this view.

On the other hand, there are those who see prostitution as sex work. According to Outshoorn (2005):

> For those adhering to the sex work position, women can be victims of trafficking, but not all women sex workers crossing borders are victims of forced prostitution. Many women migrate to work in the sex industry to make a living. Here the unequal distribution of wealth on a global scale is seen as the causal factor for sex commerce. (147)

The Global Alliance Against Traffic in Women subscribes to this perspective. Founded in 1994 and based in Thailand, the organization has embraced the sex workers' rights movement and has called for the decriminalization of prostitution, asserting that the trafficking of women is not about prostitution, but rather about the conditions of coercion, deception, and abuse around the global sex trade.

In 2000, the United Nations Protocol to Prevent, Suppress and Punish Trafficking in Persons, Especially Women and Children was passed and it is an important milestone because it appears to delink prostitution from trafficking. According to the protocol:

> 'Trafficking in persons' shall mean the recruitment, transportation, transfer, harbouring or receipt of persons, by means of the threat or use of force or other forms of coercion, of abduction, of fraud, of deception, of the abuse of power or of a position of vulnerability or of the giving

> or receiving of payments or benefits to achieve the consent of a person having control over another person, for the purpose of exploitation. Exploitation shall include, at a minimum, the exploitation of the prostitution of others or other forms of sexual exploitation, forced labour or services, slavery or practices similar to slavery, servitude or the removal of organs. (United Nations 2000)

The delinking of prostitution from trafficking is evident in two ways. First, there is recognition of "the threat or use of force or other forms of coercion," thus apparently making it easier to differentiate between forced and free prostitution. Second, there is recognition of trafficking for purposes other than for prostitution, including "forced labour or services, slavery or practices similar to slavery, servitude or the removal of organs." Human trafficking, then, is more broadly understood than sex trafficking. Not only is there acknowledgement of exploitation beyond sexual purposes, but there is also recognition that men are trafficked as well, particularly for forced labour. However, trafficking for the purposes of sexual exploitation, specifically for prostitution, or sex trafficking, has become what most people understand to be trafficking, not only because vast numbers of trafficked victims are placed in sexual servitude (and these victims are primarily women and children), but also because of the United States' important role in redefining what trafficking means. Moreover, as Kempadoo (2012) points out, sex trafficking "is attached to a particular narrative about violence to women and carries a specific meaning," which has fuelled the abolitionist perspective on prostitution (viii).

When the UN adopted the trafficking protocol in 2000, the United States passed its own domestic legislation, entitled the Trafficking Victims Protection Act (TVPA), that same year. The TVPA contains a definition of sex trafficking that does not include the requirement of coercion as found in the UN protocol, defining it as "the recruitment, harboring, transportation, provision, or obtaining of a person for the purpose of a commercial sex act," thus equating trafficking with prostitution. In order to deal with the coercive aspect, the United States has distinguished between "sex trafficking" and "severe forms of sex trafficking," thus essentially eliminating the notion of prostitution as being freely chosen. The TVPA has had wide impact beyond American borders. Not only has the United Nations adopted the United States' "tier designations," as found in the State Department's annual *Trafficking in Persons Report*, which categorizes countries based on their anti-trafficking efforts, but the abolitionist perspective on prostitution has arguably supplanted the international consensus reached in distinguishing between free and forced prostitution in the trafficking protocol.

Although the UN trafficking protocol is not technically a human rights document, it was arguably an important step forward for the global community. Supplementing the United Nations Convention against Transnational Organized Crime (so the threat coming from transnational criminal organizations was the primary concern of states), the trafficking issue can nevertheless be framed as one of human rights, as many international women's groups have argued. Women's rights, after all, are human rights. In 2002, the Office of the High Commissioner for Human Rights (OHCHR) presented a document, entitled "Recommended Principles and Guidelines on Human Rights and Human Trafficking," to the UN Economic and Social Council. The OHCHR states unequivocally: "Violations of human rights are both a cause and a consequence of trafficking in persons. Accordingly, it is essential to place the protection of all human rights at the centre of any measures taken to prevent and end trafficking. Anti-trafficking measures should not adversely affect the human rights and dignity of persons."

What sorts of rights of trafficked victims need to be recognized and protected? The United Nations Office on Drugs and Crime, along with the Inter-Parliamentary Union (UNODC-IPU 2009), has outlined a "bill of rights of victims of trafficking" (48–63). These rights include: the right to safety; the right to privacy; the right to information; the right to legal representation; the right to be heard in court; the right to compensation for damages; the right to assistance; the right to seek residence; and the right to return. The point of recognizing these rights has been to ensure that trafficked victims will not be doubly victimized. These rights should be upheld regardless of the individual's immigration status or willingness to testify in court against her or his traffickers.

However, as many scholars, such as Doezema (2010), have pointed out, what about the rights of prostitutes who have freely chosen to be in the global sex trade? What about the rights of women who migrate for sex work out of a desire for a better life free from political prosecution or economic destitution? In this case, we need to understand the differences between trafficking and smuggling. There were two protocols supplementing the Convention against Transnational Organized Crime: one on human trafficking and the other on human smuggling. The Protocol against the Smuggling of Migrants by Land, Sea and Air is one that is little discussed in news stories or academic analyses of sex trafficking, but it is important to understand the phenomenon of human smuggling because it helps to illustrate how, in some instances, women migrate for sex work. In March 2010, the RCMP released a report, entitled "Human Trafficking in Canada," which provides clear definitions between human smuggling and human trafficking. According to the report, human smuggling "involves the facilitation of illegal entry of migrants into a country for financial or material benefit, which is typically a business transaction that ends upon arrival," whereas human trafficking (drawing from the definition provided in the UN trafficking protocol) "involves any person who recruits, transports, transfers, receives, holds, conceals, or harbours a person, or exercises control, direction, or influence over the movements of a person for the purpose of exploiting them or facilitating their exploitation" (Royal Canadian Mounted Police 2010).

Human smuggling and human trafficking differ in four fundamental ways based on: (1) consent; (2) transnationality; (3) exploitation; and (4) source of profit (UNODC-IPC 2009, 22–23). In terms of consent, smuggling generally involves the consent of those being smuggled, whereas trafficked victims have never consented to being trafficked. In terms of transnationality, smuggling centres on individuals being illegally moved from one state to another. In contrast, trafficking not only occurs between and within countries (so there is both international and domestic trafficking, the latter found, for example, in the transport of victims from rural to urban areas), but also can be done through legal means. Indeed, many trafficked victims are transported across borders through the use of a worker's permit or a student visa. The differences in terms of exploitation are particularly important because smuggling ends once the migrant has reached her or his destination, whereas trafficking has no end until the victim is rescued. Finally, in terms of source of profit, smugglers make money by charging exorbitant fees to transport people, whereas traffickers make huge profits from the ongoing exploitation of their victims.

Smuggling, like trafficking, involves transnational criminal organizations, which pose challenges to the sovereign state, and states like Canada are targeting smugglers as well as traffickers in their legislation. However, consent is evident in those who turn to smugglers. There are women in dire circumstances in many parts of the world who may want to migrate for sex work but are unable to do so because of stringent immigration laws. Like many individuals throughout the world who seek a better life free from political persecution or economic destitution, these women may turn to illegal means to migrate. As Outshoorn (2005, 147) states: "Much of what is called trafficking is actually the smuggling of human beings, which enables undocumented people to migrate to other countries to make a living in better circumstances. Among those smuggled, there are women who intend to work in the sex industry." In this case, the problem is smuggling, not trafficking, unless of course one's stance on prostitution is that trafficking and prostitution are one and the same. It is because the trafficking discourse has "strong anti-migration, anti-prostitution foundations" that scholars, like Kempadoo (2012, xi), point out that migrant workers and sex workers have come together to oppose what she calls both the abolitionist and criminal justice approaches to anti-trafficking.

DISENTANGLING PROSTITUTION FROM TRAFFICKING

Given the global influence of the United States on the trafficking issue, combined with heart-wrenching and stark images and stories of what has become commonly referred to as "modern sex slavery," where academics and activists, politicians and journalists, Hollywood celebrities and everyday people alike have been moved to action, the acceptance of prostitution as work is becoming less, rather than more, of a reality. Not only is this seen in Canada's new prostitution law, but in February 2014 the European Parliament voted in favour of a resolution to criminalize the buying of sex, effectively endorsing the Nordic model for European Union (EU) states to adopt. This is problematic from a feminist liberal perspective because, by essentially outlawing prostitution, the choices of women, particularly poor women, are further limited. Martha Nussbaum (1999) and Christine Overall (1992) have taken opposing positions on prostitution, but they both recognize that prostitution is not a unique profession, either in terms of "taking money for bodily services" (Nussbaum) or selling labour power in a capitalist society (Overall). Indeed, both compare the work of prostitutes to university professors (which they both are). Nussbaum argues that the prostitute and the philosophy professor "[both] provide bodily services in areas that are generally thought to be especially intimate and definitive of selfhood" (283). The prostitute is paid for her body; the professor for her mind. According to Nussbaum, philosophers historically were seen as degrading their work "by receipt of a wage" because doing so "alienates her mind, or turns her thoughts into commodities" (283). Moreover, living in a capitalist society, according to Overall (1992), necessitates that individuals must sell their labour power, and although there may be different reasons as to why professors choose their profession (a desire for knowledge, a love of teaching, a sense of service), economic gain may be their primary motive just as it is for prostitutes. Prostitution, as defined by Overall, is "a commercial enterprise, and evidence strongly suggests that the women who engage in it do so primarily, and often exclusively, for economic gain" (709).

At the same time, Overall asserts that prostitution "differs in a crucial way from other forms of women's labor [because] while women's work of cooking, child care or nursing is often commoditized, these forms of labor can and do also exist independently of any form of commercialization or exchange" (716). Women grow and prepare food, take care of children, and nurse the ill without these tasks being bought and sold, but "sex work is by definition the commoditization of sex [so that] what is essential about prostitution is not sexual activity itself but the buying of sexual activity" (717). This buying of sexual activity is what makes prostitution objectionable. It "is a classist, ageist, racist, and sexist industry, in which the disadvantaged sell services to those who are more privileged" (717). Prostitution is grounded in both capitalism and patriarchy, and as such, it rests not only on primarily women selling their bodies to men (there are instances of men selling their bodies to men, but this is not the norm), but also on social constructions of gender roles of male dominance and female submission. Overall uses an infamous sexist joke in which a man asks a woman if she would sleep with him for $1 million, to which she replies in the affirmative. When asked subsequently if she would sleep with him for $5, she replies indignantly, "What do you take me for?" He responds, "We've already established that; now we're just negotiating your price." This joke illustrates, as Overall argues, "the notion that all women are whores at heart ... that there is something inherent in women and independent of sexist cultural conditions that makes us want to sell sexual services to men" (719).

These sorts of objections to prostitution raised by Overall stem from the fundamental inequalities between women and men, which, in turn, are grounded in capitalist conditions that perpetuate these gender inequalities. The buyers, who are men, are the only beneficiaries of prostitution. Overall can never imagine a time when women and men would be equal buyers and sellers. "In a culture where women's sexuality is used to sell, and women learn that sex is our primary asset, sex work is not and cannot be just a private business transaction, an exchange of benefits between equals, or an egalitarian trade" (Overall 1992, 721). Prostitution in all its forms, from the high-end escort to the exploited street-based worker, is the public manifestation of capitalist patriarchy. It can never be a private sex act where monies are exchanged. Although Overall recognizes that it is important to distinguish between "[defending] prostitutes' entitlement to do their work" and condemning "prostitution itself as a practice under patriarchy," she nevertheless asserts that "the claim of a right to be a prostitute can be turned against women by those who merely want to preserve men's entitlement to buy women's bodies" (723–24).

The focus on the buyers—the men who feel entitled "to buy women's bodies"—has been a crucial part of the abolitionist feminist position, and the conflation between trafficking and prostitution rests in part on the "demonization of the client" because "the initial focus on traffickers has steadily expanded to include the customers ('the demand'), who are seen as the root cause of trafficking" (Weitzer 2010, 72). The prostituted/trafficked woman, now seen as "good" because she is victimized, is counterposed to the "bad" customer or john. When then justice minister MacKay introduced Bill C-36 in June 2014, he referred to buyers of sex as "perverts," leading observers to wonder if that would be his choice of words in describing Mike Allen, the MLA from Alberta—a fellow Conservative—who was caught soliciting for prostitution. Former Alberta premier Alison Redford conflated prostitution and trafficking when she expressed her disgust about Allen's behaviour, stating: "When I was justice minister, we started doing work with respect to the sexual exploitation of women and human trafficking. This is an issue that is very close to my heart" (as quoted in Drinkwater 2013). In their factums to the Supreme Court, both the Evangelical Fellowship of Canada (2013) and the Women's Coalition for the Abolition of Prostitution (2013) draw from the arguments of well-known radical feminist and legal scholar Catherine MacKinnon on trafficking and prostitution (see MacKinnon 2011). The Evangelical Fellowship (2013) pointed out its acceptance of "a high correlation between the legalization of prostitution related activities and an increase in human trafficking," arguing that "the demand for sex workers is not met by the indigenous population for the most part, but fulfilled by forcible recruitment into the industry via trafficking." This is part of what some call a "moral crusade," which has been dominated by a coalition of the religious right and abolitionist feminists, and although abolitionist feminists focus on prostitution as the exploitation of women, "religious conservatives have long denounced prostitution as perverse and sinful, a source of moral decay in society, and a threat to marriage" (Weitzer 2010, 70). The idea that prostitution is immoral, grounded in the strict morality of marital sex, so that any sex outside of marriage (premarital, extramarital, non-marital) is considered immoral, drives conservative thinking. This sort of thinking, evident in parts of Western society and other conservative regions throughout the world, can only lead to the stigmatization of a profession predicated on the buying and selling of sex.

The stigmatization of prostitution stems from the idea that what is being sold is "unacceptable in polite society" (Nussbaum 1999, 286). What is considered unacceptable (and therefore stigmatized) has changed historically so that at one point actors, singers, and dancers were stigmatized because it was "shameful to display one's body to strangers in public, especially in the expression of passionate emotion" (Nussbaum 1999, 280). The stigmatization of prostitution goes beyond this to a "gender hierarchy" where "the dangerous sexuality of women is controlled by men … [and] the prostitute, a sexually active woman, [is] a threat to male control of women" (286). The prostitute must be left outside of polite society either by repressing her profession through the criminalization of her behaviour or, if her services are necessary to satisfy men's sexual needs, through the regulation of her behaviour. The stigmatization of prostitution has led to women being shunned.

Unlike Overall, Nussbaum accepts that prostitution can be a private sex act between consenting adults, albeit as part of a monetary exchange, and this crucial difference leads her to support the decriminalization of prostitution. The case of a high-end escort, like Ashley Dupre, is easier to defend as a woman choosing to be a sex worker, but what about women in economically impoverished situations? What about street-based workers, or women engaged in survival sex? Isn't there something wrong with women selling their bodies for monetary gain, not only for poor and/or racialized women throughout the West, but also in many parts of the world where very few economic options exist for women? Nussbaum asserts that "there is nothing wrong per se with taking money for the use of one's body" (297), and that this should not be seen as an issue of choice, but as a matter of poverty. According to Nussbaum, "many poor people's lives are nonautonomous … [that] they may fulfill internal conditions of autonomy, being capable of making bargains … but none of this counts for a great deal, if in fact the struggle for survival gives them just one unpleasant option" (296). However, Nussbaum argues that criminalizing prostitution only further limits poor women's choices. Thus, isn't it better to focus on women's conditions of work? Where do they work (because outdoor prostitution is generally more dangerous than indoor prostitution, i.e., homes, hotels, brothels, etc.)? How much control do they have in choosing their customers? How much of their earnings are theirs to keep? What kinds of health checks are they subjected to, and are they fully informed about mitigating the health risks in their trade? These sorts of questions are even more pertinent to poor, often racialized women in the sex trade because they are the ones who are the most marginalized throughout society.

Although prostitution as work should not be glorified, outlawing prostitution is not the answer.

> This does not mean that we should not be concerned about ways in which prostitution as currently practiced, even in the absence of force and fraud, undermines the dignity of women, just as domestic service in the past undermined the dignity of members of a given race or class. But the correct response to this problem seems to be to work to enhance the economic autonomy and personal dignity of members of that class, not to rule off limits an option that may be the livelihood for many poor women and to further stigmatize women who already make their living this way. (Nussbaum 1999, 297)

Of the three types of prostitution systems, decriminalization is the best way to address the impoverished situations of many women who end up in the sex trade, to deal with the stigmatization of sex work often grounded in the control of women's sexuality, and to protect the rights of sex workers who continue to live on the margins of society. In August 2015, Amnesty International joined a broad range of groups worldwide calling for the decriminalization of sex work: from UN agencies, such as the World Health Organization, UN Women, UNAIDS, the UNDP's Global Commission on HIV and the Law, and the International Labour Organization, to anti-trafficking and human rights groups, such as the Global Alliance Against Trafficking in Women, the Global Network of Sex Work Projects, Human Rights Watch, the Open Society Foundations, and Anti-Slavery International (Murphy 2015).

By choosing to adopt an abolitionist system or the Nordic model, the Conservative government under Stephen Harper effectively outlawed prostitution even though the focus is on the criminalization of the buyers of sex. According to the preamble of Canada's law, "the Parliament of Canada recognizes the social harm caused by the objectification of the human body and the commodification of sexual activity [and] it is important to protect human dignity and the equality of all Canadians by discouraging prostitution, which has a disproportionate impact on women and children." Women in prostitution are constructed as victims, which is characteristic of the Nordic model, but the Canadian law still allows some criminalization of the selling of sexual services if done near schools, playgrounds, or daycare centres. There was actually an even broader understanding of what would be criminalized in Bill C-36, and it was the only part of the bill that was amended as it went through the legislative process. Before the amendment, the bill was not clear exactly where the selling of services would be criminalized, stating only "in locations where individuals under 18 might reasonably be present." With greater clarity, the Conservative government deemed that women are victims unless they sell sex near schools, playgrounds, or daycare centres. In that case, according to the law, they must have *chosen* to engage in prostitution and therefore their actions are criminalized. Thus, the women are not victims after all because the "protection of communities," a conservative ideal, trumps "the protection of exploited persons." This, alone, should have given radical or abolitionist feminists pause in supporting the former Conservative government's new prostitution law. Given the Liberal Party's opposition to that law when, as the third party in Parliament, it was composed of only 37 members, the question after the October 2015 election is whether the new government under Prime Minister Trudeau will use its newfound majority of 184 seats to repeal the law and decriminalize prostitution in Canada. Let us hope so.

RECOMMENDED FILMS, VIDEO CLIPS, AND WEBSITES

Canada's New Prostitution Law Explained with Toys. 2014. Produced by the *National Post*. Published on December 16, 2014. www.youtube.com/watch?v=a05IYvDF1vc.

Enslaved and Exploited: The Story of Sex Trafficking in Canada. 2010. Documentary produced by Hope for the Sold (Canada). www.ligi.ubc.ca/?p2=/modules/liu/news/view.jsp&id=395. See also: hopeforthesold.com/.

The Exhibition. 2013. Documentary directed by Damon Vignale, featuring Pamela Masik (Canada). www.theexhibitionmovie.com/.

Hope in Heaven. 2007. Documentary directed by Meredith Ralston (Canada). www.hopein-heavenfilm.com/.

Selling Sex. 2015. Documentary directed by Meredith Ralston (Canada). www.msvu.ca/en/home/programsdepartments/artsandscience/womensstudies/facultyprofiles/meredithralston.aspx.

ADDITIONAL READINGS

Abel, Gillian, Lisa Fitzgerald, and Catherine Healy, with Aline Taylor, eds. 2010. *Taking the Crime Out of Sex Work: New Zealand Sex Workers' Fight for Decriminalisation*. Bristol: Policy Press.

Agustin, Laura Maria. 2007. *Sex at the Margins: Migration, Labour Markets and the Rescue Industry*. London: Zed Books.

Andrijasevic, Rutvica. 2010. *Migration, Agency, and Citizenship in Sex Trafficking*. London: Palgrave Macmillan.

Chuang, Janie. 2006. "The United States as Global Sheriff: Using Unilateral Sanctions to Combat Human Trafficking." *Michigan Journal of International Law* 27, no. 2: 437–94.

Kempadoo, Kamala, with Jyoti Sanghera and Bandana Pattanik. 2012. *Trafficking and Prostitution Reconsidered: New Perspectives on Migration, Sex Work, and Human Rights*. 2nd ed. Boulder: Paradigm Publishers.

Lowman, John. 2011. "Deadly Inertia: A History of Constitutional Challenges to Canada's Criminal Code Sections on Prostitution." *Beijing Law Review* 2, no. 2: 33–54.

Parent, Collette, Chris Buckert, Patrice Corriveau, Maria Nengah Mensah, and Louise Toupin, eds. 2013. *Sex Work: Rethinking the Job, Respecting the Workers*. Translated by Kathe Roth. Vancouver: UBC Press.

Spector, Jessica, ed. 2006. *Prostitution and Pornography: Philosophical Debate about the Sex Industry*. Stanford: Stanford University Press.

Weitzer, Ronald. 2012. *Legalizing Prostitution: From Illicit Vice to Lawful Business*. New York: New York University Press.

Concluding Comments
POLITICS AND SEX REVISITED

THE IMPORTANCE OF EDUCATION

If there is a common theme in all six topics examined in this text, it is "education, not (further) legislation," an observation made explicitly in Chapter 4 on laws banning female genital mutilation/cutting (FGM/C) in the West. Legal remedies to deal with inequality are necessary but clearly insufficient. Inequalities persist long after the achievement of formal legal equality, but instituting more laws is often not the answer for countries like Canada and the United States. That is why from a feminist liberal perspective the identification and eradication of systems of dominance prevalent in society are crucial if individual autonomy is to be realized. Laws alone are not enough to achieve gender equality. In the case of FGM/C, UNICEF (2013, 89) points out that legislative changes may have little effect on attitudes and beliefs on FGM/C if legal and social norms are at odds. The UNICEF report discusses the social norms approach as a way to illustrate how families who may decide not to cut their daughters misperceive the extent to which this decision will lead to social disapproval and exclusion, and these perceptions are evident in families in both the African region and immigrant communities in the

West. Families end up cutting their daughters despite apparently successful educational and intervention programs (i.e., attitudinal changes have occurred in these families) because they think FGM/C is the norm in their communities.

The social norms approach has been used for over a decade by practitioners interested in alcohol abuse and violence prevention, specifically in American universities (Fabiano et al. 2003; Berkowitz 2005). It is founded on arguments of "pluralistic ignorance," where the misperceptions of individuals lead them to see the views of peers and others as different from their own, and "false consensus," where their false beliefs lead them to believe the attitudes of others are similar when they are not.

> False consensus and pluralistic ignorance are mutually reinforcing and self-perpetuating.... The majority is silent because it thinks it is a minority and the minority is vocal because it believes that it represents the majority.... The term *social norms approach* refers to the corrections of social norms ... rather than attempts to change norms that are unhealthy or problematic. Thus, the goal is to reveal and enhance already existing healthy norms that have been underestimated and weakened. (Berkowitz 2005, 194–95)

The social norms approach is grounded in the acknowledgement that progress has been made, for example, in terms of gender equality, but the norms around it are weakened by attitudes and behaviours that individuals misperceive as dominant in their society or community. The overwhelming majority of men throughout the West are non-violent, and as progress has occurred, it is evident that they reject problematic constructions of masculinity, which, as discussed in Chapter 1, are grounded in sexism and homophobia. In the case of violence prevention in universities, educational efforts can be directed to "men who may misperceive both the norms of male peers and the norms of female peers in ways that could encourage problematic behaviours and limit men's capacity to reduce sexual assault and to intervene against other men's harmful attitudes and coercive behaviors" (Fabiano et al. 2003, 106). By dealing with men's misperceptions, they can be seen, according to Fabiano and her colleagues (2003), as "social justice allies" in violence prevention. In other words, the overwhelming majority of men in university do not have sexist attitudes, but some of them end up exhibiting sexist behaviours because they misperceive other men's (and women's) beliefs. A social norms approach corrects these misperceptions by directing programs to male students. This is in keeping with efforts that prevent victim-blaming because the focus is on potential offenders as opposed to potential victims of sexual assault, such as the "Don't Be That Guy" campaign, first launched in 2010 by the Sexual Assault Voices of Edmonton with the support of the Edmonton Police Services (Butterfield 2012).

Rape myths persist despite legislative changes, and further education for all students undertaken as part of a university's mission, particularly in cases of acquaintance rape where consent is central, is much needed. That is why institutionalizing affirmative consent in universities makes sense. For Canada, this is already the law throughout the country and every university should explicitly adopt it as part of its disciplinary process. For the United States, this is already occurring regardless of whether state legislation requires universities to adopt affirmative consent (as discussed in Chapter 5, the definition of consent in sexual assault cases differs from state to state) because of federally mandated Title IX requirements. The disturbing rape chants made by Canadian university students demonstrated the extent to which sexist attitudes about rape, rape victims, and rapists can become embedded in individual thinking so that chanting about rape can become uncritically accepted and normalized. These chants were not, as some conservative commentators argued, harmless acts of immature university students, but rather indications that further education about sexual violence is needed. For Saint Mary's University, this will come in the form of online training modules on safety and respect, modelled on a program by the University of Montana, that will feature the university's policies and procedures, definitions of consent and sexual assault, the effects of alcohol and drug use, the importance of being an effective bystander, and understanding response procedures in the event of an incident on or off campus (Saint Mary's University 2014, 10). The intent is to make these online training modules a requirement for all students to take. For the University of Ottawa, the university president has accepted the task force's recommendation to provide funding for new undergraduate courses that address sexual violence from an interdisciplinary perspective. As the report of the task force points out, "the University is uniquely placed to foster a community where students can develop critical thought and engagement" (University of Ottawa 2015, 38). In addition, the report makes a specific recommendation that every course syllabus contain a section stating the university's zero tolerance for sexual violence in the same way that every syllabus has a section on plagiarism.

The importance of education is also clearly important in overcoming the deleterious effects of the feminine body-as-object both on the sense of self and on attitudes in society. The focus on appearance has become even more pronounced with the pathologizing of fat in the West, but efforts to rightly end fat-shaming need to occur alongside efforts to end "fit-shaming," namely by critiquing the view that being fit means being thin. There is no shame in wanting to take care of one's body, particularly in living a healthy, active lifestyle, one that becomes increasingly important as individuals age. Women have taken control of their lives, particularly through the attainment of independent economic means, and education about body-as-process, leading to the recognition of a fit and strong body ideal, can not only increase a woman's body confidence, but also impact Western societal attitudes that focus on appearance. Prominent women in politics, including Michelle Obama and Hillary Rodham Clinton, illustrate how body confidence can be part of the creation of a viable sense of self, and this is crucial to confluent love, which arguably characterizes both the Obama and Clinton marriages. For Clinton, this would mean that her reasons for staying with Bill after the Lewinsky scandal are predicated not on political calculation (which has a derogatory connotation, especially for women), but more on her control of her sexuality and the ongoing monitoring and negotiation of an egalitarian "pure relationship" because intimacy is part of self-development (this is the part of the feminist liberal perspective to which I return at the end of this chapter).

Moreover, as Nicola Lacey (1993, 110) has argued, we do not "have to find legal solutions to all the problems identified by feminist critique," particularly when legal solutions become counterproductive if they lead to problematic alliances with social conservatives. In the case of bans on the niqab and the burqa in the West, veil bans cannot easily be disentangled from anti-immigrant and anti-Muslim sentiments that exist in Western society, so the best way to deal with women wearing face-concealing veils (assuming that they are forced) is not to ban them, but to educate women and men about equality. It would be the same sorts of arguments for women who purportedly objectify themselves to pursue what seem to be unattainable body ideals to the point of pursuing any cosmetic surgery, including genital modifications (assuming that this is false consciousness of choice). Disturbing political partnerships are also evident in efforts to condemn pornography and prostitution where the relationship between radical feminists and social conservatives has been long-standing. Sex-radical feminists have condemned what they refer to as unholy alliances since the feminist sex wars, but more contemporary connections with social conservatives are found in the conflation of sexualization and objectification by anti-porn feminists and the conflation of prostitution and trafficking by abolitionist feminists. Changes can come about by mainstreaming egalitarian pornography, specifically feminist porn, but this may require changes to sex education curricula in high schools. Although this is highly unlikely because students are minors, educational efforts can be directed at the university level (such as arguments found in Chapter 6), recognizing that this would not be acceptable to anti-porn feminists because of their particular perspective that pornography is inherently bad for women. Adult consensual prostitution, like pornography, should be decriminalized, recognizing that here, too, abolitionist feminists who see all sex workers as sexually exploited, and therefore all victims, hold a particular viewpoint that is not necessarily good for women in the sex trade. Difficulties in changing political discourse around prostitution as exploitation are certainly evident in Canada's decision to adopt the Nordic model after the Supreme Court struck down the country's existing prostitution law because it violated the rights of sex workers. Canada's new law is, however, not wholly faithful to the Nordic model, not only because there are few legislated social supports for sex workers, but also because some of their activities remain criminalized, making it even more problematic as legislation purportedly to protect women in prostitution. The new Liberal government under Trudeau, elected in October 2015, now has the opportunity to rectify this and decriminalize prostitution.

LEGAL RECOGNITION OF SAME-SEX MARRIAGE

In looking at how power infuses gender in ways that focus on sexuality, there has been clear progress in undermining the valorization of the heterosexual conjugal bond that not only disempowers women but also marginalizes sexual minorities. Although the focus of this book has been on the continuing challenges that women face, this focus also makes sense for those concerned with injustices perpetuated against sexual minorities. Weeks (2007) argues that changes in gender relations have been crucial because, as he stresses, "the starting point has to be the full human equality of men and women, and from this flows all the other forms of equality" (7). In other words, by paying attention to women's equality, the stage is set for equality in other ways. There is no better example than same-sex marriage where the severing of "the automatic unity between sexual activity and reproduction, between sex and marriage, and between marriage and parenting," which has empowered women, has led to the severing of "the automatic link between marriage and heterosexuality" (Weeks 2007, 15), which has taken gay and lesbian partnerships from the margins to the mainstream. The recognition of same-sex marriage is where legislation in the contemporary context remains crucial in ensuring equality, and largely due to court decisions upholding individual rights, progress has occurred in a significant handful of sovereign states throughout the world.

Marriage has traditionally been a male-dominated institution where historically women were the property of men, including husbands' unlimited and unequivocal access to sexual intercourse with their wives. As discussed in Chapter 5 on rape and sexual violence, the recognition of marital rape has been an important step forward in women's rights because the spousal exemption in rape law undermined a woman's right to be free from sexual violence. A husband's use of force against his wife or to have sex without her consent was simply perceived as within *his* right. That has changed. Violence within marriage is within the legal purview of the state, and governments can prosecute husbands who rape their wives.

Marriage continues to be a heterosexual-dominated institution throughout the world, but as of February 2016 same-sex marriage is legal in 21 sovereign states (counting the United Kingdom as one sovereign state as opposed to dividing England/Wales from Scotland; and Greenland, although an autonomous entity, as part of Denmark). Canada became the fourth country in the world to legalize same-sex marriage (after the Netherlands, Belgium, and days after Spain) with the passage of the Civil Marriage Act in July 2005 under the Liberal minority government of Prime Minister Paul Martin. Ten years later the United States became the 20th sovereign state to recognize same-sex marriage with the historic *Obergefell v. Hodges* decision handed down by the US Supreme Court in June 2015. In both Canada and the United States, the role of the courts has been crucial in the movement to legalize same-sex marriage. In Canada, the process began after provincial courts ruled that the restriction of marriage to a union between a man and woman violated the equality provisions (Section 15) of the Charter of Rights and Freedoms. The Supreme Court of Canada did not hear appeals of lower court decisions, but rather was asked by the Liberal government of the time to make a "reference decision" on the federal government's wording of Bill C-38 (the legislation that would become the Civil Marriage Act). A reference decision is a unique function undertaken by the court system in Canada to consider important questions of law, such as the constitutionality or interpretation of federal or provincial legislation, and to provide an opinion without a case per se. In other words, the Supreme Court of Canada is not only the final court of appeal, but also a body that the federal government can ask to provide an opinion on a piece of legislation in question, such as the one on same-sex marriage. In handing down its reference decision in December 2004, the Supreme Court ruled that the federal government had exclusive jurisdiction over marriage (so federal law would take precedence over provincial laws), and that the bill conformed with the Charter, particularly in terms of protecting religious freedom because religious officials would not be forced to perform same-sex marriages if doing so would be against their religious beliefs.

Although the Conservative minority government under Stephen Harper, which took power in January 2006, reopened the issue of same-sex marriage, it did so only as a motion in the House of Commons on December 7 of that year. The 2006 motion "call[ed] on the government to introduce legislation to restore the traditional definition of marriage," and the motion was easily defeated. Although the Harper Conservatives went on to win a majority government in May 2011, there was no indication that matters would change. Indeed, when questions arose on whether same-sex marriages of non-Canadians performed in Canada were legal, the Harper government quickly acted to eliminate any loopholes in Canada's same-sex marriage legislation. Moreover, under former foreign affairs minister John Baird, the protection of same-sex rights abroad had become one of Canada's stated foreign policy priorities.

In the United States, same-sex marriage had been legalized at the state (or sub-national) level. Marriage is under state, not federal, jurisdiction, and this was reaffirmed by the US Supreme Court in its June 2013 decision (*United States v. Windsor*) striking down the Defense of Marriage Act (DOMA). DOMA was passed by the federal government in 1996, and it not only defined marriage as a union between a man and a woman, but also denied federal benefits, such as Social Security survivor benefits, federal health care, and estate tax exemptions, to same-sex couples whose marriages are recognized in the states in which they live. Federal courts found these sections of DOMA unconstitutional, and in 2011, the Obama administration decided not to defend DOMA in court. Supporters of DOMA, including the Republican-controlled House of Representatives, appealed to the Supreme Court to reverse lower court rulings. Referred to as the *Windsor* decision, the Supreme Court ruled that legally married same-sex couples were entitled to federal benefits, upholding the unconstitutionality of DOMA. It was a 5–4 decision, and although Justice Kennedy, writing for the majority, asserted that DOMA "disparage[d] and injure[d] those whom the state, by its marriage laws sought to protect in personhood and dignity," he stated that the court's ruling applied only to marriages from states that allowed same-sex couples to wed. In other words, the Supreme Court did not declare same-sex marriage a constitutional right in 2013, thus keeping in place state laws that banned same-sex marriage.

The Supreme Court not only ruled on DOMA, but also on California's Proposition 8 in June 2013. It is crucial to understand that the historic passage of state ballot initiatives in the 2012 election supporting same-sex marriage was in marked contrast to the 2008 election, particularly in the case of California where the state initiative, Proposition 8, asked voters to change the California constitution to eliminate the right of same-sex couples to marry in the state after court decisions allowed them to do so. In other words, the 2008 proposition was to reverse the recognition of same-sex marriage in California. Alarmingly, the proposition passed, leading same-sex advocates to challenge its constitutionality. Both the trial and appeals courts in California struck down Proposition 8, with the appeals court declaring that it "serves no purpose, and has no effect, other than to lessen the status and human dignity of gays and lesbians in California and to officially reclassify their relationship and families as inferior to those of opposite-sex couples."

Supporters of Proposition 8 appealed to the Supreme Court to reverse the rulings of the lower courts, but the state of California did not appeal to the Supreme Court, nor did state authorities make the case to the appeals court when the trial court declared Proposition 8 invalid. Rather, proponents of Proposition 8 appealed on the state's behalf. It was on this technicality that the majority of the Supreme Court, in a 5–4 decision, declared that the case was improperly before the court as it was improperly before the appeals court in California. The Supreme Court ruled that only state authorities could appeal the trial court's decision, and because they did not, the trial court's decision would stand. In other words, the proponents of Proposition 8 had no standing before the courts.

The June 2013 decisions by the US Supreme Court on both DOMA and California's Proposition 8 were immediately seen as important victories by same-sex marriage advocates. Because the Supreme Court effectively dismissed the Proposition 8 case, its ruling on DOMA, or the *Windsor* decision, set into motion court challenges in *all* states where same-sex marriage had been banned. In the first 17 months after the *Windsor* decision (June 2013 to November 2014), dramatic changes happened in the United States. During that period, there were 52 legal victories for same-sex marriage advocates in state courts (15 of 16 cases), federal courts (32 of 34 cases), and federal appellate courts (5 of 6 cases). At the federal appellate level, the Court of Appeals for the Sixth Circuit with its decision on November 6, 2014, to uphold state bans on same-sex marriage created a "circuit split," which resulted in the Supreme Court having to fully weigh in on the issue. Just a month earlier in October 2014, the Supreme Court had refused to hear any appeals on same-sex marriage, effectively allowing lower court decisions to stand. The five federal appellate courts had declared bans on same-sex marriage as unconstitutional, so there was no disagreement at the time at the federal appellate level. The November 6, 2014, decision by the Sixth Court of Appeals changed the legal landscape, and the Supreme Court had to rule on the constitutionality of same-sex marriage. On June 26, 2015, the Supreme Court handed down its decision in a 5–4 vote, reversing the judgment of the Court of Appeals for the Sixth Circuit. Justice Kennedy, who was seen as the pivotal vote, wrote for the majority once again. His closing paragraph went viral, generating extraordinary emotions online and bringing tears of joy to many activists and supporters of same-sex marriage (Weissmann 2015). It bears repeating verbatim here:

> No union is more profound than marriage, for it embodies the highest ideals of love, fidelity, devotion, sacrifice, and family. In forming a marital union, two people become something greater than once they were. As some of the petitioners in these cases demonstrate, marriage embodies a love that may endure even past death. It would misunderstand these men and women to say they disrespect the idea of marriage. Their plea is that they do respect it, respect it so deeply that they seek to find its fulfillment for themselves. Their hope is not to be condemned to live in loneliness, excluded from one of civilization's oldest institutions. They ask for equal dignity in the eyes of the law. The Constitution grants them that right. (United States Supreme Court 2015)

However, as the promotion of sexual freedoms and the acceptance of same-sex relationships have become more the norm throughout the West, there have been forces of resistance that, under the guise of protecting traditional family values or preserving traditional culture, undermine women's rights and the rights of sexual minorities. According to the International Lesbian, Gay, Bisexual, Trans and Intersex Association (ILGA), which has kept track of the status of same-sex rights throughout the world, the persecution of gays and lesbians has been ongoing. There is no better example than Russia, which passed a law in June 2013 banning the "propaganda of non-traditional sexual relations to minors," which built on regional bans in the country on "propagation of homosexuality" and "promotion of gay lifestyles" passed since 2006. Although the Russian anti-gay law caused some controversy during the Sochi 2014 Olympics, including President Obama's decision not to attend the games, these types of laws are characteristic of homophobic arguments framed in terms of protecting traditional values. As Graeme Reid, director of the Lesbian, Gay, Bisexual and Transgender Rights Program of Human Rights Watch, has argued, the Russian government has condemned sexual minorities under the sponsorship of "traditional values" resolutions in the United Nations Human Rights Council. For example, a resolution in fall 2012 focused on the "traditional values of humankind" as the way to protect and promote human rights, and as Reid (2012) points out, "underpinning this is an argument that homosexuality is a moral issue and not a rights issues at all." Russia continues to persecute sexual minorities and, more alarmingly, its laws have given vigilante groups and individuals a "license to harm," according to Human Rights Watch (2014), evident in increasing attacks on LGBTQ people and activists throughout the country.

Throughout parts of Eastern Europe, Central Asia, and Africa, laws are being passed or being considered to criminalize "homosexual propaganda," if not homosexuality, under the guise of "protecting children" and the family while, at the same time, countries in North America. Latin America, and the European Union have become more accepting of sexual minorities. According to the ILGA and the Pew Research Center, the world is becoming more divided on same-sex issues and the rights of sexual minorities. In addition, in countries like Uganda, the anti-gay movement has gained ground partly by what are perceived as the neo-colonial attitudes of the West because countries like the United States, the United Kingdom, and Canada are placing greater foreign policy priority on the protection of the rights of sexual minorities, and are seen as imposing it on others as Western cultural imperialism, an argument that should be familiar to those who have fought for the universality of women's rights. The role of American evangelicals has also been evident in fuelling the anti-gay movement, leading to concerns that the culture wars are being exported abroad. The challenges are real not only to the rights of sexual minorities, but also to the rights of women through the control of their sexuality. These are the same evangelicals who hold "purity balls" in the United States. As Amy Derogatis (2014) explains:

> Purity balls stand out as a dramatic form of pledging virginity within American evangelicalism. The emphasis placed on the father's role in protecting his daughter's chaste body until marriage, and the daughter's

> commitment to her father as well as God, raises important questions about female autonomy and the value being placed on young girls' virginity. It also raises troubling questions about a young woman's ability to make informed sexual choices.

It is clear that with conservative forces at work throughout the world seeking to curb, reverse, or reject sexual reforms, all those concerned with individual rights and with social justice for women and sexual minorities alike must work together to realize equality.

SEX, GENDER, AND GENDER IDENTITY

As evident by the work of the International Lesbian, Gay, Bisexual, Trans and Intersex Association, concerns about sexual minorities extend beyond injustices perpetrated based on sexual orientation. In Chapter 1, two significant considerations were raised regarding the categories of sex and gender: one, that male and female are not immutable categories given that there are intersex people; and two, that men (namely those with male physical attributes such as a penis) and women (namely those with female physical attributes such as a vagina) are not immutable categories given that that there are transgender people. The Intersex Society of North America points out that intersex and transgender people are assumed to be the same, but the distinction between them is important. "Most people with intersex conditions come to medical attention because *doctors or parents notice something unusual about their bodies* [and thus their sense of difference is often precipitated externally]. In contrast, people who are transgendered [*sic*; see below] *have an internal experience of gender identity* that is different from most people" (Intersex Society of North America, n.d.). Intersex people have clearly faced injustices, particularly as children, because so many have been subject to genital modifications to force conformity with either male or female genitalia. That is why those in the West who seek to end male infant circumcision have found common cause with not only those who condemn FGM/C, but also those who oppose medical interventionist procedures on intersex children because they argue that no genitals (male, female, or intersex) should be cut before the age of consent (Earp 2014).

This section is concerned primarily with transgender people in large part because of the controversial arguments of some radical feminists, pejoratively called TERFs (trans exclusionary radical feminists), who question whether transgender women are *women*. Evident in the works of Janice Raymond (1979) and Sheila Jeffreys (2014), this line of thinking has polarized the debate around sex, gender, and gender identity. Given the relatively recent attention to transgender issues in the public arena, the use of terminology is a crucial part of understanding the topic. GLAAD, which formerly stood for the Gay and Lesbian Alliance Against Defamation when it was established in 1985 in the United States, dropped that referential understanding in 2013 in order to demonstrate that its work is much broader because GLAAD advocates for the entire LGBTQ community. The organization exclusively goes by GLAAD with no reference to what the acronym originally stood for because it is concerned with injustices perpetuated based not only on sexual orientation but also on gender identity. GLAAD (n.d.) provides an excellent primer on terminology relevant to transgender issues in the contemporary context, and excerpts are found below.

> *Gender Identity*: One's internal, deeply held sense of one's gender. For transgender people, their own internal gender identity does not match the sex they were assigned at birth. Most people have a gender identity of man or woman (or boy or girl). For some people, their gender identity does not fit neatly into one of those two choices. Unlike gender expression … *gender identity is not visible to others* [italics added].
>
> *Gender Expression*: External manifestations of gender, expressed through one's name, pronouns, clothing, haircut, behavior, voice, or body characteristics. Society identifies these cues as masculine and feminine, although what is considered masculine and feminine changes over time and varies by culture. Typically, transgender people seek to make their gender expression align with their gender identity, rather than the sex they were assigned at birth.
>
> *Sexual Orientation*: Describes an individual's enduring physical, romantic and/or emotional attraction to another person. Gender identity and sexual orientation are not the same. Transgender people may be straight, lesbian, gay, or bisexual. For example, a person who transitions from male to female and is attracted solely to men would identify as a straight woman.

Transgender [this is an adjective; it is inappropriate to use "transgendered" because "gayed" or "lesbianed" are not used as adjectives]: An umbrella term for people whose gender identity and/or gender expression differs from what is typically associated with the sex they were assigned at birth. People under the transgender umbrella may describe themselves using one or more of a wide variety of terms—including transgender.... *Use the descriptive term preferred by the individual* [italics added]. Many transgender people are prescribed hormones by their doctors to change their bodies. Some undergo surgery as well. But not all transgender people can or will take those steps, and *a transgender identity is not dependent upon medical procedures* [italics added].

Transsexual [this is also an adjective]: An older term that originated in the medical and psychological communities. Still preferred by some people who have permanently changed—or seek to change—their bodies through medical interventions (including but not limited to hormones and/or surgeries). Unlike transgender, transsexual is not an umbrella term. Many transgender people do not identify as transsexual and prefer the word transgender.

Transgender man: [People] ... assigned female at birth but identify and live as a man.... Some may also use FTM, an abbreviation for female-to-male.

Transgender woman: [People] ... assigned male at birth but identify and live as a woman.... Some may also use MTF, an abbreviation for male-to-female.

Cisgender: A term used by some to describe people who are not transgender. "Cis-" is a Latin prefix meaning "on the same side as," and is therefore an antonym of "trans-." [This is gaining popular usage to describe the overwhelming majority of individuals whose gender identity align with their sex assigned at birth.]

> *Gender Non-Conforming*: A term used to describe some people whose gender expression is different from conventional expectations of masculinity and femininity.... Not all gender non-conforming people identify as transgender; nor are all transgender people gender non-conforming.... The term is not a synonym for transgender or transsexual and should only be used if someone self-identifies as gender non-conforming.
>
> *Genderqueer*: A term used by some people who experience their gender identity and/or gender expression as falling outside the categories of man and woman. They may define their gender as falling somewhere in between man and woman, or they may define it as wholly different from these terms. The term is not a synonym for transgender or transsexual and should only be used if someone self-identifies as genderqueer. (GLAAD, n.d.)

According to GLAAD, it is important to be careful using the terms *cross-dresser* and *drag queen*, and not to use the outdated word *transvestite*. As well, a transgender person's chosen names should be always used along with the appropriate pronoun. Individuals altering their birth sex undergo a process called "transition," and this process differs from individual to individual. The point is that the identity of a transgender person is dependent on the individual's internal understanding of her or his gender identity. Although many transgender people are outwardly feminine or masculine, the outward manifestation of their identity is about their gender expression, not their gender identity, which recognizes that often the inability to express themselves stems from the disapprobation, if not persecution, of transgender people by family, friends, and society at large. They have been closeted in ways only too familiar to many gays and lesbians who have fought for the recognition of same-sex rights. In addition, regardless of their gender expression, transgender people may not have undergone hormone treatments or genital modifications to conform to their gender identity. Many transgender women have penises and many transgender men are able to become pregnant, challenging commonly understood biological sex differences between women and men. As discussed in Chapter 1, male and female are sex categories while masculinity and femininity are gender categories, and they relate to each other because men (namely those with male physical attributes such as a penis) are expected to be masculine and women (namely those with female physical attributes such as a vagina) are expected to be feminine. Although it is crucial to question binary thinking and to understand that categories are not fixed or immutable, the idea of gender-as-power (as opposed to merely gender-as-difference) illustrates the unequal relationship between men and women where men dominate women. Gender is not only about socially constructed understandings of masculinity and femininity but also about the continuing hierarchical relationship between the two. Gender is the primary system of dominance with which this book has been concerned because the linkages between politics, gender, and sexuality draw attention to continuing challenges that women face in heterosexual relationships. Unfortunately, some well-meaning groups in their attempts to be inclusive of transgender people end up making ill-advised decisions that appear to question gender exercised as power, such as a small liberal arts college in the United States cancelling a performance of the *Vagina Monologues*, a well-known feminist play by Eve Ensler, because not all women who identify as women have vaginas, or an abortion rights group changing its name from Fund Texas Women to Fund Texas Choice because it is not only women who get pregnant and therefore would need abortion services. As Elinor Burkett (2015) argues:

> The insult and outright fear that trans men and women live with is all too familiar to [women], and a cruelly marginalized group's battle for justice is something [women] instinctively want to rally behind. But as the movement becomes mainstream, it's growing harder to avoid asking pointed questions about the frequent attacks by some trans leaders on women's right to define ourselves, our discourse and our bodies.

The problem is power continues to be exercised in ways that link the category of women to their reproductive and productive capabilities, so that sex differences cannot be wholly disregarded in terms of gender. For radical feminists who criticize the practice of "transgenderism," a problematic term used by Sheila Jeffreys (2014), the linkages between sex and gender translate to suspicion, if not rejection, of transgender women because, they argue, women born female have had to bear oppression by men throughout their lives. These radical feminists do not see gender as an internally defined identity but as a mode of oppression. As Michelle Goldberg (2014) has pointed out in what has become a controversial article, entitled "What Is a Woman? The Dispute between Radical Feminism and Transgenderism":

> [According to a particular view of radical feminism] gender is less a category than a caste position. Anyone born a man retains male privilege in society; even if he chooses to live as a woman—and accept a correspondingly subordinate social position—the fact that he has a choice means that he can never understand what being a woman is really like. By extension, when trans women demand to be accepted as women they are simply exercising another form of male entitlement.

Transgender activists have condemned Goldberg for giving voice to essentially a transphobic group (Wilkins 2014), but her article details how radical feminists who espouse these views, such as Jeffreys and Janice Raymond, have faced widespread condemnation, from having their talks and conference venues cancelled to being subjected to Internet abuse and even death threats. Labelled as TERFs who see themselves as being silenced (Jeffreys 2012; Macdonald 2015), they are at the extreme margins of feminist thinking. Indeed, their problematic arguments about the relationship between women and men, far from being compelling, illustrate the progress that has been made in society, particularly in the West. Transgender rights are ascendant. From the rallying cries resulting from the December 2014 death of an Ohio transgender teen, Leelah Acorn, whose suicide note (posted on her Tumblr blog) pointed out the need to "fix society," to the April 2015 *Vanity Fair* cover of Caitlyn Jenner, which details her "saying goodbye" to the 1976 US Olympic athlete, Bruce Jenner, and ex-husband of Kris Jenner and father figure of the Kardashian clan, transgender women, in particular, have led the struggle for recognition.

For feminist liberals, "women" is a political category, not a metaphysical or biological one, and the extent to which sex and gender are linked is when women face discrimination because of their particular bodily needs. As Abbey (2011, 274) points out, "If women were not disadvantaged by pregnancy relative to men, for example, this need not remain a feminist concern." The concern about reproductive rights for women stems from societal control of women's bodies, and not from women being born female. Abbey argues that feminist liberals, like Nussbaum, "would agree that sexed bodies need not manifest the gendered behaviours that social norms attach to them (because) the creative and even transgressive possibilities for personal identity opened up by the sex-gender separation mesh with [the] anticipation of gender's elimination" in terms of power (271).

TRANSFORMATION OF INTIMACY

In one of her interviews after her *Vanity Fair* cover, Caitlyn Jenner was asked whether coming out as transgender has affected her sexual desires because "one of the most common questions [faced by transgender people, especially if they choose to transition medically] is how it affects whom they are attracted to and whom they love" (Burke 2015). It is a question that speaks to sexuality and not only identity. To illustrate the difference, Norman Spack, the co-director of a special gender management clinic at Boston Children's Hospital, states that "gender identity is who you to go bed as," whereas "sexual orientation is who you go to bed with" (quoted in Burke 2015). For Jenner, her transition did not affect her sexual attraction to women, and although she may now be regarded as lesbian instead of straight, the fluidity of her gender and sexuality is emblematic of progress in contemporary Western society. This sort of fluidity is becoming more commonplace among young people in the West, evident from the pages of Facebook to the declarations of young celebrities, such as Miley Cyrus. Whether identifying as a woman, man, or genderqueer; heterosexual, gay, lesbian, bisexual, or pansexual; cisgender, transgender, or gender non-conforming, many young people in the West are at the forefront of challenging binary thinking. Neither woman nor man, but genderqueer; neither homosexual nor heterosexual (or bisexual because even that assumes same-sex or opposite-sex attraction), but pansexual; neither transgender nor cisgender, but gender non-conforming, individuals are being accepted for who they are and whomever they desire.

The idea that individuals should be able to exercise capabilities in these fundamental ways is rooted in respect for human dignity and the fostering of individual autonomy. Politics is about power, and the challenge is to continually identify systems of dominance that undermine individual autonomy and to work toward the realization of every individual's capabilities. For many women, gender remains about power, but women's sexual freedoms resulting from the sexual revolution in the West have led to both intimacy and masculinity being redefined, undermining the valorization of the heterosexual conjugal bond and creating the conditions for Giddens's "pure relationship," which rests on confluent, as opposed to romantic, love. As Giddens argues, passionate love—namely, pair bonding based on both emotional and sexual connections—is particularly subversive of society. Passionate love is usually contrasted with companionate love, the latter based solely on an emotional bond. For Giddens, the emotional and sexual bond between two individuals has been transformed with women's sexual freedoms where passionate love in Western society has become confluent rather than romantic. Confluent love is rooted in an egalitarian partnership where an individual *chooses* to be with another. This choice is often crucial not only to an individual's personal happiness, but also to an individual's public (workplace) success. As Sheryl Sandberg (2014) argues, choosing a life partner is the most important decision a woman can make because having a supportive partner is key to a woman's success. She credits her husband, David Goldberg, as instrumental to her success, which made his unexpected death in May 2015 at the age of 47 a testimony to both the breadth of their partnership and the depth of her individual fortitude. As she stated in an essay posted on Facebook a month after his death:

> I think when tragedy occurs, it presents a choice. You can give in to the void, the emptiness that fills your heart, your lungs, constricts your ability to think or even breathe. Or you can try to find meaning. These past thirty days, I have spent many of my moments lost in that void. And I know that many future moments will be consumed by the vast emptiness as well. But when I can, I want to choose life and meaning. (Sandberg as quoted in Shontell 2015)

By illustrating that intimacy is part of self-development, confluent love is subversive not only in undermining heterosexuality as the norm, but also in validating a feminist liberal understanding of privacy as a continuing ideal. The public-private is crucial to liberal thinking, and the private as understood by feminist liberals is a reference to the domestic or household sphere. The home is where women have historically been relegated, but it is also where the ideals of individual autonomy and equality can be realized in intimate relationships. If the private or home domain can indeed be about (confluent) love, and not power, then it should no longer be a concern of government or the society at large. Women will prosper because of their relationships with men, and couples will include all those who love regardless of sexual orientation or gender identity.

RECOMMENDED FILMS, VIDEO CLIPS, AND WEBSITES

Edie and Thea: A Very Long Engagement. 2009. Documentary directed by Susan Muska and Gréta Olafsdóttir (United States). http://ediewindsor.com/ediethea1.html.

International Lesbian, Gay, Bisexual, Trans and Intersex Association. www.ilga.org/.

InterSEXion. 2012. Documentary directed by Grant Lahood (New Zealand). www.intersexion-film.com/.

Pew Research Center—Religion and Public Life. Gay Marriage and Homosexuality. www.pew-forum.org/topics/gay-marriage-and-homosexuality/.

The Problem with Same-Sex Marriage. 2012. Produced by the Family Research Council (United States). Published on May 10, 2012. www.youtube.com/watch?v=egxB0dTajb4.

Transforming Gender. 2015. Documentary directed by Marc de Guerre (Canada). www.cbc.ca/doczone/episodes/transforming-gender.

Who We Become. 2014. Documentary directed by Adam Perez and Jan Hendrik Hinzel (United States). www.findingfamilydoc.com/.

ADDITIONAL READINGS

Anderson, Eric. 2012. *The Monogamy Gap*. New York: Oxford University Press.

Cutrona, Carolyn. 2004. "A Psychological Perspective: Marriage and the Social Provisions of Relationships." *Journal of Marriage and Family* 66, no. 4 (November): 992–99.

Kaplan, Roberta (with Lisa Dickey). 2015. *Then Comes Marriage: United States v. Windsor and the Defeat of DOMA*. New York: W.W. Norton and Company.

Krucks, Sonia. 2012. *Simone de Beauvoir and the Politics of Ambiguity*. New York: Oxford University Press.

Nussbaum, Martha C. 2010. *From Disgust to Humanity: Sexual Orientation and Constitutional Law*. New York: Oxford University Press.

REFERENCES

AAP (American Academy of Pediatrics). 2010a. "Policy Statement—Ritual Genital Cutting of Female Minors." *Pediatrics* 125, no. 5 (May): 1088–93. pediatrics.aappublications.org/content/125/5/1088.full.

———. 2010b. "Policy Statement—AAP Publications Reaffirmed and Retired." *Pediatrics* 126, no. 1 (July): 177. pediatrics.aappublications.org/content/126/1/177.short.

Abbey, Ruth. 2011. *The Return of Feminist Liberalism*. Montreal and Kingston: McGill-Queen's University Press.

Aboriginal Legal Services of Toronto. 2013. "Factum of the Intervener." SCC File no. 34788: *Attorney General of Canada, et al. v. Terri Jean Bedford, et al.* www.scc-csc.gc.ca/factums-memoires/34788/FM055_Intervener_ALST.pdf.

Abraham, Tamara. 2011. "Michelle Obama Exercises Her Right to Bare Arms—Twice in Three Days." *Daily Mail Online*, May 2. www.dailymail.co.uk/femail/article-1382790/Michelle-Obama-exercises-right-bare-arms--twice-days.html.

Akintunde, Dorcas Olubanke. 2010. "Female Genital Mutilation: A Socio-Cultural Gang Up Against Womanhood." *Feminist Theology* 18, no. 2: 192–205.

Albury, Kath. 2014. "Porn *and* Sex Education, Porn *as* Sex Education." *Porn Studies* 1, no. 1–2: 172–81.

Altemimei, Dannia. 2013. "Prostitution and the Right to Privacy: A Comparative Analysis of

Current Law in Canada and the United States." *Illinois Law Review* 2: 625–59. illinoislawreview.org/wp-content/ilr-content/articles/2013/2/Altemimei.pdf.

American Psychological Association, Task Force on the Sexualization of Girls. 2007. *Report of the APA Task Force on the Sexualization of Girls*. (Updated in 2010.) www.apa.org/pi/women/programs/girls/report-full.pdf.

Andreassen, Rikke, and Doujte Lettinga. 2012. "Veiled Debates: Gender and Gender Equality in European National Narratives." In *Politics, Religion and Gender: Framing and Regulating the Veil*, eds. Sieglinde Rosenberger and Brigit Sauer, 17–36. London: Routledge.

Andrijasevic, Rutvica. 2010. *Migration, Agency and Citizenship in Sex Trafficking*. Houndsmills, UK: Palgrave Macmillan.

Auerbach, David. 2014. "How a (Canadian-Founded) Company You've Never Heard of Took Control of the Porn Industry." *Slate*, October 24. news.nationalpost.com/2014/10/24/how-a-canadian-founded-company-youve-never-heard-of-took-control-of-the-porn-industry/.

Bachman, Ronet, and Raymond Paternoster. 1993. "A Contemporary Look at Effects of Rape Law Reform: How Far Have We Really Come?" *Journal of Criminal Law and Criminology* 84, no. 3: 554–74.

Baehr, Amy. 2004a. "Introduction." In *Varieties of Feminist Liberalism*, edited by Amy Baehr, 1–20. Lanham, MD: Rowman and Littlefield.

———, ed. 2004b. *Varieties of Feminist Liberalism*. Lanham, MD: Rowman and Littlefield.

Baker, Jennifer. 2015. "Campus Rape Skepticism: How Not to 'Debunk' Research." *Psychology Today*, March 6. www.psychologytoday.com/blog/the-love-wisdom/201503/campus-rape-skepticism.

Bakht, Natasha. 2012. "Veiled Objections: Facing Public Opposition to the Niqab." In *Reasonable Accommodation: Managing Religious Diversity*, edited by Lori Beaman, 70–108. Vancouver: UBC Press.

Barry, Kathleen. 1979. *Female Sexual Slavery*. New York: New York University Press.

Barthel, Margaret. 2014. "I Wasn't a Fan of Sheryl Sandberg—Until I Couldn't Find a Job." *Atlantic*, April 8. www.theatlantic.com/business/archive/2014/04/i-wasnt-a-fan-of-sheryl-sandbergs-until-i-couldnt-find-a-job/360343/.

Bazelon, Emily. 2014. "The Word You Are Searching for Is *Rape*." *Slate*, February 13. www.slate.com/articles/double_x/doublex/2014/02/rape_sexual_abuse_molestation_the_terms_have_become_interchangeable_but.html.

Becker, Jo. 2014. "How the President Got to 'I Do' on Same-Sex Marriage." *New York Times*, April 16. www.nytimes.com/2014/04/20/magazine/how-the-president-got-to-i-do-on-same-sex-marriage.html.

Beckman, Peter, and Francine D'Amico, eds. 1994. *Women, Gender, and World Politics*. Westport, CT: Bergin and Garvey.

Beggan, James, and Scott Allison. 2003. "Reflexivity in the Pornographic Films of Candida Royalle." *Sexualities* 6, no. 3–4: 301–24.

Bellamy, Richard. 2000. *Rethinking Liberalism*. New York: Pinter.

Berer, Marge. 2010. "Editorial: Cosmetic Surgery, Body Image and Sexuality." *Reproductive Health Matters* 18, no. 35: 4–10.

Bergen, Raquel Kennedy, and Paul Bukovec. 2006. "Men and Intimate Partner Rape: Characteristics of Men Who Sexually Abuse Their Partner." *Journal of Interpersonal Violence* 21, no. 10 (October): 1375–84.

Berger, Peter L., ed. 1999. *The Desecularization of the World*. Washington, DC: Ethics and Public Policy Center.

Berkowitz, Alan. 2005. "An Overview of the Social Norms Approach." In *Changing the Culture of College Drinking: A Socially Situated Health Communication Campaign*, edited by Linda C. Lederman and Leah P. Sewart, 193–214. Cresskill, NJ: Hampton Press.

Bernstein, Jacob. 2013. "What's in a Name: Family and More." *New York Times*, December 6. www.nytimes.com/2013/12/08/fashion/Same-sex-and-straight-couples-alike-discuss-changing-last-names-after-marriage.html?pagewanted=all&_r=0.

Bertone, Andrea. 2009. "Trafficking for Sexual Exploitation." In *Human Rights: Politics and Practice*, edited by Michael Goodhart, 201–18. New York: Oxford University Press.

Bien-Aimé, Taina. 2014. "Eradicating Female Genital Mutilation in Our Lifetime: The Vision of Efua Dorkenoo (1949–2014)." *Huffington Post*, December 5. www.huffingtonpost.com/taina-bienaime/post_8672_b_6259134.html.

Bilge, Sirma. 2010. "Beyond Subordination vs. Resistance: An Intersectional Approach to the Agency of Veiled Muslim Women." *Journal of Intercultural Studies* 32, no. 1: 9–28.

Blackwell, Tom. 2014. "Wave of Popularity for Cosmetic Surgery on Female Genitalia Worries Some Critics." *National Post*, January 30. news.nationalpost.com/2014/01/30/wave-of-popularity-for-cosmetic-surgery-on-female-genitalia-worries-some-critics/.

Blumberg, Antonia. 2014. "Ultra-Orthodox Jewish Men Cause Flight Delay by Refusing to Sit Next to Women." *Huffington Post*, September 30. www.huffingtonpost.com/2014/09/30/orthodox-jewish-flight-delay_n_5902078.html?cps=gravity.

Boesveld, Sarah. 2012. "Women as the Breadwinners: Turning the Traditional Model of Gender Roles in Marriage on Its Head." *National Post*, February 25. news.nationalpost.com/2012/02/25/womean-as-the-breadwinners-turning-the-traditional-model-of-gender-roles-in-marriage-on-its-head/.

———. 2014. "Canadian Law Decisive on What Constitutes Sexual Consent: There's Nothing 'Implied' or 'Implicit' About It." *National Post*, November 26. news.nationalpost.com/news/canada/canadian-law-decisive-on-what-constitutes-sexual-consent-theres-nothing-implied-or-implicit-about-it.

Bordo, Susan. 2003. *Unbearable Weight: Feminism, Western Culture, and the Body*. 10th anniversary edition. Berkeley: University of California Press.

Bramadat, Paul. 2000. *The Church on the World's Turf: An Evangelical Christian Group at a Secular University*. New York: Oxford University Press.

Bramadat, Paul, and Lorne Dawson. 2014. *Religious Radicalization and Securitization in Canada and Beyond*. Toronto: University of Toronto Press.

Breakenridge, Rob. 2014. "Pornography—Canada's Other Sex Trade." *National Post*, June 23. fullcomment.nationalpost.com/2014/06/23/rob-breakenridge-pornography-canadas-other-sex-trade/.

British Columbia Civil Liberties Association. 2006. "BCCLA Position Paper: Sexuality and Civil Rights: Freedom from Government Reprisal." bccla.org/wp-content/uploads/2012/04/2006-BCCLA-Paper-BDSM.pdf.

Bromley, Victoria L. 2012. *Feminisms Matter: Debates, Theories, Activism*. Toronto: University of Toronto Press.

Brown, Alyssa. 2014. "Michelle Obama Maintains Positive Image." *Gallup*, March 3. www.gallup.com/poll/167696/michelle-obama-maintains-positive-image.aspx.

Burke, Mark Kathryn. 2015. "Gender Identity Versus Attraction: 'It's Apples and Oranges' Says Bruce Jenner." *ABC News*, April 24. abcnews.go.com/Health/gender-identity-versus-attraction-apples-oranges-bruce-jenner/story?id=30570293.

Burkett, Elinor. 2015. "What Makes a Woman?" *New York Times*, June 6. www.nytimes.com/2015/06/07/opinion/sunday/what-makes-a-woman.html?emc=edit_tnt_20150606&nlid=55025100&tntemail0=y&_r=0.

Butterfield, Michelle. 2012. "Edmonton Sexual Assault Awareness Campaign: 'Don't Be That Guy' So Effective City Relaunches with New Posters." *Huffington Post*, December 1. www.huffingtonpost.ca/2012/12/01/edmonton-sexual-assault-awareness-campaign-dont-be-that-guy_n_2224228.html.

Cahill, Ann J. 2010. "Getting to My Fighting Weight." *Hypatia* 25, no. 2 (Spring): 485–92.

Carlson, Kathryn Blaze. 2013. "Don't Call Her First Lady: A Rare Sit-down Chat with Laureen Harper." *Globe and Mail*, March 9. www.theglobeandmail.com/news/politics/dont-call-her-first-lady-a-rare-sit-down-chat-with-laureen-harper/article9561792/?page=all.

Carter, S. Daniel. 2014. "The Campus Sexual Violence Elimination Act." www.cleryact.info/campus-save-act.html.

CBC News. 2011. "Parties, Laureen Harper Focus of WikiLeaks Cables." April 28. www.cbc.ca/news/politics/parties-laureen-harper-focus-of-wikileaks-cables-1.1025490.

———. 2012. "Pickton Inquiry Slams 'Blatant Failures' by Police." December 17. www.cbc.ca/news/canada/british-columbia/pickton-inquiry-slams-blatant-failures-by-police-1.1191108.

———. 2014. "Toronto Police Investigating Jian Ghomeshi Allegations." October 31. www.cbc.ca/news/canada/toronto-police-investigating-jian-ghomeshi-allegations-1.2820337.

Cesari, Jocelyne. 2005. "Islam, Secularism and Multiculturalism After 9/11: A Transatlantic Comparison." In *European Muslims and the Secular State*, edited by Jocelyne Cesari and Sean McLoughlin, 39–51. Aldershot, UK: Ashgate.

Chafe, William. 2012. *Bill and Hillary: The Politics of the Personal*. New York: Farrar, Straus and Giroux.

Chozik, Amy. 2014. "Hillary Clinton Says She Has 'Moved on' from Lewinsky Scandal." *New York Times*, June 4. www.nytimes.com/2014/06/05/us/politics/hillary-clinton-says-she-has-moved-on-from-lewinsky-scandal.html.

Chrisafis, Angelique. 2009. "Nicolas Sarkozy Says Islamic Veils Are Not Welcome in France." *Guardian*, June 22. www.theguardian.com/world/2009/jun/22/islamic-veils-sarkozy-speech-france.

Clarke, Laura Hurd. 2010. *Facing Age: Women Growing Older in Anti-Aging Culture*. Lanham, MD: Rowman and Littlefield.

Claxton, Shannon, and Manfred van Dulmen. 2013. "Casual Sexual Relationships and Experiences in Emerging Adulthood." *Emerging Adulthood* 1, no. 2: 138–50.

Clinton, Hillary Rodham. 2003. *Living History*. New York: Simon and Schuster.

———. 2014. *Hard Choices*. New York: Simon and Schuster.

Conroy, Scott. 2008. "Palin Breaks with McCain on Gay Marriage Ban." *CBS News*, October 20. www.cbsnews.com/news/palin-breaks-with-mccain-on-gay-marriage-ban/.

Cooper, Brittney. 2010. "A'n't I a Lady?: Race, Women, Michelle Obama, and the Ever-Expanding Democratic Imagination." *MELUS* 35, no. 4 (Winter): 39–57.

———. 2013. "Lay off Michelle Obama: Why White Feminists Need to Lean Back." *Salon*, November 29. www.salon.com/2013/11/29/lay_off_michelle_obama_why_white_feminists_need_to_lean_back/.

Coronel, Sheila, Steve Coll, and Derek Kravitz. 2015. "An Anatomy of a Journalistic Failure." *Rolling Stone*, April 5. www.rollingstone.com/culture/features/a-rape-on-campus-what-went-wrong-20150405?page=13.

Cossman, Brenda. 2014. "The Ghomeshi Question: The Law and Consent." *Globe and Mail*, October 27. www.theglobeandmail.com/globe-debate/the-ghomeshi-question-the-law-and-consent/article21315629/.

Cottle, Michelle. 2013. "How Michelle Obama Became a Feminist Nightmare." *Politico*, November 21. www.politico.com/magazine/story/2013/11/leaning-out-michelle-obama-100244.html#.U-vsfONdU9p.

Coy, Maddy, ed. 2012. *Prostitution, Harm, and Gender Inequality*. Surrey: Ashgate.

Crenshaw, Kimberle. 2011. "Demarginalising the Intersection of Race and Sex: A Black Feminist Critique of Anti-discrimination Doctrine, Feminist Theory, and Anti-racist Politics." In *Framing Intersectionality*, edited by Helma Lutz, Maria Teresa Herrera Vivar, and Linda Supik, 25–42. Surrey: Ashgate.

Cudd, Ann E. 2011. "For Capitalism as a Feminist Ideal and Reality." In *Capitalism, For and Against: A Feminist Debate*, by Ann E. Cudd and Nancy Holmstrom, 3–130. New York: Cambridge University Press.

Dagnes, Alison, ed. 2011. *Sex Scandals in American Politics*. New York: Continuum.

Davis, Kathy. 1991. "Remaking the She-Devil: A Critical Look at Feminist Approaches to Beauty." *Hypatia* 6, no. 2 (Summer): 21–43.

———, ed. 1997. *Embodied Practices*. London: Sage Publishers.

Derogatis, Amy. 2014. "Sex and the Single Evangelical: Purity Balls, Odd Daddy Roles, and Saving It for Jesus Christ." *Salon*, November 2. www.salon.com/2014/11/03/sex_and_the_single_evangelical_purity_balls_odd_daddy_roles_and_saving_it_for_jesus_christ/.

Dewey, Caitlin. 2013. "7 Ridiculous Restrictions on Women's Rights around the World." *Washington Post*, October 27. www.washingtonpost.com/blogs/worldviews/wp/2013/10/27/7-ridiculous-restrictions-on-womens-rights-around-the-world/.

Dines, Gail. 2006. "The White Man's Burden: Gonzo Pornography and the Construction of Black Masculinity." *Yale Journal of Law and Feminism* 18, no. 1: 283–97. gaildines.com/2009/09/the-white-mans-burden/.

———. 2010. *Pornland: How Porn Has Hijacked Our Sexuality*. Boston: Beacon Press.

Dobrowolsky, Alexandra, ed. 2009. *Women and Public Policy in Canada: Neo-liberalism and After?* Don Mills, ON: Oxford University Press.

Doezema, Jo. 2010. *Sex Slaves and Discourse Masters*. London: Zed Books.

Donaghue, Ngaire. 2009. "Body Satisfaction, Sexual Self-Schemas, and Subjective Well-being in Women." *Body Image* 6, no. 1: 37–42.

Donovan, Kevin, and Jesse Brown. 2014. "CBC Fires Jian Ghomeshi over Sex Allegations." *Toronto Star*, October 26. www.thestar.com/news/canada/2014/10/26/cbc_fires_jian_ghomeshi_over_sex_allegations.html?utm_medium=twitter&utm_source=twitterfeed.

Drinkwater, Rob. 2013. "Alberta Premier 'Disgusted' by MLA's Arrest in Prostitution Sting." *CTV News*, July 18. www.ctvnews.ca/canada/alberta-premier-disgusted-by-mla-s-arrest-in-prostitution-sting-1.1372436.

Duhaime-Ross, Arielle. 2014. "Rolling Stone Just Wrecked an Incredible Year of Progress for Rape Victims." *Verge*, December 5. www.theverge.com/2014/12/5/7342317/rolling-stone-retraction-rape-blame-consent.

Du Mont, Janice, and Deborah Parnis. 1999. "Judging Women: The Pernicious Effects of Rape Mythology." *Canadian Women Studies* 19, no. 2: 102–9.

Earp, Brian D. 2014. "Female Genital Mutilation (FGM) and Male Circumcision: Should There Be a Separate Ethical Discourse?" February 18. blog.practicalethics.ox.ac.uk/2014/02/female-genital-mutilation-and-male-circumcision-time-to-confront-the-double-standard/.

Eaton, A. W. 2007. "A Sensible Antiporn Feminism." *Ethics* 117, no. 4 (July): 674–715.

———. 2008. "A Reply to Critics." *Symposia on Gender, Race, and Philosophy* 4, no. 2 (Spring 2008). web.mit.edu/sgrp/2008/no2/Eaton0508.pdf.

Eberle, Christine. 2013. "Will Quebec's Charter of Values Withstand Constitutional Scrutiny?" Centre for Constitutional Studies, University of Alberta, October 17. ualawccsprod.srv.ualberta.ca/ccs/index.php/constitutional-issues/the-charter/fundamental-freedoms-section-2/718-will-quebec-s-charter-of-values-withstand-constitutional-scrutiny.

Eggertson, Laura. 2012. "Bill and Hillary: The Politics of the Personal by William H. Chafe: Review." *Toronto Star*, September 29. www.thestar.com/entertainment/books/2012/09/29/bill_and_hillary_the_politics_of_the_personal_by_william_h_chafe_review.html.

Elliott, Charlene. 2007. "Big Persons, Small Voices: On Governance, Obesity, and the Narrative of the Failed Citizen." *Journal of Canadian Studies* 41, no. 3 (Fall): 134–49.

Ellis, Mark. 2006/2007. "Breaking the Silence: Rape as an International Crime." *Case Western Reserve Journal of International Law* 38, no. 2: 225–47.

Eltahawy, Mona. 2010. "Is France Right to Ban Wearing the Burka in Public?" *Observer*, March 21. www.theguardian.com/theobserver/2010/mar/21/debate-on-french-burka-ban.

Enloe, Cynthia. 1989. *Making Feminist Sense of International Politics*. London: Pandora Press.

Evangelical Fellowship of Canada. 2013. "Factum of the Intervener." SCC File no. 34788: *Attorney General of Canada, et al. v. Terri Jean Bedford, et al.* www.scc-csc.gc.ca/factums-memoires/34788/FM085_Intervener_Evangelical.pdf.

Fabiano, Patricia, Wesley Perkins, Alan Berkowitz, Jeff Linkenbach, and Christopher Stark. 2003. "Engaging Men as Social Justice Allies in Ending Violence Against Women: Evidence for a Social Norms Approach." *Journal of American College Health* 52, no. 3: 105–12.

Farrell, Amy Erdman. 2011. *Fat Shame: Stigma and the Fat Body in American Culture*. New York: New York University Press.

Fayner, Scott. 2010. "Down the Tubes: How Free Streaming Video Threatens the Porn Industry." *MIT Technology Review*, August 25. www.technologyreview.com/review/420419/down-the-tubes/.

Fitz-Morris, James. 2015. "Conservatives' Niqab Ban Shaped by Quebec's Secular Charter Battle." *CBC News*, June 21. www.cbc.ca/news/politics/conservatives-niqab-ban-shaped-by-quebec-s-secular-charter-battle-1.3120072.

Flanagan, Tom. 2014. *Persona Non Grata, The Death of Free Speech in the Internet Age*. Toronto: Signal (McClelland & Stewart).

Foerster, Amy. 2009. "Contested Bodies: Sex Trafficking NGOs and Transnational Politics." *International Feminist Journal of Politics* 11, no. 2: 151–73.

Franzoi, Stephen. 1995. "The Body-as-Object Versus Body-as-Process: Gender Differences and Gender Considerations." *Sex Roles* 33, no. 5/6: 417–37.

Friedman, Jaclyn, and Jessica Valenti. 2008. *Yes Means Yes!: Visions of Female Sexual Power and a World Without Rape*. Berkeley, CA: Seal Press.

Garvey, Marianne, Brian Niemietz, Lachlan Cartwright, and Molly Friedman. 2013. "Ashley Dupre, the One-Time Escort Who Helped Sock It to Former Gov. Eliot Spitzer, Marries Construction Honcho in Paris." *New York Daily News*, October 26. www.nydailynews.com/entertainment/gossip/confidential/ashley-dupre-marries-construction-honcho-paris-article-1.1497765.

Ghomeshi, Jian. 2014. "Full Statement" on CBC Fan Club Facebook Page. October 26. www.facebook.com/cbcfanclub/posts/10152563915028842.

Giddens, Anthony. 1992. *The Transformation of Intimacy*. Stanford: Stanford University Press.

Gimlin, Debra L. 2002. *Body Work*. Berkeley, CA: University of California Press.

GLAAD. n.d. "GLAAD Media Reference Guide—Transgender Issues." www.glaad.org/reference/transgender.

Globe and Mail. 2010. Editorial. "No Reason to Be Tolerant of Female Genital Mutilation." June 20. www.theglobeandmail.com/globe-debate/editorials/no-reason-to-be-tolerant-of-female-genital-mutilation/article1373491/.

Goldberg, Michelle. 2014. "What Is a Woman? The Dispute between Radical Feminism and Transgenderism." *New Yorker*, August 4. www.newyorker.com/magazine/2014/08/04/woman-2.

Golden, Claudia, and Maria Shim. 2004. "Making a Name: Women's Surnames at Marriage and Beyond." *Journal of Economic Perspectives* 18, no. 2 (Spring): 143–60.

Gordon, Bonnie, and Martha Feldman. 2006. *The Courtesan's Arts: Cross-cultural Perspectives*. New York: Oxford University Press.

Grayson, Paul. 2014. "York Professor at Centre of Religious Rights Furor: Rights Code Is the Issue." *Globe and Mail*, January 16. www.theglobeandmail.com/globe-debate/my-quarrels-not-with-york-but-ontarios-rights-code/article16350272/.

Grinberg, Emanuela. 2014. "Schools Preach 'Enthusiastic' Yes in Sex Consent Education." *CNN News*, September 3. www.cnn.com/2014/09/03/living/affirmative-consent-school-policy/.

Gulli, Cathy. 2012. "The Richer Sex." *Maclean's*, March 6. www.macleans.ca/society/life/the-richer-sex/.

Gunn, Alexandra. 2012. "The Natural: Laureen Harper Talks Family, Fitness, and Canadian Pride." *Ottawa Life*, May 12. www.ottawalife.com/2012/05/the-natural-laureen-harper-talks-family-fitness-and-canadian-pride/#sthash.LfjvbcIC.dpuf.

Gurney, Matt. 2014. "Cyberbullying Will Not Be Tolerated. Except for the Porno Teacher." *National Post*, October 21. fullcomment.nationalpost.com/2014/10/21/matt-gurney-cyber-bullying-will-not-be-tolerated-except-for-the-porno-teacher/.

———. 2014. "America's Largest Rape Prevention Group Dodges 'Victim Blaming' Bullet." *National Post*, March 27. news.nationalpost.com/full-comment/matt-gurney-americas-largest-rape-prevention-group-dodges-victim-blaming-bullet.

Hakim, Catherine. 2010. "Erotic Capital." *European Sociological Review* 26, no. 5 (March): 499–518.

Hamblin, James. 2014. "How Not to Talk About the Culture of Sexual Assault." *The Atlantic*, March 29. www.theatlantic.com/health/archive/2014/03/how-not-to-talk-about-the-culture-of-sexual-assault/359845/.

Harris, Lynn. 2010. "Female Genital Mutilation in the US: No Compromise." *Salon*, June 2. www.salon.com/2010/06/02/fgm_genital_nick/.

Hartley, Nina. 2013. "Porn: An Effective Vehicle for Sexual Role Modeling and Education." In *The Feminist Porn Book: The Politics of Producing Pleasure*, edited by Tristan Taormino, Celine Parrenas Shimizu, Constance Penley, and Mireille Miller-Young, 228–36. New York: The Feminist Press at the City University of New York.

Human Rights Watch. 2014. "License to Harm: Violence and Harassment against LGBT People and Activists in Russia." December 14. www.hrw.org/report/2014/12/15/license-harm/violence-and-harassment-against-lgbt-people-and-activists-russia.

Hurd, Elizabeth. 2008. *The Politics of Secularism in International Relations*. Princeton: Princeton University Press.

Immen, Wallace. 2010. "The Skinny on Weight Discrimination." *Globe and Mail*, January 22.www.theglobeandmail.com/report-on-business/careers/career-advice/the-skinny-on-weight-discrimination/article4311089/.

Intersex Society of North America. n.d. "What's the Difference between Being Transgender or Transsexual and Having an Intersex Condition?" www.isna.org/faq/transgender.

Ishaq, Zunera. 2015. "Why I Intend to Wear a Niqab at My Citizenship Ceremony." *Toronto Star*, March 16. www.thestar.com/opinion/commentary/2015/03/16/why-i-intend-to-wear-a-niqab-at-my-citizenship-ceremony.html.

Jeffreys, Sheila. 2012. "Let Us Be Free to Debate Transgenderism without Being Accused of 'Hate Speech.'" *Guardian*, May 29. www.theguardian.com/commentisfree/2012/may/29/transgenderism-hate-speech.

———. 2014. *Gender Hurts: A Feminist Analysis of the Politics of Transgenderism*. New York: Routledge.

Jirovsky, Elena. 2010. "Views of Women and Men in Bobo-Dioulasso, Burkina Faso, on Three Forms of Genital Modification." *Reproductive Health Matters* 18, no. 35: 84–93.

Johnsdotter, Sara. 2012. "Projected Cultural Histories of the Cutting of Female Genitalia: A Poor Reflection as in a Mirror." *History and Anthropology* 23, no. 1 (March): 91–114.

Johnsdotter, Sara, and Birgitta Essen. 2010. "Genitals & Ethnicity: The Politics of Genital Modifications." *Reproductive Health Matters* 18, no. 35: 29–37.

Johnson, Zach. 2014. "Angelina Jolie Kicks Off Global Summit to End Sexual Violence in Conflict—Watch Her Moving Speech." *EOnline*, June 10. www.eonline.com/news/549679/angelina-jolie-kicks-off-global-summit-to-end-sexual-violence-in-conflict-watch-her-moving-speech.

Johnston, Josee, and Judith Taylor. 2008. "Feminist Consumerism and Fat Activists: A Comparative Study of Grassroots Activism and the Dove Real Beauty Campaign." *Signs* 33, no. 4 (Summer): 941–66.

Kaminer, Wendy. 1992. "Feminists Against the First Amendment." *Atlantic*, November 1. www.theatlantic.com/magazine/archive/1992/11/feminists-against-the-first-amendment/305051/.

Kantor, Jodi. 2012. *The Obamas*. New York: Back Bay Books.

Kay, Barbara. 2014. "'Values' Return to Quebec in More Sensible Liberal Version." *National Post*, September 18. news.nationalpost.com/full-comment/barbara-kay-values-return-to-quebec-in-more-sensible-liberal-version.

Keeble, Edna. 2005. "Immigration, Civil Liberties, and National/Homeland Security." *International Journal* 60, no. 2 (Spring): 359–72.

Keeble, Edna, and Meredith Ralston. 2003. "Discourses and Feminist Dilemmas." In *Feminist Perspectives on Canadian Foreign Policy*, edited by C. T. Sjolander, H. A. Smith, and D. Stienstra, 136–54. Don Mills, ON: Oxford University Press.

Kempadoo, Kamala. 2012. "Introduction: Abolitionism, Criminal Justice, and Transnational Feminism: Twenty-First-Century Perspectives on Human Trafficking." In *Trafficking and Prostitution Reconsidered: New Perspectives on Migration, Sex Work, and Human Rights*, 2nd ed., edited by Kamala Kempadoo with Jyoti Sanghera and Bandana Pattanik, vii–xlii. Boulder: Paradigm Publishers.

Khattab, Moushira. 2013. "Reflections on the Adoption of UNGA Resolution Banning Female Genital Mutilation." Middle East Program, Woodrow Wilson Center for Scholars, *Viewpoints* 13 (January). www.intact-network.net/intact/cp/files/1387188941_Reflections%20on%20the%20Adoption%20of%20UNGA%20Resolution%20Banning%20Female%20Genital%20Mutilation.pdf.

Kimmel, Michael S. 2005. *The Gender of Desire*. Albany: State University of New York Press.

Kingkade, Tyler. 2014a. "How a Title IX Harassment Case at Yale in 1980 Set the Stage for Today's Sexual Assault Activism." *Huffington Post*, June 10. www.huffingtonpost.com/2014/06/10/title-ix-yale-catherine-mackinnon_n_5462140.html.

———. 2014b. "Males Are More Likely to Suffer Sexual Assault Than to Be Falsely Accused of It." *Huffington Post*, December 8. www.huffingtonpost.com/2014/12/08/false-rape-accusations_n_6290380.html.

Kingston, Anne. 2007. "Wife of the Party." *Maclean's*, August 13. EBSCO.

———. 2012. "Veils: Who Are We to Judge?" *Maclean's*, January 17. www.macleans.ca/society/life/who-are-we-to-judge/.

———. 2015. "Sophie Grégoire-What? It May Be 2015, But Not for Political Wives." *Maclean's*, November 27. www.macleans.ca/society/life/sophie-gregoire-what-it-may-be-2015-but-not-for-political-wives/.

Kirkland, Anna. 2008. "Think of the Hippopotamus: Rights Consciousness in the Fat Acceptance Movement." *Law and Society Review* 42, no. 2 (June): 397–432.

———. 2011. "The Environmental Case for Obesity: A Case for Feminist Skepticism." *Signs* 36, no. 2 (Winter): 463–85.

Kitchens, Caroline. 2014. "It's Time to End 'Rape Culture' Hysteria." *Time*, March 20. time.com/30545/its-time-to-end-rape-culture-hysteria/.

Kucinich, Jackie, and Nia-Malika Henderson. 2014. "Sarah Palin's Remarkable Staying Power." *Washington Post*, April 15. www.washingtonpost.com/blogs/she-the-people/wp/2014/04/05/sarah-palins-remarkable-staying-power/.

Lacey, Nicola. 1993. "Theory into Practice? Pornography and the Public/Private Dichotomy." *Journal of Law and Society* 20, no. 1 (Spring): 93–113.

Langlois, Anthony J. 2009. "Normative and Theoretical Foundations of Human Rights." In *Human Rights: Politics and Practice*, edited by Michael Goodhart, 11–25. New York: Oxford University Press.

Larson, Leslie. 2014. "Silda Wall Spitzer Gets $7.5 Million Divorce Payout." *New York Daily News*, April 28. www.nydailynews.com/news/politics/silda-spitzer-7-5-million-divorce-payout-article-1.1771309.

Lehmann, Claire. 2014. "Hijab Selfies Make a Mockery of Spiritual Identity." *ABC [Australian Broadcasting Corporation] News*, October 7. www.abc.net.au/religion/articles/2014/10/07/4102009.htm.

Lerum, Kari, and Shari Dworkin. 2009. "'Bad Girls Rule': An Interdisciplinary Commentary on the Report of the APA Task Force on the Sexualization of Girls." *Journal of Sex Research* 46, no. 4: 250–63.

Levitz, Stephanie. 2013. "Laureen Harper: Sophie Gregoire, Justin Trudeau's Wife, 'Could Give Me Lessons.'" *Huffington Post*, April 23. www.huffingtonpost.ca/2013/04/23/laureen-harper-sophie-gregoire_n_3137006.html.

Lewinsky, Monica. 2014. "Shame and Survival." *Vanity Fair*, June. www.vanityfair.com/style/society/2014/06/monica-lewinsky-humiliation-culture.

Lincoln, Bruce. 2002. *Holy Terrors: Thinking about Religion after September 11*. Chicago: University of Chicago Press.

Lyon, Matthew. 2004. "No Means No? Withdrawal of Consent During Intercourse and the Continuing Evolution of the Definition of Rape." *Journal of Criminal Law and Criminology* 95, no. 1: 277–314.

Macdonald, Terry. 2015. "Are You Now or Have You Ever Been a TERF?" *New Statesman*, February 16. www.newstatesman.com/politics/2015/02/are-you-now-or-have-you-ever-been-terf.

MacGillis, Alec, and Karl Vick. 2008. "'First Dude' Todd Palin Illustrates Alaska's Blend of Private and Public." *Washington Post*, September 22. www.washingtonpost.com/wp-dyn/content/story/2008/09/22/ST2008092200075.html.

MacKinnon, Catherine. 1989. *Towards a Feminist Theory of the State*. Cambridge: Harvard University Press.

———. 2011. "Trafficking, Prostitution, and Inequality." *Harvard Civil Rights-Civil Liberties Law Review* 46, no. 2 (Summer): 271–309. harvardcrcl.org/wp-content/uploads/2009/06/MacKinnon.pdf.

Macpherson, Don. 2014. "PQ's Values Charter Was All Just a Big Political Ploy." *Montreal Gazette*, May 4. www.montrealgazette.com/news/Macpherson+values+charter+just+political +ploy/9801356/story.html.

Makarechi, Kia. 2013. "CNN's Steubenville Coverage Focuses on Effect Rape Trial Will Have on Rapists, Not Victim." *Huffington Post*, March 17. www.huffingtonpost.com/kia-makarechi/cnn-steubenville-coverage_b_2896948.html.

Makin, Kirk. 2013. "How Canada's Sex Assault Laws Violate Rape Victims." *Globe and Mail*, October 5. www.theglobeandmail.com/news/national/how-canadas-sex-assault-laws-violate-rape-victims/article14705289/?page=all.

Malone, Noreen, and (portfolio by) Amanda Demme. 2015. "'I'm No Longer Afraid': 35 Women Tell Their Stories About Being Assaulted by Bill Cosby, and the Culture That Wouldn't Listen." *New York* [magazine], July 26. nymag.com/thecut/2015/07/bill-cosbys-accusers-speak-out.html.

Marshall, Katherine. 2006. "Converging Gender Roles." *Perspectives on Labour and Income*. Statistics Canada, Catalogue no. 75-001-XIE. July. www.statcan.gc.ca/pub/75-001-x/10706/9268-eng.pdf.

Massola, James. 2014. "Tony Abbott to Kill off Parliament House Burqa Ban." *Sydney Morning Herald*, October 2. www.smh.com.au/federal-politics/political-news/tony-abbott-to-kill-off-parliament-house-burqa-ban-20141002-10pjoh.html.

McDermott, Vincent. 2014. "Disgraced MLA Mike Allen back in Alberta Tory Caucus." *Edmonton Sun*, July 7. www.edmontonsun.com/2014/07/07/disgraced-mla-mike-allen-back-in-alberta-tory-caucus.

McGinley, Ann C. 2009. "Hillary Clinton, Sarah Palin, and Michelle Obama: Performing Gender, Race, and Class on the Campaign Trail." *Denver University Law Review* 86 (Special issue): 709–25.

McGregor, Jaynce, and Kady O'Malley. 2015. "Stephen Harper Makes His Case for New Powers to Combat Terror." *CBC News*, January 30. www.cbc.ca/news/politics/stephen-harper-makes-his-case-for-new-powers-to-combat-terror-1.2937602.

McKenzie, Michelle, and Patricia Rozee. 2010. "Rape: A Global Perspective." In *Feminism and Women's Rights Worldwide*, vol. 3, edited by Michelle A. Paludi, 177–208. Santa Barbara, CA: Praeger.

McNally, Siobhan. 2014. "Fatkini Trend Inspiring and Empowering Curvy Women Everywhere." *Mirror*, August 18. www.mirror.co.uk/news/real-life-stories/fatkini-trend-inspiring-empowering-curvy-4070813.

McTeer, Maureen. 2003. *In My Own Name*. Toronto: Random House.

Mehta, Diana. 2016. "Women's Advocates Say Ghomeshi Trial Shows What Sex Assault Complainants Face." *Winnipeg Free Press*, February 3. www.winnipegfreepress.com/canada/womens-advocates-say-ghomeshi-trial-shows-what-sex-assault-complainants-face-367554861.html.

Mirhashem, Molly. 2015. "What Young Feminists Think of Hillary Clinton." *National Journal*, May 16. www.nationaljournal.com/magazine/2016-hillary-clinton-feminists-20150515.

Mottier, Veronique. 2008. *Sexuality: A Very Short Introduction*. Oxford: Oxford University Press.

Murphy, Catherine. 2015. "Here's Why We at Amnesty Backed the Decriminalisation of Sex Work." *Independent* [UK], August 13. www.independent.co.uk/voices/comment/heres-why-amnesty-backed-the-decriminalisation-of-sex-work-and-our-response-to-the-criticisms-10453954.html.

Murray, Jacqueline. 2012. "Todd Akin's Views Are, Literally, Medieval." *Globe and Mail*, August 23. www.theglobeandmail.com/commentary/todd-akins-views-are-literally-medieval/article4494067/.

Muslim Council of Britain. 2014. "Muslim Council of Britain Speaks Out Against Female Genital Mutilation," June 19. www.mcb.org.uk/muslim-council-of-britain-speaks-out-against-female-genital-mutilation/.

Narayan, Uma. 1998. "Essence of Culture and a Sense of History: A Feminist Critique of Cultural Essentialism." *Hypatia* 13, no. 2: 86–106.

Nasaw, Daniel. 2014. "In Toronto with the World's Feminist Pornographers." *BBC News*, May 9. www.bbc.com/news/magazine-27192724.

National Post. 2014. "Lots of 'Rape Culture' Rhetoric. But Not Much Evidence." Editorial, March 13. news.nationalpost.com/full-comment/national-post-editorial-board-lots-of-rape-culture-rhetoric-but-not-much-evidence.

Naugler, Diane, ed. 2012. *Canadian Perspectives in Sexualities Studies: Identities, Experiences, and the Contexts of Change*. Don Mills, ON: Oxford University Press.

Nelson, Sara. 2015. "Vaginal Piercings to Be Classed as FGM under New NHS Guidelines." *Huffington Post*, March 18. www.huffingtonpost.co.uk/2015/03/18/vaginal-piercings-classed-fgm-new-nhs-guidelines_n_6892376.html.

Nussbaum, Martha C. 1999. *Sex and Social Justice*. New York: Oxford University Press.

———. 2011. *Creating Capabilities: The Human Development Approach*. Cambridge, MA: Belknap Press of Harvard University Press.

———. 2012. *The New Religious Intolerance: Overcoming the Politics of Fear in an Anxious Age*. Cambridge, MA: Harvard University Press.

Okin, Susan Moller. 1999. "Is Multiculturalism Bad for Women?" In *Is Multiculturalism Bad for Women?*, edited by Joshua Cohen, Matthew Howard, and Martha C. Nussbaum, 9–24. Princeton: Princeton University Press.

Orbach, Susie. 1978. *Fat is a Feminist Issue*. New York: Paddington Press.

Outshoorn, Joyce. 2005. "The Political Debates on Prostitution and Trafficking of Women." *Social Politics: International Studies in Gender, State & Society* 12, no. 1 (Spring): 141–55.

———. 2011. "The Politics of Prostitution Revisited: Trends in Policy and Research." In *Sexuality, Gender, and Power: Intersectional and Transnational Perspectives*, edited by Anna G. Jonasdottir, Valerie Bryson, and Kathleen B. Jones, 127–41. New York: Routledge.

Overall, Christine. 1992. "What's Wrong with Prostitution? Evaluating Sex Work." *Signs* 17, no. 4: 705–24.

Page, Clarence. 1993. "What's in a Name? Plenty, When It's Hillary Clinton's." *Chicago Tribune*, February 3. articles.chicagotribune.com/1993-02-03/news/9303175032_1_americans-feel-president-clinton-hillary-clinton-s-first-lady.

Palin, Sarah. 2009. *Going Rogue*. New York: HarperCollins.

Palmer, Brian. 2011. "What's the Difference Between 'Rape' and 'Sexual Assault'?" *Salon*, February 17. www.slate.com/articles/news_and_politics/explainer/2011/02/whats_the_difference_between_rape_and_sexual_assault.html.

Payton, Laura. 2011. "Face Veils Banned for Citizenship Oaths." *CBC News*, December 12. www.cbc.ca/news/politics/face-veils-banned-for-citizenship-oaths-1.1048750.

Penley, Constance, Celine Parrenas Shimizu, Mireille Miller-Young, and Tristan Taormino. 2013. "Introduction: The Politics of Producing Pleasure." In *The Feminist Porn Book: The Politics of Producing Pleasure*, edited by Tristan Taormino, Celine Parrenas Shimizu, Constance Penley, and Mireille Miller-Young, 9–20. New York: The Feminist Press at the City University of New York.

Peoples, Steve, and Ken Thomas. 2013. "'He's Got the Rifle, I Got the Rack': Sarah Palin Explains Relationship with Her Husband in CPAC Speech." *National Post*, March 16. news.nationalpost.com/2013/03/16/sarah-palin-cpac-speech/.

Peritz, Ingrid. 2015. "Sophie Grégoire-Trudeau's Tandem Surname is Everybody's Business." *Globe and Mail*, December 10. www.theglobeandmail.com/news/national/sophie-gregoire-trudeaus-tandem-surname-is-everybodys-business/article27701792/.

Peterson, V. Spike, and Anne Sisson Runyan. 2010. *Global Gender Issues in the New Millennium*. 3rd ed. Philadelphia: Westview Press.

Plaxton, Michael. 2014. "Should We Reintroduce 'Rape'?" *Huffington Post*, January 24. www.huffingtonpost.ca/michael-plaxton/rob-anders-rape-bill_b_4661698.html?utm_hp_ref=canada-politics.

Plummer, Ken. 2008. "Studying Sexualities for a Better World? Ten Years of *Sexualities*." *Sexualities* 11, no. 1/2: 7–22.

Public Health Agency of Canada. 2008. *Canadian Guidelines for Sexual Health Education*. Ottawa. www.sieccan.org/pdf/guidelines-eng.pdf.

Purdy, Chris. 2014. "Women Bare Bellies in Bikinis to Support Edmonton Mom Mocked over Stretch Marks." *Edmonton Journal*, August 7. www.edmontonjournal.com/women+bare+bellies+bikinis+-support+Edmonton+mocked+over+stretch+marks+with+video/10095727/story.html.

Quebec Charter of Values. 2013. www.assnat.qc.ca/en/travaux-parlementaires/projets-loi/projet-loi-60-40-1.html.

Rahman, Momin, and Stevi Jackson. 2010. *Gender and Sexuality: Sociological Approaches*. Cambridge: Polity Press.

Ralston, Meredith, and Edna Keeble. 2009. *Reluctant Bedfellows: Feminism, Activism, and Prostitution in the Philippines*. Sterling, VA: Kumarian Press.

Raymond, Janice. 1979. *The Transsexual Empire: The Making of the She-Male*. Boston: Beacon Press.

Reed, Theresa AKA Darklady. 2006. "Private Acts versus Public Art: Where Prostitution Ends and Pornography Begins." In *Prostitution and Pornography: Philosophical Debate about the Sex Industry*, edited by Jessica Spector, 249–57. Stanford: Stanford University Press.

Reese, Diana. 2012. "Sarah Palin to Pen Book on Fitness." *Washington Post*, October 15. www.washingtonpost.com/blogs/she-the-people/wp/2012/10/15/sarah-palin-to-pen-book-on-fitness/.

Reid, Graeme. 2012. "'Traditional Values' Code for Human Rights Abuse?" *CNN*, October 12. globalpublicsquare.blogs.cnn.com/2012/10/17/traditional-values-code-for-human-rights-abuse/.

Reiman, Jeffrey. 2012. *As Free and as Just as Possible: The Theory of Marxian Liberalism*. Chichester: Wiley-Blackwell.

Richard, Joanne. 2014. "Move over Metrosexual, Spornosexual Is Here." *Vancouver 24 Hrs*, June 23. vancouver.24hrs.ca/2014/06/19/move-over-metrosexual-spornosexual-is-here.

Richtel, Matt. 2013. "Intimacy on the Web, with a Crowd." *New York Times*, September 21. www.nytimes.com/2013/09/22/technology/intimacy-on-the-web-with-a-crowd.html?_r=0.

Rosenberger, Sieglinde, and Brigit Sauer. 2012. "Framing and Regulating the Veil: An Introduction." In *Politics, Religion, and Gender: Framing and Regulating the Veil*, edited by Sieglinde Rosenberger and Brigit Sauer, 1–14. London: Routledge.

Rothblum, Esther. 2012. "Why a Journal on Fat Studies?" *Fat Studies* 1, no. 1: 3–5.

Royal Canadian Mounted Police. 2010. *Human Trafficking in Canada*. March (Unclassified). publications.gc.ca/collections/collection_2011/grc-rcmp/PS64-78-2010-eng.pdf.

Royalle, Candida. 2013. "What's a Nice Girl Like You ..." In *The Feminist Porn Book: The Politics of Producing Pleasure*, edited by Tristan Taormino, Celine Parrenas Shimizu, Constance Penley, and Mireille Miller-Young, 58–69. New York: The Feminist Press at the City University of New York.

Rudd Center for Food Policy and Obesity. 2013. "Weight Discrimination Legislation." www.yaleruddcenter.org/what_we_do.aspx?id=121.

Rukavina, Steve. 2015. "Quebec Judge Wouldn't Hear Case of Woman Wearing Hijab." *CBC News*, February 26. www.cbc.ca/news/canada/montreal/quebec-judge-wouldn-t-hear-case-of-woman-wearing-hijab-1.2974282.

Rustici, Camille. 2011. "France Burqa Ban Takes Effect; Two Women Detained." *Huffington Post*, November 4. www.huffingtonpost.com/2011/04/11/france-burqa-ban-takes-ef_n_847366.html.

Rutter, Virginia, and Pepper Schwartz. 2012. *The Gender of Sexuality: Exploring Sexual Possibilities*. 2nd ed. Lanham, MD: Rowman and Littlefield Publishers.

Saguy, Abigail, and Anna Ward. 2011. "Coming Out as Fat: Rethinking Stigma." *Social Psychology Quarterly* 74, no. 1 (March): 53–75.

Saint Mary's University. 2013. Report from the President's Council. "Promoting a Culture of Safety, Respect, and Consent at Saint Mary's University and Beyond." December 15. www.smu.ca/webfiles/PresidentsCouncilReport-2013.pdf.

———. 2014. "An Update from the President Council's Action Team." December. www.smu.ca/webfiles/ActionTeamReport-December.pdf.

Sampert, Shannon. 2010. "Let Me Tell You a Story: English-Canadian Newspapers and Sexual Assault Myths." *Canadian Journal of Women and Law* 22, no. 2: 301–28.

Sandberg, Sheryl, with Nell Scovell. 2014. *Lean in (for Graduates)*. New York: Alfred A. Knopf.

Saner, Emine. 2013. "Waris Dirie: 'Female Genital Mutilation Is Pure Violence against Girls.'" *Guardian*, October 14. www.theguardian.com/lifeandstyle/2013/oct/14/waris-dirie-female-genital-mutilation-fgm.

Sassi, Franco. 2010. *Obesity and the Economics of Prevention: Fit Not Fat*. Paris: OECD Publishing.

Schreiber, Ronnee. 2008. *Righting Feminism*. New York: Oxford University Press.

Seltzer, Leon. 2011. "What Distinguishes Erotica from Pornography?" *Psychology Today*, April 6. www.psychologytoday.com/blog/evolution-the-self/201104/what-distinguishes-erotica-pornography.

Shane, Scott. 2015. "Faulted for Avoiding 'Islamic' Labels to Describe Terrorism, White House Cites a Strategic Logic." *New York Times*, February 18. www.nytimes.com/2015/02/19/us/politics/faulted-for-avoiding-islamic-labels-white-house-cites-a-strategic-logic.html.

Shontell, Alyson. 2015. "Sheryl Sandberg Wrote a Beautiful Essay about the Sudden Death of Her Husband and Dealing with Grief." *Business Insider*, June 3. www.businessinsider.com/sheryl-sandbergs-essay-on-dave-goldbergs-death-and-grief-2015-6.

Shrage, Laurie. 1994. *Moral Dilemmas of Feminism: Prostitution, Adultery, and Abortion*. London: Routledge.

———. 2005. "Exposing the Fallacies of Anti-porn Feminism." *Feminist Theory* 6, no. 1: 45–65.

———. 2008. "Comments on A. W. Eaton's 'A Sensible Antiporn Feminism.'" *Symposia on Gender, Race, and Philosophy* 4, no. 2 (Spring 2008). web.mit.edu/sgrp/2008/no2/Shrage0508.pdf.

Simpson, Mark. 2014. "The Metrosexual Is Dead. Long Live the 'Spornosexual.'" *Telegraph*, June 10. www.telegraph.co.uk/men/fashion-and-style/10881682/The-metrosexual-is-dead.-Long-live-the-spornosexual.htm.

Slaughter, Anne-Marie. 2012. "Why Women Still Can't Have It All." *Atlantic*, July/August. www.theatlantic.com/magazine/archive/2012/07/why-women-still-cant-have-it-all/309020/.

———. 2013. "Yes, You Can: Sheryl Sandberg's 'Lean In.'" *New York Times*, March 7. www.nytimes.com/2013/03/10/books/review/sheryl-sandbergs-lean-in.html?pagewanted=all.

Smith, Clarissa. 2010. "Pornographication: A Discourse for All Seasons." *International Journal of Media and Cultural Politics* 6, no. 1: 103–8.

Smith, Clarissa, and Feona Attwood. 2013. "Emotional Truths and Thrilling Slide Shows: The Resurgence of Antiporn Feminism." In *The Feminist Porn Book: The Politics of Producing Pleasure*, edited by Tristan Taormino, Celine Parrenas Shimizu, Constance Penley, and Mireille Miller-Young, 41–57. New York: The Feminist Press at the City University of New York.

Sneed, Tierney. 2015. "'The Hunting Grounds' Subjects Defend Title IX Campaign." *US News and World Report*, February 27. www.usnews.com/news/articles/2015/02/27/the-hunting-ground-subjects-defend-title-ix-campaign.

Squires, Judith. 2003. "Public and Private." In *Political Concepts*, edited by Richard Bellamy and Andrew Mason, 131–44. Manchester: Manchester University Press.

The Starr Report: The Independent Counsel's Complete Report to Congress on the Investigation of President Clinton. 1998. Introduction by Phil Kuntz. New York: Simon and Schuster.

Statistics Canada. 2008. "Sexual Assault in Canada." (Archived Content.) www.statcan.gc.ca/pub/85f0033m/85f0033m2008019-eng.htm.

Steans, Jill. 2006. *Gender and International Relations*. 2nd ed. Cambridge: Polity Press.

Stein, Sam. 2008. "Palin on Abortion: I'd Oppose Even If My Own Daughter Was Raped." *Huffington Post*, October 2. www.huffingtonpost.com/2008/09/01/palin-on-abortion-id-oppo_n_122924.html.

Stuart, Hunter. 2013. "Pope Francis Excommunicates Australian Priest Who Advocated for Gay Marriage and Female Clergy." *Huffington Post*, September 24. www.huffingtonpost.com/2013/09/24/pope-francis-excommunicates-priest-greg-reynolds_n_3983059.html.

Sullivan, Oriel. 2006. *Changing Gender Relations, Changing Families*. Lanham, MD: Rowman and Littlefield Publishers.

Supreme Court of Canada. 2013. *Canada (Attorney General) v. Bedford*, 2013 SCC 72, [2013] 3 S.C.R. 1101. scc-csc.lexum.com/scc-csc/scc-csc/en/item/13389/index.do.

Tanabe, Karin. 2011. "Hillary Clinton Sits Down with *Harper's Bazaar*." *Politico*, February 15. www.politico.com/click/stories/1102/hillary_clinton_dishes_to_harpers_.html.

Tang, Kwong-Leung. 1998. "Rape Law Reform in Canada: The Success and Limits of Legislation." *International Journal of Offender Therapy and Comparative Criminology* 42, no. 3: 258–70.

Taormino, Tristan. 2013. "Calling the Shots: Feminist Porn in Theory and Practice." In *The Feminist Porn Book: The Politics of Producing Pleasure*, edited by Tristan Taormino, Celine Parrenas Shimizu, Constance Penley, and Mireille Miller-Young, 255–64. New York: The Feminist Press at the City University of New York.

Tickner, J. Ann. 2005. "What Is Your Research Program? Some Feminist Answers to International Relations Methodological Questions." *International Studies Quarterly* 49, no 1: 1–21.

———. 2011. "Gender in World Politics." In *The Globalization of World Politics*, 5th ed., edited by John Baylis, Steve Smith, and Patricia Owens, 262–77. New York: Oxford University Press.

Tong, Rosemary. 1989. *Feminist Thought: A Comprehensive Introduction*. Boulder: Westview Press.

Trudeau, Justin. 2015. "Canadian Liberty and the Politics of Fear." Speech delivered at the McGill Institute for the Study of Canada, March 9. www.liberal.ca/canadian-liberty-and-the-politics-of-fear/.

Turkewitz, Julie. 2014. "A Fight as US Girls Face Genital Cutting Abroad." *New York Times*, June 10. www.nytimes.com/2014/06/11/us/a-fight-as-us-girls-face-genital-cutting-abroad.html.

Tyler, Meaghen. 2012. "Theorizing Harm through the Sex of Prostitution." In *Prostitution, Harm, and Gender Inequality*, edited by Maddy Coy, 87–101. Surrey: Ashgate.

Tyrrell, R. Emmett. 2013. "Sarah Palin's Rack." *American Spectator*, May. spectator.org/articles/55781/sarah-palins-rack.

UNFPA-UNICEF (United Nations Population Fund–United Nations Children's Fund). 2013. Joint Programme on Female Genital Mutilation/Cutting: Accelerating Change. "Summary Report of Phase I 2008-2013." www.unfpa.org/sites/default/files/admin-resource/FGM-report%2012_4_2013.pdf.

UNICEF (United Nations Children's Fund). 2013. *Female Genital Mutilation/Cutting: A Statistical Overview and Exploration of the Dynamics of Change*. New York: UNICEF. www.unicef.org/cbsc/files/UNICEF_FGM_report_July_2013_Hi_res.pdf.

United Nations. 1948. "The Universal Declaration of Human Rights." Paris: United Nations. www.un.org/en/universal-declaration-human-rights/.

———. 2000. "Protocol to Prevent, Suppress, and Punish Trafficking in Persons, Especially Women and Children." www.unodc.org/documents/treaties/UNTOC/Publications/TOC%20Convention/TOCebook-e.pdf.

United Nations General Assembly. 1994. "Declaration on the Elimination of Violence against Women." https://documents-dds-ny.un.org/doc/UNDOC/GEN/N94/095/05/PDF/N9409505.pdf?OpenElement

United Nations Security Council (UNSC). 2000. "Resolution 1325(2000)." https://documents-dds-ny.un.org/doc/UNDOC/GEN/N00/720/18/PDF/N0072018.pdf?OpenElement.

———. 2008. "Resolution 1820(2008)." http://www.securitycouncilreport.org/atf/cf/%7B65B-FCF9B-6D27-4E9C-8CD3-CF6E4FF96FF9%7D/CAC%20S%20RES%201820.pdf.

United States Department of Justice. n.d. "Overview of Title IX of the Education Amendments of 1972." www.justice.gov/crt/overview-title-ix-education-amendments-1972-20-usc-1681-et-seq.

United States Supreme Court. 2015. *Obergefell et al. v. Hodges, Director, Ohio Department of Health et al.*, no. 14-556 [Decided June 26, 2015]. www.supremecourt.gov/opinions/14pdf/14-556_3204.pdf.

University of British Columbia. 2014. "Transforming UBC and Developing a Culture of Equality and Accountability: Confronting Rape Culture and Colonialist Violence." Report of the UBC President's Task Force on Gender-Based Violence and Aboriginal Stereotypes, March 28. equity2.sites.olt.ubc.ca/files/2014/05/Task-Force-on-IGBVAS-Final-Report-March-28-2014.pdf.

University of Ottawa. 2015. "Report of the Task Force on Respect and Equality: Ending Sexual Violence at the University of Ottawa." January 29. www.uottawa.ca/president/sites/www.uottawa.ca.president/files/report-of-the-task-force-on-respect-and-equality.pdf.

UNODC-IPU (United Nations Office on Drugs and Crime–Inter-Parliamentary Union). 2009. *Combating Trafficking in Persons: A Handbook for Parliamentarians*. www.unodc.org/documents/human-trafficking/UN_Handbook_engl_core_low.pdf.

Urbach, Robyn. 2015. "On a Day about Inclusivity, Anti-bullying Activists Protest Laureen Harper's Support." *National Post*, April 10. news.nationalpost.com/full-comment/robyn-urback-on-a-day-about-inclusivity-anti-bullying-activists-protest-laureen-harpers-support.

Vickers, Jill. 1997. *Reinventing Political Science: A Feminist Approach*. Halifax: Fernwood Publishing.

Vincent, Donovan. 2015. "Canadians Oppose Niqab During Citizenship Ceremony, Poll Suggests." *Toronto Star*, March 17. www.thestar.com/news/canada/2015/03/17/canadians-oppose-niqab-during-citizenship-ceremony-poll-suggests.html.

Wade, Lisa. 2009. "Defining Gendered Oppression in Newspapers: The Strategic Value of 'Female Genital Mutilation.'" *Gender and Society* 23, no. 3 (June): 293–314.

———. 2011. "The Politics of Acculturation: Female Genital Cutting and the Challenges of Building Multicultural Democracies." *Social Problems* 58, no. 4: 518–37.

Waltman, Max. 2010. "Rethinking Democracy: Legal Challenges to Pornography and Sex Inequality in Canada and the United States." *Political Research Quarterly* 63, no. 1: 218–37.

Wasylkiw, L., A. A. Emms, R. Meuse, and K. F. Poirier. 2009. "Are All Models Created Equal? A Content Analysis of Women in Advertisements of Fitness Versus Fashion Magazines." *Body Image* 6, no. 2: 137–40.

Weeks, Jeffrey. 1985. *Sexuality and Its Discontents*. London: Routledge.

———. 2007. *The World We Have Won*. London: Routledge.

Weiss, Margot. 2011. *Techniques of Pleasure: BDSM and the Circuits of Sexuality*. Durham, NC: Duke University Press.

Weissmann, Jordan. 2015. "The Beautiful Closing Paragraph of Justice Kennedy's Gay Marriage Ruling." *Slate*, June 26. www.slate.com/blogs/the_slatest/2015/06/26/supreme_court_legalizes_gay_marriage_here_is_the_beautiful_last_paragraph.html.

Weitzer, Ronald. 2007. "Prostitution: Facts and Fictions." *Contexts* 6, no. 4: 28–33.

———. 2010. "The Movement to Criminalize Sex Work in the United States." *Journal of Law and Society* 37, no. 1: 61–84.

White House Task Force. 2014. *Not Alone*. The First Report of the White House Task Force to Protect Students from Sexual Assault. April. www.notalone.gov/assets/report.pdf.

Whiting, Natalie. 2014. "Women in Solidarity with Hijabs Campaign Aims to Unite Muslim and Non-Muslim Australians." *ABC [Australian Broadcasting Corporation] News*, October 3. www.abc.net.au/news/2014-10-02/campaign-uniting-muslims-and-australian-women-launched/5786814.

WHO (World Health Organization). 2002. *World Report on Violence and Health*. Edited by Etienne Krug, Linda Dahlberg, James Mercy, Anthony Zwi, and Rafael Lozano. Geneva: World Health Organization. whqlibdoc.who.int/hq/2002/9241545615.pdf.

———. 2008. *Eliminating Female Genital Mutilation: An Interagency Statement.* Geneva: OHCHR, UNAIDS, UNDP, UNECA, UNESCO, UNFPA, UNHCR, UNICEF, UNIFEM, and WHO.

Wilkins, Riki. 2014. "Op-ed: Antitrans RadFems Are on the Wrong Side of History." *Advocate*, August 12. www.advocate.com/commentary/riki-wilchins/2014/08/12/op-ed-antitrans-radfems-are-wrong-side-history.

Willsher, Kim. 2014. "France's Burqa Ban Upheld by Human Rights Court." *Guardian*, July 1. www.theguardian.com/world/2014/jul/01/france-burqa-ban-upheld-human-rights-court.

Winter, Bronwyn. 2001. "Fundamental Misunderstandings: Issues in Feminist Approaches to Islamism." *Journal of Women's History* 13, no. 1: 9–41.

Woertman, Liesbeth, and Femke van den Brink. 2012. "Body Image and Female Sexual Functioning and Behavior: A Review." *Journal of Sex Research* 49, no. 2–3: 184–211.

Wolf, Naomi. 1991. *The Beauty Myth.* Toronto: Vintage Books.

Women's Coalition for the Abolition of Prostitution. 2013. "Factum of the Intervener." SCC File no. 34788: *Attorney General of Canada, et al. v. Terri Jean Bedford, et al.* www.scc-csc.gc.ca/factums-memoires/34788/FM075_Intervener_Coalition.pdf.

Yeung, Lisa. 2014. "#BeenRapedNeverReported: Powerful Stories and Conversation." *Huffington Post*, November 1. www.huffingtonpost.ca/2014/11/01/beenrapedneverreported-sexual-assault-rape_n_6087478.html.

Yoffe, Emily. 2014. "The College Rape Overcorrection." *Slate*, December 7. www.slate.com/articles/double_x/doublex/2014/12/college_rape_campus_sexual_assault_is_a_serious_problem_but_the_efforts.html.

Yousafzai, Malala, with Christina Lamb. 2013. *I Am Malala: The Girl Who Stood Up for Education and Was Shot by the Taliban*. New York: Little; Brown and Company.

Zabjek, Alexandra. 2014. "Edmonton Mom of Five Fights Back after Being Ridiculed for Stretch Marks." *Edmonton Journal*, August 2. www.edmontonjournal.com/Edmonton+five+fights+back+after+being+ridiculed+stretch+marks+with+video/10083088/story.html.

Zebroff, Petra. 2012. "What NOT to Learn from Pornography: A Guide for Men." *Huffington Post*, November 1. www.huffingtonpost.ca/petra-zebroff/pornography-lessons-men-sexuality-_b_2041287.html.